GUIDES.
AS EASY AS IT GETS!

Personal Finance in Your 20s and 30s

Fifth Edition

by Sarah Young Fisher and Susan Shelly McGovern

ALPHA
A member of Penguin Random House LLC

Publisher: Mike Sanders
Associate Publisher: Billy Fields
Acquisitions Editor: Jan Lynn
Cover Designer: Lindsay Dobbs
Book Designer: William Thomas
Compositor: Ayanna Lacey
Proofreader: Lisa Starnes
Indexer: Tonya Heard

Fifth American Edition, 2016
Published in the United States by DK Publishing
6081 E. 82nd Street, Indianapolis, Indiana 46250

Copyright © 2016 Dorling Kindersley Limited
A Penguin Random House Company
16 17 18 19   10 9 8 7 6 5 4 3 2 1
002-296406-OCTOBER2016

Published in the United States by Dorling Kindersley Limited.

IDIOT'S GUIDES and Design are trademarks of Penguin Random House LLC

ISBN: 9781465454621
Library of Congress Catalog Card Number: 2016935181

DK books are available at special discounts when purchased in bulk for sales promotions, premiums, fund-raising, or educational use. For details, contact: DK Publishing Special Markets, 345 Hudson Street, New York, New York 10014 or SpecialSales@dk.com.

Printed and bound in the United States of America

idiotsguides.com

Contents

Introduction

Learning to handle your finances wisely and responsibly is an ongoing process that requires your time and attention at every stage of your life. Personal finance is a big-picture event, not just a day-to-day or month-to-month process.

When you're just starting out, learning to budget and make your money last can be a daunting process—especially if you're not earning as much as you'd like to be. You have bills to pay, student loans to repay, a car payment to make, and that long weekend at the beach you and your friends are planning.

By learning the basics of personal finance now, you position yourself for financial success later in life. You'll have money to put aside for retirement, to help your kids with their college costs, and to live comfortably into your golden years.

This book provides a base to help you get started with saving money, paying back what you owe, and establishing a favorable credit history. It helps you understand how to stretch the dollars you have and put something aside for your future. When you finish the last part, you'll have a basic, sound understanding of how your personal finances work in various stages of your life. You won't quite be an expert, but you'll have a lot more confidence when it comes to handling your money and building a financially secure future.

How you handle your personal finances now affects nearly every aspect of your life in the future, so it's essential that you get started on the right foot.

How This Book Is Organized

We wrote this book in five parts:

Part 1, Your Financial Foundation, discusses how a good foundation can be your start to a successful financial future. Understanding what kind of bank accounts you need and getting a handle on your income and expenses helps you get an overview of your finances and learn to manage them with confidence.

In **Part 2, Building Your Credit,** we discuss credit cards and how to use them properly. What you do with your credit card or cards can be helpful or detrimental to your future credit score. Using your card responsibly and paying off your debt each month helps your credit score and makes it easier for you to borrow money in the future. Fixing your credit once it's been damaged can be very difficult, so it's important to build good credit from the beginning.

If you're saddled with student loans, you're by no means alone. Paying back all that debt can put a lot of pressure on your budget and make it difficult to think about saving. **Part 3, Paying Off Your Student Loans and Debt,** shares some strategies you can employ to pay less on your loans and have some money left over to pay off credit cards or start your emergency fund.

Hopefully you've found a good-paying job that offers benefits. The job market is improving, but many people still find themselves in jobs for which they're overqualified and not making as much money as they would like. If you're in that position or are unemployed, **Part 4, Your Money and Your Career,** gives you some tips for stretching your paycheck or using your unemployment benefits wisely.

Starting to save money when you're young can help ensure your financial comfort and stability for the future. As you learn in **Part 5, Your Savings,** even small savings can add up when they're invested wisely and have time to grow. To get your money working for you, you'll need to know the best kinds of accounts for saving and ways you might invest your money.

Throughout your life, it will be necessary for you to spend money—sometimes a lot of money. **Part 6, Big-Ticket Purchases,** is where to turn if you're planning to buy a new car or a house in the future. In these chapters, you learn what you should be starting to think now and also discover the best ways to accomplish your goals. And once you've made a major investment, you'll need insurance to protect it.

As we discuss in **Part 7, Relationships and Money,** your financial situation is tied to your personal situation in many ways, and your life circumstances affect your financial circumstances. Being single has different financial implications from being married and having children. It's important to understand how your financial situation changes along with your relationships and learn how to keep your money safe and working for your future.

Retirement probably seems like a different lifetime at this point, but the years pass quickly and it's important that you start thinking now about your future, as we cover in **Part 8, Looking to Your Future.** Investing money now in an employer-sponsored 401(k) plan or individual retirement account (IRA) gives your money time to grow and provide a comfortable retirement.

At the back of the book, we've included a glossary of terms, a list of further resources you can use to continue your financial education, and some other helpful forms and worksheets.

Extras

Throughout the book, you'll find sidebars that provide additional information. Here's what to look for:

DEFINITION

The language of personal finance can be a bit daunting. These sidebars give you clear explanations of some of the financial jargon you'll encounter.

DOLLARS AND SENSE

These tips offer practical information and suggestions to keep you in control of your personal finances.

MONEY PIT

Be sure to read these cautionary notes. They could keep you from making some common mistakes regarding your personal finances.

POCKET CHANGE

These snippets of information on a variety of topics give you something to talk about at your next cocktail party.

Acknowledgments

We would like to thank the many people who provided time, information, and resources for this book. Especially, we thank our editors at Alpha Books and Gene Brissie of James Peter Associates.

Your Financial Foundation

If you're just starting to get a handle on your finances, you need to start with the basics. That means taking a look at what you've got and figuring out how to make what money you have work for you by setting up the right kinds of bank accounts. You also need to start thinking about how much you spend and determine how to make your money cover everything you need.

Part 1 helps you establish a firm financial foundation upon which you can build for your future.

Your Financial Base

So you want to learn more about personal finance? That's a good thing! Your relationship with money begins when you're very young, and it's important to develop and practice good financial habits throughout your life.

If you've graduated from college or gotten a job and are just starting out, it's an exciting time in your life. It's also a time when it's really important to be smart with your money. Getting a good financial start will make your life a lot easier later on. Getting off on the wrong foot financially could result in real problems for your future, such as a poor credit score or uncontrolled debt.

In This Chapter

- Personal finance and your financial future
- Getting real about your financial position
- Learning what you're worth financially
- You might have more than you think!
- Taking care of your financial base

Understanding Personal Finance

What is *personal finance,* exactly? Simply put, it's every aspect of your life that deals with money. Personal finance is everything from buying a Netflix subscription, to finding an affordable apartment, to leasing a car, to putting money into a retirement plan. Your personal finances affect your relationships, your lifestyle, and especially your financial future.

> **DEFINITION**
>
> **Personal finance** is all about you and your money. The emphasis of the phrase is definitely on the word *personal.*

How well you accomplish your personal financial goals determines where and how you'll live, and eventually it will influence where your kids go to school and the quality of your retirement.

To understand personal finance as it relates to you, you need to first have an understanding of your financial base. Your financial base includes your income, which, incidentally, includes more than your salary. Any bank accounts you have; investments such as a 401(k); and stuff you own, like a car or personal property, are included, too. Your financial base also is based on what you owe, such as student and/or credit card debt, rent, or a monthly car payment. Getting a handle on your financial base is necessary so you can figure out how to live within your means and start saving money for your future.

Evaluating Where You Are

The economy has improved dramatically since the Great Recession, but its effects have lingered and are still being felt. The stock market remains uncertain, people who ordinarily would have retired are still working to recoup losses they experienced, and many people—especially young people—are still looking for jobs.

Maybe you graduated from college and didn't have any trouble landing a high-paying job as an engineer or computer systems analyst. But if that's not the case and you either aren't employed or you are working in a job you're overqualified for, try not to be too discouraged.

Although the national unemployment rate at the beginning of 2016 was at its lowest level since 2008 and jobs were being added every month, younger workers were disproportionately unemployed and underemployed. Forty percent of all unemployed Americans were in the 18 to 25 age group, meaning 4.6 million young people were without jobs. Among those who were working, many were earning less than $25,000 a year.

If this situation sounds too familiar, hang in there. Keep looking (you'll read some tips for landing a job in Chapter 11), and don't give up. If you're living at home, as nearly 40 percent of women and almost 50 percent of men between the ages of 18 and 34 were in 2015, you have the advantage of relatively low expenses. If you're working and living at home, you have a great opportunity to save some money. If you're already living on your own, you need to figure out how to handle all your expenses and start saving for your future.

A major concern for many millennials—the age group that in 2016 is between about 18 and 34—is student debt. If you're among the 70 percent of college graduates with student debt, you have to figure out a strategy for repaying those loans.

And your college loans might not be the only money you owe. If you have a credit card, it's likely that your average annual percentage rate hovers somewhere around 21.4 percent, according to a study of the top 50 banks by Magnify Money (magnifymoney.com). You'll learn a lot about dealing with credit cards and debt in Parts 2 and 3. For now, we'll simply advise you to keep your debt as low as possible and manage your debt payments.

 POCKET CHANGE

According to the Pew Research Center, people between the ages of 18 and 34 are, or will soon become, the largest living generation in the United States, overtaking the aging baby boomers.

Regardless of your current financial situation, it's important to be realistic about what you have and what you owe. Consider your income—or lack of thereof, if that's the case. Think about the expenses you have and how you're managing them. Take a look at how much you owe and how long it will take you to get out of debt. When you combine all those factors, you can determine your net worth.

Determining Your Net Worth

If you've got a job, you're probably bringing home a paycheck. Very few people show up at the office every morning just because they love to be there (interns excepted). The paycheck at the end of the week or every 2 weeks might not be the only thing you like about your job, but it's probably pretty high on the list.

Even if your salary isn't what you'd like it to be, it's likely to still be your primary source of income. When you begin to consider your *net worth,* or your financial situation, your salary is very important. For most of us, the salary pays the bills, boosts savings accounts, and sets up emergency funds.

DEFINITION

Your **net worth** is what you get when you add up all your financial assets and then subtract all your financial liabilities.

When you examine your financial situation, however, you might be pleasantly surprised to find out you have more than you realize. You could have overlooked some money, for example.

To determine your net worth, you have to know exactly what you have and exactly what your expenses are. After you've thought carefully about any and all funds you might have in the form of savings, bonds, mutual funds, or whatever, take a minute to fill out the following net worth worksheet (using the value of the asset as of the valuation date). A lot of the included categories won't apply to you, but some will. It should help you to get a better understanding of exactly what you have and what you're worth.

Assets

Assets	Value
Bonds	
Cash accounts	
Certificates of deposit	
Mutual funds	
Savings bonds	
Stocks	
Tax refunds	
Treasury bills	
Cash value life insurance	
Assets Subtotal:	
Personal Property	**Value**
Businesses	
Cars	
Personal property	
Personal Property Subtotal:	

Real Estate	Value
Mortgages owned	
Residences	
Income properties	
Vacation homes	
Real Estate Subtotal:	
Retirement	**Value**
Annuities	
IRAs	
Pensions	
Retirement Subtotal:	

Liabilities

Current Liabilities	Value
Alimony	
Child support	
Personal loans	
Current Liabilities Subtotal:	
Installment Liabilities	**Value**
Bank loans	
Car loans	
College loans	
Credit card bills	
Furniture loans	
Home improvement costs	
Life insurance loans	
Pension plan loans	
Installment Liabilities Subtotal:	

continues

Liabilities (continued)

Real Estate Liabilities	Value
Residences (include second mortgage/line of credit)	
Income properties	
Vacation homes	
Real Estate Liabilities Subtotal:	
Taxes	**Value**
Capital gains tax	
Income tax	
Property tax	
Taxes Subtotal:	
Other Liabilities	**Value**
Other Liabilities Subtotal:	
Total Assets:	
Total Liabilities (subtract from assets):	
Total Net Worth:	

Think carefully about what you might have. Were any savings accounts set up for you when you were a kid? What about savings bonds? Some families are great at buying U.S. savings bonds for birthdays. Have you put aside money someplace for emergencies? Do you have money saved for a car or a house?

 DOLLARS AND SENSE

According to the U.S. Bureau of Public Debt, $14 billion worth of unclaimed savings bonds are sitting in government accounts. It's estimated that 55 million Americans own these bonds. If you think you may have been given savings bonds but aren't sure, you can check by entering your Social Security number on this U.S. Treasury Department website at treasurydirect.gov/indiv/tools/tools_treasuryhunt.htm.

If you have any bonds or savings accounts on which you're earning interest, the interest on them counts as income. Your income tax refund, bonuses, and any monetary gifts you receive also count as assets and must be included when you're considering what you have. If you have a cash value life insurance policy, the amount of cash value is counted toward your net worth. (Read more about cash value life insurance in Chapter 19.) Generally, though, when we talk about income, we're primarily talking about your salary.

Looking for Hidden Financial Assets

Most people start working pretty much from the ground up when it comes to accruing money. When you first start out on your own, it usually isn't very hard to figure out what you have. Sometimes, though, you might overlook money you've accumulated or that other people have accumulated for you. Hardly anybody has a long-lost rich uncle who dies and leaves behind a fortune, but many people do have well-meaning relatives who try to help them along by setting up bank accounts or buying bonds in their name. Consider whether you may have any of the following assets. If you do, they'll affect your net worth.

Accounts

Relatives often set up bank accounts in a child's name, which, for one reason or another, sometimes get forgotten and overlooked. Or maybe you have some money left over in a 529 college savings plan.

Mutual Funds

Mutual funds, including stock funds, bond funds, hybrid funds, U.S. funds, money market funds, and so forth, should be included when calculating your net worth. If you get statements from a company such as The Vanguard Group, Charles Schwab Corporation, Jack White and Company, or Fidelity Investments, you have mutual funds to consider.

 DEFINITION

> **Mutual funds** enable you to pool your money with that of a large group of investors. Professionals invest the pool of money in stocks, bonds, and other securities, and you own shares that represent the investments.

Stocks (Equities)

Some families give shares of certain stock, such as Disney or Apple, to kids to introduce them to the stock market or as gifts.

Bonds

Bonds sometimes are given as contest prizes, birthday presents, or as part of scholarship packages in schools. If you know of any bonds you have, or think you might have, track them down and include them in the "what you have" category of your personal finances.

Emergency Money

Financial experts recommend keeping an emergency fund of 3 to 6 months' salary to use if you lost your job, got sick and couldn't work, or faced any other emergency circumstances. If you have emergency money, it should be included among your assets. If you don't have any set aside, you should start building that fund.

After you've carefully considered all your sources of income and other financial assets, add them up and determine what you have. Only when you've fully explored what you have will you have a better idea of how you might address your wants and needs, as discussed in the next chapter.

> **DOLLARS AND SENSE**
>
> As you take inventory of what you have, using an app that helps determine net worth can make tracking and tallying your assets easier.

Protecting Your Financial Base

If you're financially strapped at the moment, consider it a temporary situation and focus on the future. If you have a job and are making enough money to support yourself, you're off to a great start. Sure, there will be things you'd like to have but can't afford right now, but that's okay. Keep telling yourself you'll be in better financial shape next year, and enjoy the experience of being out on your own.

To stay on the right financial track, remember these three things:

- Resist the temptation to use credit cards to buy what you want but can't afford. You'll get yourself in trouble if you do this and end up with less money in the future. Be patient, and know that eventually you'll have more buying power.

- Be aware of financial opportunities, and take advantage of them when they're available.

- Save even small amounts of money, starting as early as you can, to yield larger results for your future. Putting away even $10 a week gives you nearly $500 saved at the end of a year. If you invest that amount of money each year beginning in your 20s, you'll be surprised at the amount of money you'll have when you reach your 50s or 60s.

Many people miss chances to improve their financial positions because they simply don't know what's available to help them do so. By reading this book, you've shown that you're interested in your personal finances and are willing to take the initiative to learn how to get—and keep—your finances healthy. The sooner you start making the most of your money, the more money you'll have later.

We look closer at the following areas of financial opportunity later in the book, but it's important that you know what opportunities to look for.

401(k) Plans

We get into more detail about these little gold mines in Chapter 21, but suffice it to say, 401(k)s are a great way to save money. If you're eligible to participate at work, be sure you do. Individual retirement accounts (IRAs), Roth IRAs, and other retirement plans also are good vehicles for saving.

Compound Interest

Starting to save even a little money when you're young will pay off big time after a few years. The longer your money is invested, the faster it grows. That's called *compounding*, and it's a great way to see your money grow. We cover this more in Chapter 13.

Lower Interest Rates

If you're paying 18 or 20 percent interest on your credit card, you might be able to get a significantly lower rate just by shopping around and asking. A couple points can make a big difference. Check out Chapter 5 for more on credit cards.

The Best Possible Bank Accounts

If you're paying big bucks in bank fees, you're not making the most of your money. It takes some work, but it's worth it to look around and compare what's available. We get into this in more detail in Chapter 2.

A Budget

Most people wouldn't consider a budget a financial opportunity, but it definitely is. Preparing and using a budget gives you a chance to see where your money goes and offers an opportunity to cut back and save. We explore budgets in Chapter 3.

Learning Opportunities

A wealth of financial information is available for anyone willing to take the time to find and study it. The internet is full of smart websites and financial blogs offering information and advice, and free personal financial planning websites abound online. Apps are available to help you save, invest, bank, and shop, too. Many of the most informative resources are mentioned throughout this book, and Appendix B lists additional ones you can check out.

If you resist credit card debt and take advantage of financial opportunities, you'll be taking a giant step toward your financial goals. Ask for help if you're confused about a financial matter. Many issues concerning money, investments, and so on can be complex, even to people who study them on a daily basis, so don't be discouraged if some financial issues seem baffling at first. They'll become clearer as you learn more.

If you seek advice from a friend or family member, you're likely to hear what's worked best for them. What worked best for them, however, might not be what will work best for you. Nobody wants to sound like a complete idiot, so you're likely to hear about the great financial move your brother made when he started his first job, while he completely skips over the bonehead deal he made when buying a car.

MONEY PIT

Be sure you take all the financial advice you get with a large grain of salt. If you follow the advice of every financial guru who comes along, promising on one talk show or another to quadruple your investment in 6 months or less, you're likely to end up losing some serious money along the way.

The Least You Need to Know

- Personal finance affects nearly every aspect of your life.
- Regardless of your financial situation, it's important to be realistic about what you have and what you owe.
- Your net worth is all your financial assets minus all your financial liabilities.
- When you think and research carefully, you might discover you have overlooked some financial assets.
- There are important steps you can take to stay on track financially.

CHAPTER 2

Choosing the Right Bank Accounts

If you've been on your own for any length of time, either at college or living on your own and working, you've probably had some association with a bank or credit union. It used to be that people chose their bank based mostly on convenience and availability. Plenty of automated teller machines (ATMs) or branch offices made it easy to take care of business and made a bank attractive to prospective customers, even those who do most of their banking online.

Surveys show that these days, however, younger clients are being more discerning about choosing banks. They're passing by the big regional and national banks and looking for local institutions they believe will be more attentive to their needs, charge lower fees for services, and offer plenty of access to ATMs.

In This Chapter

- Shopping around for the best bank bargains
- Comparing banks and credit unions
- Taking advantage of online banking
- Balancing interest rates with bank fees
- Cutting ATM costs

Professional services company Accenture PLC reported that in 2014, community banks saw a 5 percent increase in customers ages 18 to 34, while big regional and national banks lost 16 percent of customers in the same age group. Business at credit unions increased by 3 percent.

The fact that younger customers are studying their options and being deliberate when choosing banks is good news. Let's review what customers are looking for and how banking institutions differ.

Do You Have the Accounts You Need?

Chances are pretty good you already have savings and checking accounts. You've probably been keeping some money in a checking account to pay for things such as books, rent, the cable bill, your car payment, and any other bills that come along. Money in checking accounts used to be accessed by paper checks, but they've mostly been replaced by *debit cards* and credit cards.

> **DEFINITION**
>
> **Debit cards** give you the convenience of a credit card without the debt because the money used to pay for purchases comes out of your checking account—money already available to you. An ATM card may or may not be a debit card. An ATM card accesses your account through an ATM; a debit card accesses your account from almost anywhere.

It's possible you've managed to get through life so far *without* checking and savings accounts. If that's the case, it's time to get them established. If you already have these accounts, take a good look at them to see if you're getting the best deal you can.

Checking Accounts

The concept of a checking account is simple. You keep money in an account and use a debit card, or write a check, to access money from the account instead of paying with cash. This eliminates the need to carry large amounts of cash or send cash through the mail to pay bills in the event you aren't set up for online payments.

Finding a checking account that makes sense for you isn't quite as easy as getting on a bank's website and filling out a form or two. You'll need to do some research to ensure you get an account that won't charge a lot of fees yet offers the most advantages. Remember, banks are competing for customers, so they're willing to offer some perks to get your business. Don't forget, however, to look at the flip side and consider all the fees and conditions you'll have to pay when you open an account.

DOLLARS AND SENSE

There's still a place for paper checks, but more and more bank customers—especially younger ones—are using mobile deposit and photo bill payment apps. A mobile deposit app enables you to scan the front and back of your check and send it to your bank electronically as a deposit. With a photo bill payment app, you can scan a paper bill and transmit the image to your bank, which generates an electronic payment from your account.

In today's competitive banking environment, you can find a checking account that doesn't come with monthly maintenance fees and surcharges. That's more likely to happen if you're willing to go with a community bank or credit union instead of a major bank.

If you're sold on big banks and not willing to change, be prepared to pay a fee, as only 38 percent of checking accounts at larger banks are free, according to Bankrate. However, 72 percent of credit unions offer free checking, and many smaller banks and credit unions even offer rewards checking accounts if you meet certain conditions.

To get those rewards, you might have to agree to use your debit card a certain number of times a month or have your paycheck directly deposited into your account. Or you might have to agree to online banking or maintaining a minimum balance.

In exchange, many banks offer interest on checking accounts or rewards such as free overdraft protection, travel miles, or a small rebate on your debit purchases.

Although these are conditions that might be daunting to older customers, most millennials already do direct deposit, bank online, and use their debit cards. So be sure to look for free checking, and compare the perks that might accompany it.

POCKET CHANGE

One checking rewards program that's getting a lot of buzz is the Kasasa checking account, offered by hundreds of community banks and credit unions across the country. Depending on the participating institution, a Kasasa account offers 2, 3, or even 4 percent interest on checking accounts up to $10,000. Or you can get cash rebates on debit card purchases or other perks. Find out more at kasasa.com.

While you're looking for free checking or a rewards programs, however, also remember to check into any fees associated with the account. Even if you're not being charged any monthly maintenance fees, you still could be looking at fees for ATM transactions, overdrafts, and so forth.

Here are some common checking account fees to be aware of:

- **Minimum balance fees**   If you're sure you can maintain the required balance, this isn't a problem. If you have doubts, keep looking.

- **ATM fees**   More about these in a bit, but if you're a frequent ATM user and your bank is an ATM wasteland, think about a change.

- **Overdraft charges**   These can be killers, so be sure to keep track of what you have and what you spend. Download a budgeting app, or see if your bank offers an automatic alert when your balance falls below a certain level to avoid incurring this charge.

- **Lost card fees**   If your debit card is lost or stolen, you'll likely be charged for a new one.

- **Hard-copy statement fees**   This probably isn't an issue, but if for some reason your statements aren't available online, you could be charged for the printouts.

- **Account closing fees**   Your bank wants to keep your business and may charge you if you close your account. Ask about this when you're considering opening an account.

- **Foreign transaction charges**   If you travel abroad frequently, be sure to talk to someone at your bank about these fees and how you can minimize them.

If you're just getting a checking account set up or are looking to find a new bank, be sure to get a complete listing of all account fees and regulations, and take the time to read it carefully. Compare the information with that from other institutions, too, because there may be significant differences. If you come across rules you don't understand, ask someone to explain them to you. Also inquire about fees, minimum balances, interest rates, overdraft protection, and anything else you can think of that might be helpful to know.

 DOLLARS AND SENSE

If your employer offers direct deposit of your paycheck, consider taking advantage of it. Some banks offer perks for signing up for direct deposit, including waived fees on checking accounts and direct deposit signing bonuses. Direct deposit usually results in you getting your paycheck sooner, too.

After you've opened a checking account, or changed your account to a bank that offers a better deal, there are a few other things to keep in mind.

One simple but important rule is to keep your checkbook and debit card in a safe place and report the loss or theft of either immediately. Federal law limits liability for a lost or stolen bank debit card if you report the loss to your bank or credit union within 2 days. If you do that, the most fraudulent charges you can be responsible for is $50. If you don't report the lost card within 2 days of it going missing, you'll be liable for $500 of fraudulent charges. And if you really slack off and don't report the loss for more than 60 days after you get your next statement, you're responsible for *all* charges.

You also must keep track of how much money you have in your account to avoid overdraft fees. At the beginning of 2016, the average overdraft fee was $34. A couple of those fees a month can take a big chunk out of a paycheck.

An easy way to avoid these fees is to download your bank's mobile app. The app allows you to log in to your account from anywhere, so you can check your account balance, transfer funds, track transactions, and keep an eye out for suspicious activity wherever you are.

If your bank doesn't offer a mobile app, check out some of the free apps you can download such as these:

- Balance (cwakamo.com/balance)

- Mint (mint.com)

- Checkbook (appxy.com/checkbook)

If you write checks, be sure to keep a record of the check number, amount, and to whom it was written. This is important in the event your landlord claims he didn't receive your rent payment, for example.

Also, always review your statement each month and confirm all deposits, ATM transactions, and withdrawals. If you notice something that doesn't look right, call your bank right away. Banks do make mistakes, and they're not always in your favor.

 **MONEY PIT**

Gone are the days when you could wait until the end of the month to review your bank statements. With hacking and security breaches at an all-time high, it's important to check your accounts frequently. If you find suspicious activity in one of your accounts, notify your bank immediately.

When deciding on the checking account that's best for you, ask yourself some questions:

- Will my paycheck be deposited directly into my checking account?

- How will I keep track of my transactions and balances?

- Will I be writing any checks or paying all my bills online?

- Do I want to know that I can walk into a branch and ask someone for help, or will I handle my checking account online?

Savings Accounts

Many of the same points covered in the "Checking Accounts" section apply when you're looking to open a savings account, too. You need to figure out your savings habits and find a bank that offers a deal that will best suit you.

Most banks charge a monthly or quarterly maintenance fee unless you meet certain criteria, and some might tack on an additional fee if your balance falls below a required minimum. In addition, you might be required to keep a savings account active for a specified time or face penalties.

When you're looking for a place to set up your account, review the list of questions suggested in the earlier "Checking Accounts" section, and ask if those apply to savings accounts, too.

You also need to ask a few other questions specifically geared toward savings accounts:

- Does the bank use a *tiered account system?*

- Will I be penalized if I close the account before a certain time?

- Is the account federally insured?

- How much interest will I get on my savings?

 DEFINITION

With a **tiered account system,** you earn higher interest if your account balance is consistently over a certain amount set by the bank, usually at least $1,000 but many times higher. Generally, it's better to have your money somewhere other than in a savings account if you have a large amount.

Back in the day, banks were required to pay 5 percent interest on savings accounts—something practically unthinkable today. That required interest ended with banking deregulation in 1986. At the beginning of 2016, the national average for interest banks pay on savings accounts is 0.26 percent, according to MyBankTracker, an independent resource that lets consumers compare banks.

That being said, however, it pays to shop around because the amount of interest varies significantly from bank to bank. Some banks were offering 0.01 percent interest on savings in February 2016, but others came in as high as 1 percent with no minimum deposit. Check out MyBankTracker (mybanktracker.com) for a comparison of rates.

Money Market Accounts

Money market accounts (MMAs), a type of savings account, generally pay higher interest than regular savings accounts. You can write a minimum number of checks (usually three) on the account each month. As with checking accounts, some online banks are offering relatively high interest rates on MMAs.

If you write only a couple checks a month, a money market account might be worth considering. But there's usually a hefty fee if you write more than the number of checks permitted, and the bank may require a higher minimum balance than with a savings account. Any additional interest is quickly chewed up if you have to pay for extra checks or a low-balance fee. You learn more about these accounts in Chapter 13

Certificates of Deposit

If your savings account balance becomes substantial—that is, if it contains more money than you think you'll need anytime really soon—consider putting some of it in a certificate of deposit (CD). With a CD, you deposit money for a specified amount of time, usually from 3 months to a number of years. The longer you leave your money in the account, the more interest you should get on it.

Interest rates on CDs generally are higher than those on savings and money market accounts, but there's usually a penalty if you need to get the money out of the account before the agreed-upon time.

Although variable (changeable) rate CDs are available, CD rates are usually set for the term of the certificate, unlike money market rates, which are changeable at any time. More information about CDs is included in Chapter 13.

All Banks Are Not Created Equal

Take a look around your local area sometime, and notice the difference in the brick-and-mortar financial institutions. You'll probably find quite a few, ranging in size from something as large as the Bank of America to a small local bank or credit union. And then there are online banks, which provide services exclusively via the internet.

Traditionally, there were three types of financial institutions:

- Banks

- Credit unions

- Thrifts, or savings and loans

Let's take a quick look at the similarities and differences of these.

Commercial Banks

Also known as full-service banks, commercial banks are the most widely used financial institutions in the United States, with about 5,440 in operation. There used to be a lot more commercial banks, but for a variety of reasons—including mergers, failures, and a steep decline in the number of new banks—the number has dropped significantly.

Commercial banks are permitted to take deposits, loan money, and provide other banking services. They can have either a federal or state charter and are regulated accordingly.

The size of commercial banks varies greatly, from huge mega-banks to small community banks.

 POCKET CHANGE

The U.S. banking system is federally operated, but it has 50 state jurisdictions, each with its own regulatory and operating procedures. The name of a bank can help you figure out whether it's state or federally regulated. If it's federally regulated, its name will include *National* or *N.A.*

Credit Unions

With more than 100 million members, credit unions have been growing in popularity in recent years. They offer many of the same services as commercial banks—checking accounts, savings accounts, vacation clubs, ATM services, mobile apps, and online banking. Credit unions generally can offer better rates on loans and savings because as not-for-profit organizations, they don't pay federal taxes.

It used to be that only people with a common occupation, association, or geographical area could form and join credit unions. These days, however, practically everyone can join a credit union in one capacity or another.

Before joining a credit union, be sure it's federally insured. Federally insured credit unions are insured by the National Credit Union Share Insurance Fund, which is backed by U.S. government. Those that are not federally insured may not have government backing.

Thrifts

Thrifts are the financial institutions commonly known as savings and loans (S&Ls). S&Ls took a hit in the late 1980s, when many of them failed and had to be bailed out by Uncle Sam (that is, taxpayer dollars). Legislative changes that followed improved the quality of thrifts, making them good options for depositors once again.

 DEFINITION

Thrifts is the collective name for savings banks and savings and loans associations. They generally accept deposits from and extend credit primarily to individuals.

S&Ls were developed for the purpose of providing loans to residential customers, meaning their business line is designed to meet the needs of local customers. A relatively small number of S&Ls still operate, as their numbers have greatly declined, but today they're run pretty much like any other bank.

Regardless of the type of institution you choose, be sure to do your homework. Look into its history, and check its financial soundness by using Bankrate's "Safe and Sound" calculator at bankrate.com/rates/safe-sound/bank-ratings-search.aspx.

If you ever get into a situation in which you believe your bank has treated you unfairly or is not conducting business properly, you can contact the Federal Reserve System's Consumer Help site. Find out more at federalreserveconsumerhelp.gov.

Banking Online Versus Online Banking

As with many other aspects of business and society, the banking world has changed dramatically due to technology. Most people perform at least some of their banking online, with more and more leaning toward mobile banking.

Technology makes it possible—and very easy—to make deposits, pay bills, transfer money from one account (or person) to another, and perform other tasks, and fewer people are venturing out to visit their banks. Banking analysts predict this will mean fewer bank branches in the future, and those that remain will be smaller with fewer tellers.

Today, most people conduct at least some of their banking online—paying bills, transferring money, depositing checks, taking care of other tasks, etc.—with a computer, tablet, or smartphone.

Using your bank's mobile app to bank online, however, is not the same as being a customer of an online bank.

Online banks, nearly all of which are backed by the Federal Deposit Insurance Corporation (FDIC), operate exclusively via the internet. No brick-and-mortar branches exist.

If your bank is an online bank, you can't swing through the drive-thru to pick up some cash or stop by a branch to ask the teller a question or sign a form. And not having to maintain that drive-thru or lobby, or pay a lot of tellers to help you with that question or form, saves online banks a serious amount of money.

Because of that, online banks can afford to pay higher interest rates to their customers, and that makes them very appealing. It's not unusual for online banks to pay upward of 1 percent interest on savings accounts, which is far better than many traditional banks can offer.

Lower costs for the banks also can translate into lower fees for you—another benefit. And most online banks offer free ATM use and other perks. In addition, you don't have to think about waiting in line at a branch, shuffling through paper statements, or having your branch close for the day before you can deposit your check.

DOLLARS AND SENSE

As with any bank, it's important to do your research and choose the online bank that best meets your needs.

Here are some highly rated online banks for 2016:

- Ally Bank (ally.com)

- Nationwide Bank (nationwide.com)

- Discover Bank (discover.com)

- Connexus Credit Union (connexuscu.org)

- First Internet Bank of Indiana (firstib.com)

No matter how you decide to conduct your banking, interest rates probably will be a factor in deciding what financial institution you choose. These days, interest rates are pretty much low across the board, although you'll probably find higher rates with a virtual bank. Still, you should look around and see where you can get the most interest on your money. Even a fraction of a percentage point adds up over time. And as you get more money, it makes even more of a difference.

Beware of Bank Fees

It used to be that most of the profits financial institutions realized came from the spread between the interest they'd pay on deposits and the interest they charged on loans. But now, more than half of the average bank's earnings is generated from fees.

Overdraft Fees

Overdraft fees are the biggest money-makers for banks, representing about 60 percent of all fees charged. Banks claim they need to charge high fees because their revenue from savings, checking, and other deposit accounts has been shrinking due to increased regulations and lost interest due to years of low mortgage rates. Many banks, however, make huge profits by letting customers spend more than what they have in their checking accounts and then charging them up to $40 in penalty for doing so.

The Consumer Financial Protection Bureau (CFPB) has taken banks to task for overdraft and other fees, but it doesn't appear that banks will be backing down.

ATM Fees

ATM fees are another big source of revenues for banks. Every time you use an ATM that isn't part of your bank's network, you pay an average fee of $4.35. Part of that fee goes to your bank, and part goes to the owner of the ATM.

ATMs were first introduced in the late 1960s and became increasingly popular over the decades that followed. Today, you can find them anywhere you might need some cash: restaurants, bars, coffee shops, department stores, movie theaters, gas stations, etc.

As convenient as ATMs can be, they can be expensive. Some cynics have stated that, considering the fees levied at cash machines, *ATM* should not stand for "automated *teller* machine," but "automated *theft* machine." Think about it. If you use an out-of-network ATM twice a week at even $4 a transaction, in a year, you will have paid more than $200 just to access your own money.

MONEY PIT

If you live in Atlanta, you have the distinction of having to pay the highest ATM fees in the country—$5.15 per transaction.

You can minimize or avoid those high fees in several ways. MyBankTracker's (mybanktracker. com) mobile app can help you locate in-network ATMs wherever you are. You also can get cash back in many retail stores, as well as at most U.S. Post Office branches.

If you have to withdraw money at an ATM, think ahead and get enough so you won't be back in a day or two. It doesn't make sense to pay $4 to get $30 out of your checking account. Also limit your visits to the ATM to avoid excessive fees.

Or consider opening a no-ATM-fee checking account at an online bank such as Schwab Bank (schwab.com) or Ally Bank (ally.com). Both offer free checking accounts with unlimited ATM fee reimbursements. Opening one of these accounts doesn't mean you have to give up your current checking account. You can use the no-ATM-fee account when an in-network ATM is not available.

The best thing to do concerning fees is to go to your bank and get a copy of its fee disclosure statement. If you're a customer at an online bank, you should be able to find an explanation of all fees online. Look it over carefully, and see how many of the fees apply to you. If it seems like too many, you might want to think about finding a new bank.

The Least You Need to Know

- Understanding your options in financial institutions helps you make a good choice when deciding where to put your money.
- You've got to know the questions to ask when trying to find the best checking and savings accounts.
- Interest rates on checking and savings accounts aren't much to talk about these days, but it's important to find the best rates you can, which actually may be from online banks.
- Online banks have joined the traditional banks, credit unions, and thrifts (savings and loans) as consumer options for financial institutions.
- Being aware and smart can help you avoid some hefty bank fees.

CHAPTER 3

Budgeting Your Living Costs

The good news, according to T. Rowe Price's 2015 Retirement Saving and Spending Study, is that the majority of millennials pay attention to how much they spend and are concerned about budgeting their money—more so than their baby boomer counterparts. The bad news is that boomers didn't set the bar all that high, and millennials still could be doing better regarding spending and saving.

The need for budgeting is rarely a popular topic. Mention the word *budget* when you're with a group of people, and you're likely to hear a collective groan. Used as either a noun or a verb, the B word is not a favorite in most people's vocabularies. Making a budget or sticking to one probably ranks right up there with going to the dentist or buying a new transmission for your car.

In This Chapter

* Why nobody likes a budget
* Accepting that a budget is the way to go
* Knowing what to include in your budget
* Deciding whether you need to earn more or spend less
* Staying on budget with websites and apps

Most people understand the need to figure out how much money they have and how they'll spend it, yet they remain reluctant to work out a budget and commit to sticking to it. Why is that? Businesses use budgets. Schools use budgets. Governments use budgets (or at least claim to). It's clear that budgets are sensible, necessary things to have. We'll even go a step further and say budgets are desirable because they keep us out of trouble, if used properly.

Why Budgets Have Such a Bad Rep

A *budget* is simply a schedule of income and expenses. It's a way of keeping track of the money you earn and planning how you spend it. See, that's not so bad, is it?

> **DEFINITION**
>
> A **budget** is a schedule of income and expenses, usually broken into monthly intervals and covering a 1-year period.

If budgets are sensible, necessary, and even desirable, why do they have such a bad reputation? The reason is that making a budget, or working within one, implies having to use restraint or, worse yet, having to do without. As a society, restraint and denial are things we have a lot of trouble dealing with.

As mentioned previously, marketers and advertisers have been bombarding you since you were old enough to understand them, telling you what you want and what you need. And although many millennials seem to be less enamored with stuff than those of other generations, that doesn't mean it's not easy to spend more money than you should, especially if you see something you like and have a couple credit cards in your wallet.

Working within a budget at the very least holds you accountable for what you earn and what you spend. A good budget tells you to the dollar how much you can spend on things such as food, restaurants, clothes, makeup, drinks with friends, movies, and more.

And although it sometimes will be difficult to stick to a budget, in the long run, it's the smartest thing you can do.

Everybody Needs a Budget

To avoid the traps so many people fall into—too much debt, too little savings, too much spending—you've got to have a budget. A budget helps you live within your means while also saving for your long-term goals.

It takes a little time to set up a good budget that's comfortable for you to use, but it's well worth it to get a clear picture of your financial situation. You can use the sample budget we've included in the next section, or adapt it for your own purposes, but know that there's no one way to set up a perfect budget. It depends on your needs and how detailed you want your budget to be.

 POCKET CHANGE

About 1.5 million Americans file for bankruptcy each year, according to U.S. bankruptcy court statistics. Among those filings, almost 97 percent are made by individuals, not businesses. The most-cited reasons for filing include medical expenses, job loss, credit card debt, divorce, and reduced income.

What Your Budget Should Include

You can start your budget simply by identifying spending categories and listing all the money you spend in each category each month, either estimated or exact. Try to include everything you spend money on, right down to toothpaste and coffee.

Chances are you'll use an app or budget software to track your income and expenses, but take a look at the following sample budget worksheet. It can help you think about your categories of spending and see just where your money goes. Feel free to revise it to best suit your needs.

Once you've gotten all the numbers in front of you, you can start working with an app that lets you manage a budget from your smartphone.

Sample Budget Worksheet

Housing	Estimated Cost	Amount/Worth
Mortgage/rent		
Phone		
Cable		
Internet		
Electric		
Utilities		
Heat		
Furniture		
Appliances		
Maintenance		
Housing Subtotal:		
Transportation	Estimated Cost	Amount/Worth
Gas/maintenance		
Tolls		
License/taxes		
Public transportation, taxis, car services		
Transportation Subtotal:		
Taxes	Estimated Cost	Amount/Worth
Federal		
State		
Local		
Social Security		
Luxury		
Taxes Subtotal:		

Debt	Estimated Cost	Amount/Worth
Credit card		
Car loans		
Student loans		
Personal loans		
Line of credit		
Debt Subtotal:		
Entertainment	**Estimated Cost**	**Amount/Worth**
Movies, concerts, theater, etc.		
Vacations		
Hobbies		
Pets		
Magazines and books		
Streaming services		
Restaurants		
Entertainment Subtotal:		
Personal	**Estimated Cost**	**Amount/Worth**
Food		
Gifts		
Clothes		
Shoes		
Jewelry		
Dry cleaning/laundry		
Hair/makeup		
Health club		
Other		
Personal Subtotal:		

continues

Sample Budget Worksheet   (continued)

Health Care	Estimated Cost	Amount/Worth
Copayments		
Prescriptions		
Doctor visits (including eye doctors)		
Dental visits		
Health Care Subtotal:		
Insurance	**Estimated Cost**	**Amount/Worth**
Car		
Home/renter's		
Disability		
Life		
Health		
Insurance Subtotal:		
Children	**Estimated Cost**	**Amount/Worth**
Day care		
Babysitters		
Toys		
Clothes		
Children	**Estimated Cost**	**Amount/Worth**
Other		
Children Subtotal:		
Charity	**Estimated Cost**	**Amount/Worth**
Donations		
Charity Subtotal:		
Total:		

Nonroutine Expenses

Although certain things, such as your rent, groceries, and clothes, will be obvious expenditures as you start preparing your budget, be sure you include a category of less-obvious expenses. Christmas or Hanukkah gifts, the birthday party you want to give your boyfriend in May, the $100 you contributed to the Red Cross to aid hurricane disaster victims, and wedding and baby gifts are all known as *nonroutine expenses*. They aren't exactly unexpected—sure, Christmas and Hanukkah do roll around every year—but they're not expenditures that come up each month, so you're more apt to overlook them.

> **DEFINITION**
>
> **Nonroutine expenses** are expenditures often overlooked because you don't have to pay them regularly.

Car repairs also are nonroutine expenses. If you don't budget for them, they can be devastating financial news. It's hard to anticipate when your muffler is going to fall off onto the highway, but when it does, you must have some money budgeted for a new one.

Or what if you've budgeted money for routine dental checkups but learn during one of those checkups that you have a loose filling in your back tooth that needs to be replaced? A little procedure like that could set you back more than $200 and wreck your monthly budget.

The best way to anticipate nonroutine expenses is to figure out all you've had in the past year. Include car repair bills, big gifts, unexpected medical bills, the weekend at the ski resort that came up unexpectedly, and any others you can think of. Add the cost of all those things, and divide the total by 12. That's how much you should set aside each month for nonroutine expenses.

Routine Expenses

The first items to list are known as *routine expenses*. You'll need to have the following in your budget:

> **DEFINITION**
>
> **Routine expenses** include the more obvious expenditures such as rent, insurance, food, and entertainment.

Housing   Your rent or mortgage makes up the biggest chunk of your housing expenses, but don't forget the other things you pay for, too. How about your utilities bill, and the sofa and loveseat you bought? Consider the set of dishes you got at IKEA and the washer and dryer. How about your cable, phone, and internet bills? If you're paying costs for upkeep, such as having the carpets cleaned, windows washed, or painting done, be sure to include that, too.

Debt   This is probably another big expense category, unless you've been very frugal or very lucky. Include in the debt category everything for which you owe money: your student loans, your car, your credit cards, and so on. Do you have a line of credit opened anywhere? What about personal loans? If your dad loaned you $1,500 for a security deposit and the first month's rent on your apartment, include that in your debt category. Include both principal and interest payments.

Insurance   Include any insurance you pay for in this category: auto, health (don't forget your copayment if you're partially insured by your employer), renter's, and so on.

Taxes   If you don't own property, you probably don't pay many taxes other than sales taxes and those deducted from your paycheck. If you do own property, you'll need to include your local property taxes, even if you put money in escrow and your mortgage company makes the payment for you. Also include the taxes deducted from your paycheck: federal, state, Social Security, occupational privilege, and any others.

Transportation   If you don't own a car, your expenses in this category will be what you spend on public transportation, taxis, and car services. If you own a car, include routine maintenance costs such as oil changes and what you spend on gas and car insurance. Don't forget the expenses for your license and car registration. If you pay tolls regularly when driving, include those, too.

Health care   Hopefully, these costs are minimal. But don't forget to budget for dental costs if your insurance doesn't cover them, as well as eye exams, glasses, prescriptions, and routine doctor visits.

Entertainment and vacations   If you're like most people in their 20s and 30s, this category contains considerable expenses. Be sure you include everything because unfortunately this is one of the first areas we look to when cutting costs. This category covers a variety of expenses such as vacations; restaurants (even fast food); and the cost of drinks if you go to bars, clubs, or coffeehouses. Think about movies, concerts, museums, cover charges, and any costs associated with your hobbies (golf, bowling, skiing, or whatever).

Don't forget pet costs; magazines and books; video rentals; the money you spend on streaming services for music, video, and books; and any other expenses related to entertainment. Don't forget the money you spend in the office football pool and on the trip to the casino.

Be honest when you list expenses in this category. Many people don't realize how much money they spend on entertainment until they sit down and add it all up.

Personal   This category includes food; clothing; shoes; jewelry; laundry and dry-cleaning costs; your health club fees; all fitness expenses; and money spent on hair stylists, manicures, makeup, and toiletries.

Children   If you have kids, you already know they're expensive. If you don't have kids but plan to someday, it doesn't hurt to know what costs are involved. Include expenses incurred for babysitters and day care, toys, clothes, food, diapers, and shoes.

Giving   List money you contribute to your church, synagogue, or charities.

After you've listed your expenses, tally them. Think about any categories you might have to add that aren't listed here, and don't forget to include the nonroutine expenses mentioned earlier.

 DOLLARS AND SENSE

When you put together a budget, you can set aside your savings in one of two ways. Either include the money you'll save each month in your routine expenses, or deduct it from your income before you start making your budget. Paying yourself first pays off greatly down the road.

Trimming the Fat: Analyzing Your Expenses

You already have your expenses organized into spending categories, so you now can break them down further into *fixed expenses* and *variable expenses*, and *nondiscretionary expenses* and *discretionary expenses*. When you have all your expenses categorized, it'll be easier to see how you can control your budget. Analyzing different ratios within your budget also helps you determine where you should be cutting back your expenses.

 DEFINITION

You can break down your expenses into **fixed expenses,** such as rent and car payments, and **variable expenses,** such as food and entertainment. These categories can be further broken down into **nondiscretionary expenses,** which are things you can't do without such as food and rent, and **discretionary expenses,** which you *can* do without like vacations and entertainment.

Fixed Versus Variable Expenses

Some of your expenses are fixed, and others are variable. Fixed expenses include the following:

- Rent

- Car payments

- Any other payments that don't vary in amount such as dues or club membership fees

- Your mortgage, if you have one

These expenses might be necessary, like rent or mortgage payments, but they often can be scaled down. If your rent is more than you can afford, you might have to move to a smaller place or get a roommate. Or perhaps you could refinance your mortgage for a lower interest rate. (Be sure to consider the expenses involved in refinancing before deciding to go ahead.) You might really like the club you've joined, but if the membership fees are too high, you may have to consider dropping out. And don't forget the varying expenses of car ownership (see Chapter 15).

Variable expenses include the following:

- Food

- Utilities

- Entertainment

- Vacations

It's probably easier to cut back on variable expenses such as these than on fixed expenses. Utilities can be adjusted to save money, and you can pass up the pricey lobster tails and eat more affordable chicken instead.

Nondiscretionary Versus Discretionary Expenses

After you break down your expenses into variable or fixed, you can add another category: nondiscretionary or discretionary.

Nondiscretionary expenses are things you must pay for or buy, including the following:

- Food

- Rent or mortgage

- Car payments

- Utilities

Nondiscretionary expenses can't be avoided, but you might be able to control them, as discussed earlier.

Discretionary expenses, on the other hand, are those that aren't necessary, including the following:

- Vacations

- Entertainment

- Club memberships

These expenses are the most obvious ones to curtail if you're trying to cut back on expenses. Now you can organize your expenses by how they fit into both sets of categories.

Expenses

Fixed, Nondiscretionary	Variable, Nondiscretionary	Fixed, Discretionary	Variable, Discretionary
Rent/mortgage	Food	Club dues	Vacations
Car payments	Utilities	Membership fees	Entertainment

Basically, there are two ways to use this information to save money: you can control your discretionary expenses (skip the vacation this year, for example), or limit your nondiscretionary expenses (maybe find a roommate or move into a smaller apartment).

Spending Ratios

When it comes to figuring out where you need to cut expenses, *spending ratios* are useful tools. A spending ratio is simply the percentage of money, as it relates to your gross income, you use for a particular area, such as housing or entertainment. If one area of expense becomes too great, you'll see that ratio is too high and begin to cut back.

To figure out your housing payment ratio, which is one kind of spending ratio, add up all your housing costs (rent or mortgage, insurance, property taxes, and so on), and compare that number to your total income. If your housing costs are more than 28 percent of your gross income, you're paying too much for housing and should look for ways to cut your costs.

To calculate your total debt ratio, add all your monthly payments (car, credit cards, rent, and so on), and compare that number to your total income. If it's more than 36 percent of your income, these expenses are too high and you should look for ways to cut them.

Finally, you can figure out your *savings ratio,* which is the percentage of your gross income you save. Compare the amount of money you save each week or month to your income for that period. Aim for 8 percent a year. If you're not saving that much, you should look for ways to cut expenses and save more.

> **DEFINITION**
>
> **Spending ratios** are used to determine the amount of your gross income that goes toward a particular expenditure area. They can be used as tools in cutting expenses. Your **savings ratio** is the opposite of your spending ratio. It is the percentage of your gross income you're able to save within a given time.

There are other ratios, too, but these are good ones to start with. Don't get too hung up on these ratios. If your housing costs are 29 or 30 percent instead of 28 percent, you don't have to immediately sublet your apartment and move back home with Mom and Dad. But if you find your ratio is up to 35 or 40 percent, you ought to think about downsizing.

One Job, Two Jobs, Three Jobs, Four …

After you've figured out how much you're spending, you'll know exactly how much money you need to pay for that spending. You'll also have a clear picture of what you spend your money on.

Take a good, hard look at how you're doing. If you're able to meet all your expenses, make regular payments on student loans and any other debt you have, save a portion of your income, and have some money left over for discretionary purposes, good for you! You're in good financial shape.

If, however, you're spending everything you earn and not saving anything, or if you're spending *more* than you earn, you've got to change your ways. If you have credit card debt that never gets paid off, if you're having trouble keeping up with student loans, or you're in over your head with car loans or other debt, your financial condition is shaky.

There are two ways to handle this situation: you can either spend less or earn more. Those who are in a real financial bind may very well need to do both of those things. For many people, it's easier to change their mind-set and cut down their spending, and that usually makes the most sense. Some hard-core spenders, however, would rather try to earn more than spend less.

If you fall into the hard-core spender category and you don't see a big raise in your future anytime soon, you need to figure out a way to get more money. You can play the lottery every night, but statistically, your chances of getting ahead that way are pretty slim. You can hope for a big inheritance or some other windfall, but you'll probably wait a long, long time. If you can't cut down on spending, you'll need to get another job. There's no getting around it.

POCKET CHANGE

It's a bitter pill to swallow, but American workers have been working harder and earning less for years. The U.S. Bureau of Labor Statistics reported that real output per person increased nearly 2.5 percent per year between 2000 and 2011 while incomes fell. When adjusted for inflation, incomes in 2014 were about $2,100 lower than when President Barack Obama took office in 2009 and $3,600 lower than when President George W. Bush was sworn in in 2001.

You'd probably be much better off if you cut your spending rather than get another job to pay for it, but working two jobs is better than racking up big debt with no way to pay for it. Many people take a second job when they're trying to earn money for a specific expense, such as a wedding or college tuition. That's fine, as long as they're careful to put the extra money in savings so they'll have it when the expense occurs. It's easy to lose sight of a long-term goal when you suddenly have extra money to spend.

If you do decide to take a second job, consider carefully what it will do to your life. What activities would you have to give up? How much less time would you have to spend with family and friends? Keep in mind, too, that many relationships have failed because one person becomes unavailable or unapproachable when he or she works too much. When working becomes (or appears to become) more important than the relationship, you can bet there will be trouble. It's a personal decision, but being able to buy a lot of things is less than ideal if you don't have time to enjoy them.

MONEY PIT

If you think you need a second job, look carefully at what you'll make and the possible expenses you'll incur because of the job. If you'll be earning $12 an hour on a second job but spending more money on transportation costs and clothes for the job, and eating dinner out every night because you're too tired or don't have time to make something at home, it just might not be worth your time and effort.

Sticking with It

After you have your budget prepared, you need to keep track of how you're doing compared to the budget. Many people have drafted great budgets only to give up on them after a few months. But your spending habits aren't the same every month, so you need to keep track of your expenses for several years to get an accurate picture of what you're spending over the long term. An app that's easy to use and lets you link all your accounts in a centralized place can help you track what you spend over time.

Many people who neglect to budget for nonroutine expenses get discouraged and quit using their budgets when they're hit with a car repair or other major expense. That's why it's important to include money for those types of expenses when you first draft your budget.

If you slip up one month and overspend, don't be too hard on yourself, and don't give up on the budget. It's like when you're trying to lose some weight. Just because you overeat one day doesn't mean you should quit the diet and eat whatever you want the next day, too. Go back to the plan, and you'll reach your goals.

Budgeting Websites

Websites that offer advice on setting up budgets and handling other financial matters are plentiful. Check out the following sites to start.

America Saves (americasaves.org)   America Saves provides tips for savings and resources to help you prepare a budget, along with the stories of people who have committed to and succeeded at saving more.

Dollarbird (dollarbird.co)   Dollarbird employs a calendar-view approach that lets you easily see how much you spend and on what every day of the month.

Bankrate (bankrate.com)   Bankrate offers much useful information. Its budgeting calculator, for example, helps you start your own budget and provides lots of tips and suggestions. You can access it at bankrate.com/calculators/smart-spending/home-budget-plan-calculator.aspx.

Budgeting Apps

Many good apps can help you with your budget. Here are some highly rated free apps for 2016.

Personal Capital (personalcapital.com)   Personal Capital lets you link all your accounts in a centralized place and has some valuable tools that help you easily see where your money is and better understand cash flow. You can use it with your iPhone, iPad, or computer.

Level Money (levelmoney.com)   Easy to use, Level Money shows you how much money you've got available for the month, week, and even day. You can use it on an iPhone or Android phone.

Mint (mint.com)   Mint's app lets you use your iPhone, Android, or Windows phone to link to and track all activity on bank, credit card, loan, and investments accounts. You also can set up alerts for bills that come due and create a budget with detailed categories.

LearnVest (learnvest.com)   In addition to budgeting tools, LearnVest gives you access to information relevant to your personal finances.

BillGuard (billguard.com)   BillGuard automatically tracks your spending without you having to enter expenditures. It also notifies you of any suspicious activity with your accounts.

Regardless of what tools you use, the most important ingredients of successful budgeting are a willingness to make a budget and to stick to it after it's made.

 DOLLARS AND SENSE

> Keep all your receipts, either as paper copies or digitally. This lets you see everything you've purchased at the end of the month and holds you accountable if you overspend.

The Least You Need to Know

- Most people don't like to think about budgeting, much less do it, but you can and should.
- After you have a handle on what you have and what you need, you can assess your financial condition.
- If your earnings aren't greater than your expenditures, you've got to earn more or spend less.
- If you're tempted to take a second job to earn more money so you can spend more, consider cutting expenses instead.
- Regardless of what budgeting tools you use, you should have a budget to know exactly how you spend your money and how you're implementing your plan.

Building Your Credit

In Part 2, we explore the topic of credit and provide you with smart strategies for establishing and building your credit. You also learn how to establish good credit when you're young, discover what a credit score is and why it's so important, and explore how to get the best credit card rates.

It's pretty certain that you're aware of the increasing challenges of protecting your credit card from fraud and keeping your account and information safe. We give you some ideas on how that can be done and some tools that can help you.

CHAPTER 4

Your Credit History, Report, and Score

Many people don't realize their credit history is carefully documented in a credit report—which, by the way, usually contains some very personal and specific information.

So let's start at the beginning and see exactly what a credit history is, how you build it, and what it's used for. Then you'll be able to understand why it's so important and how it can affect many areas of your life.

In This Chapter

- Why you need a credit history
- Avoiding problems with credit and debt
- Getting help for and fixing credit and debt problems
- Understanding your credit report and score

Building Your Credit History

When you applied for your first credit card (probably back in high school or college), your name and a lot of personal information were entered into a computer, and your *credit history* began. Since then, every time you applied for another credit card or a store card, took a vacation loan from your bank or credit union, or applied for a car loan, information was added to your *credit report*.

Your credit history is the record of everything pertaining to any credit you've ever had or applied for, all summarized in your credit report, which lists your *credit score*.

> **DEFINITION**
>
> Your **credit history** is a record of all the credit you've ever had or applied for. Details of your credit history are documented extensively in a **credit report.** Your **credit score** is a number based on data in your credit report and represents your overall creditworthiness.

If you want to borrow money for a car, a house, a vacation, debt consolidation, college, or a business, you'll need credit. If you go to a bank to borrow money and have no history of ever having any credit, you don't stand a good chance of getting the loan. The bank will be reluctant to take a chance on you because it has no indication of whether you'll pay back the money or default on the loan.

Credit cards used to be issued freely to nearly anyone who wanted one, but card issuers have become much more selective in recent years. Due to high rates of student debt, more stringent industry regulations, and other factors, many millennials who apply for credit cards are denied—something that actually can end up hurting their credit scores.

Of those who do have cards, they tend to use them hard, often maxing out their limits, which can result in higher interest rates. All these factors can create a difficult situation if you're trying to establish a credit history.

In the next chapter, you learn about identifying and scoring a credit card or two that fits your lifestyle and financial situation. Even though many millennials seem to have complicated relationships with credit cards, you'll need to have at least one in order to establish a credit history.

After all, that old car you've had since your freshman year isn't going to last forever. And there may be a time when you'd like to trade in your apartment for your own house, or maybe even start your own business.

POCKET CHANGE

> NerdWallet, a personal financial information site that provides online credit card comparison tools, reports that many people in their 20s and 30s—about 30 percent— have never even had a credit card. That would have been unheard of a generation or two back, when getting a credit card was considered a rite of passage.

Fortunately, it's not that hard to establish a credit history. If you can get a credit card, you will build a history. The trick is to develop and maintain a healthy one.

When Enough Is Enough

When you have a credit card and have been using it and making on-time payments for a while, it's easier to get more cards. For some people, that can lead to serious problems because they can't avoid the temptation to spend and get in over their heads with debt.

If you can't keep up with the payments on all your cards, your credit history will show you as high risk. When you go to apply for loans, you won't be regarded as a good candidate, and you'll have unnecessarily put your credit rating in jeopardy. Having too many open lines of credit (credit cards) also can be harmful to you when you apply for a loan. Lenders want to feel secure that your debt is under control—that you are managing your finances responsibly.

You're much more likely to be approved for a loan if you have a good record of paying off debt on a few credit cards, or even one card, than you would after you've been bogged down with a dozen cards that got away from you. Keep in control of your credit cards and your debt, and be sure your payments are on time. Know when enough is enough, and establish a good, responsible record of repaying debt.

When to Get Help

Some people get so far into debt trouble it's extremely difficult to fix, and it negatively affects their credit score for years and years. If you think you're having trouble managing your debt, it's very important to acknowledge the problem early and take immediate steps to fix it.

Overspending has serious consequences and can be a true addiction, just like drinking or gambling. If you think you can't stop spending, and you're incurring more debt than you can handle, get some help.

You can contact Debtors Anonymous at debtorsanonymous.org or seek help from a counselor who specializes in financial recovery. Some work for nonprofit organizations, and their services can be obtained at no cost. Check online for local listings.

Your All-Important Credit Score

All the information about you and your credit history is evaluated and used to determine your credit score—a very powerful predictor of your future bill-paying ability.

The best-known and most widely used score is the FICO score, which is based on a system developed by Fair Isaac Corporation. The mathematical equation used to calculate your score takes into account 22 pieces of data from your credit report, and the resulting number identifies you either as a low-risk or high-risk candidate for a lender.

Why Your Score Matters

A potential lender looks at your credit report and your credit score when deciding whether or not to give you a loan. The lower your score, the less likely it is you'll be offered a loan. If you are offered one, it undoubtedly will come with a higher interest rate or more restrictive terms.

 DOLLARS AND SENSE

> Increasingly, employers are checking out the credit reports of prospective employees before hiring. It's standard practice in some job areas, such as the defense, banking, financial, and medical fields, but other employers also are engaging in the practice. If you're turned down for the job because of something in the report, you're required, under federal law, to be notified of your right to get a copy of the report at no charge.

FICO scores are regarded as providing the best guides to future risk based solely on credit report data. The scale ranges from 300 (the lowest) to 850 (the highest). Lenders look most favorably to those whose scores are 740 or higher. The general rule of thumb is that the higher your score, the less risk you pose to a lender. Historically, people with high FICO scores have repaid loans and credit cards more consistently than people with low FICO scores. Although there's no single "cutoff score" used by all lenders, it's important to know and understand your score.

Your credit score has quite an effect on the interest rates available to you when you want to borrow money. An example of mortgage rates available for different FICO score averages are shown in the following table.

FICO Score	Mortgage Rate
760 to 850	5.92%
700 to 759	6.142%
680 to 699	6.319%
660 to 679	6.533%
640 to 659	6.963%
620 to 639	7.509%
600 to 619	9.224%
580 to 599	9.679%
550 to 579	10.275%
500 to 549	10.612%

With many younger people saddled with significant college debt and credit still fairly tight, mortgages and other loans recently available to those with credit scores below 640 won't be as readily available in the future. Therefore, it's very important to maintain good credit or improve your credit score if necessary.

You can work to improve your score by paying off credit cards, getting rid of excess cards and using only one or two, and paying all your bills by the due date. Over time, your credit score should increase.

How Your FICO Score Is Determined

Your credit rating is calculated by compiling information in five categories:

- Your payment history constitutes 35 percent of the rating. One or two late payments won't make a difference in your score, but a pattern of late payments will.

- The duration of your credit history counts for 15 percent of the rating.

- The amount of new credit counts for 10 percent, so watch how many credit cards you sign up for.

- The types of credit you've used (think home equity as compared to an uncollaterized loan) factor in for 10 percent.

- The debt you have counts for 30 percent.

Income is not a factor in determining FICO scores.

Usually, the FICO score is given with four reason codes, in order from the strongest negative reason to impact your score, the second strongest factor, and so on. It's important to understand how you scored, so be sure to review your credit report at least once a year and especially before making a large purchase, like a house or a car. If your score isn't what you'd like it to be, work to improve your score.

Several major factors can affect your credit score:

Your level of revolving debt   This is one of the most important factors considered for the FICO score. Even if you pay off your credit cards each month, your credit card may show the last billing statement in relation to your total available credit on revolving charges. If you think your FICO score should be higher, work to pay down your revolving account balances.

Shifting balances   Don't shift your credit card balances from one card to another to make it appear that you're being diligent about paying off debt. And don't open new revolving accounts. These tactics won't improve your credit score.

The length of time your accounts have been established   This can hurt you when you're first starting out, but consumers with longer credit histories tend to be lower risk than those with shorter credit histories.

Too many accounts with balances   Too many credit card accounts with balances is a dangerous sign that you won't be able to make that many payments should your employment status change.

Too many credit inquiries within the last 12 months   Borrowers who are seeking several new credit accounts are riskier than persons who aren't seeking credit, although these have only a small impact on your FICO score. Inquiries have much less impact than late payments, the amount you owe, and the length of time you've used credit.

Your personal credit report includes information such as your name, Social Security number, date of birth, your address from the time you first got a credit card until now, everywhere you've worked during that time, and how you pay your bills. Whenever you apply for a loan or for credit, the place at which you applied will check out your report with a credit agency. In turn, it will give the credit agency any additional information it's picked up on you.

> **POCKET CHANGE**
>
> Each of the top three credit agencies, Equifax, TransUnion, and Experian, probably
> has the same information about you and your credit history. They get it from banks,
> finance companies, credit card suppliers, department stores, mail-order companies,
> and various other places that have had the pleasure of doing business with you.
> Smaller, regional credit bureaus supplement the information.

The Fair Credit Reporting Act limits who can see your credit report. Of course, the list is pretty long, but it does set some guidelines. Your credit report can be released by a reporting agency under the following circumstances:

- In response to a court order or a federal grand jury subpoena
- To anyone to whom you've given written permission
- To anyone considering you for credit or collection of an account
- To anyone who will use the report for insurance purposes
- To determine your eligibility for a government license or benefits
- To anyone with a legitimate business need for the report in connection with a business transaction with which you're involved (This includes your landlord when you apply to rent an apartment as well as the cell phone and utility companies.)

When you realize how often your credit report can be accessed, you can begin to see how important it is that you keep it clean. But even if your credit record is perfect, your report might not be, and that could affect your credit score. With so much credit information floating around out there, it's easy for mistakes to be made with that information. Human error is a big factor, and somebody who misreads some information about you can mess up your credit report royally. A study showed that one out of four people who took the time to thoroughly review their credit reports discovered a mistake that eventually was corrected.

You're going to learn more about why it's important to keep an eye on your credit report and exactly how to go about getting a copy of it.

> **POCKET CHANGE**
>
> Be aware that every time an inquiry is made for your credit report, it's automatically
> logged into your report. Although this isn't necessarily bad, numerous inquiries may
> need to be explained to a potential lender.

Getting a Copy of Your Credit Report

Even if you don't plan to apply for a car loan, mortgage, or credit card anytime soon, it's a good idea to take a look at your credit report once a year. You can get a copy of your report from Annual Credit Report (annualcreditreport.com), which summarizes your credit reports from each of the three largest credit bureaus:

- Equifax Credit Services (equifax.com)

- TransUnion Credit Information Services, Consumer Disclosure Center (transunion.com)

- Experian (experian.com)

You can get the report for free, but you'll have to pay a fee if you want to know your FICO score. Unless you've experienced credit problems, there's no need to get your score every year; the report will suffice.

> **DOLLARS AND SENSE**
>
> Experts recommend you read your credit report carefully about once a year, especially before you apply for credit or when you know the credit report will be checked (as when you rent an apartment). This is the only way to be sure no mistakes have been made that will damage your credit record.

You also can get your credit report by contacting any of the three credit agencies. When requesting your credit report from any of these agencies, be prepared to provide your name, address, Social Security number, and maybe your date of birth as identification.

When you receive your report, look it over carefully. If you discover a mistake, contact all three credit agencies by certified mail, inform them of the mistake you've discovered, and request that they investigate. If you don't get a reply within 60 days, send another letter. Remind the companies that they are required by law to investigate incorrect information or provide an updated credit report with the incorrect information removed. With financial breeches and identity theft at an all-time high, you need to be vigilant and scrutinize your report for anything that doesn't look right.

> **DOLLARS AND SENSE**
>
> You have a legal right to submit a letter up to 100 words long to the credit agency, disputing something you've discovered on your credit report. The letter must be included in your file. If you do this, be sure your letter is clear, concise, and to the point.

If you see information you don't like on your credit report that, unfortunately, isn't a mistake, don't despair. The Fair Credit Reporting Act mandates that negative information on your report be removed after a certain period of time. Even if you declare bankruptcy, that information is supposed to be removed from your report after 10 years. The trick, of course, is keeping your credit report healthy and in good shape. In this case, preventive maintenance works best.

The Least You Need to Know

- It pays to be aware of your credit history because it affects so many areas of your life.
- Despite how you feel about credit cards, you'll need one or more to establish a credit history for your future.
- It's not how much credit you have, but how you handle it, that affects your credit history.
- Recognizing credit and debt problems early and getting help if you need it can stop the situation from getting out of control.
- You should know what your credit report contains, how you can get a copy of it, and ways to correct mistakes when necessary.

CHAPTER 5

Finding the Best Credit Cards

More than 1 billion credit cards of every kind are in circulation in the United States, with more than 75 percent of all Americans holding at least one. Credit cards come in all flavors, with some offering far better rates and user advantages than others. Although credit cards are convenient and necessary for building a credit history, they have been the downfall of many who overspend and find themselves unable to pay their credit card bills.

In this chapter, we look at how to get the card (or cards) that make the most sense for you, ways to avoid the fee trap, and how to be sure you can pay off your monthly balance.

In This Chapter

- Finding the card right for you
- Getting a low- or no-fee card
- Watching out for unwanted fees
- Understanding credit card interest rates
- Paying your balance

The Invention of Credit Cards

Although the idea of buying on credit had been around for a while, credit cards really got their start during the 1960s, at the tail end of the great baby boom. Bank of America introduced the first bank credit card, BankAmericard, in 1966, and consumers liked the concept. Americans were soon charging up a storm, and a new and vibrant industry was underway. After the baby boomer market had been saturated, credit card companies began targeting young people during the 1980s, trying to get them signed up for cards. Many have opinions about what the best age is for someone to get that first card, but even high school students who have just turned 18 are, in many cases, able to obtain a credit card.

Unlike now, however, in the early days of credit cards, nearly everyone paid off their balances each month. It was considered almost a disgrace to owe on a credit card. Cards were fun and convenient, but the balance on them was rarely carried over. Somewhere along the line, the stigma of owing money on credit cards lessened and eventually disappeared. Today, it's estimated that about 44 percent of American households that have credit cards hold balances.

Getting a Card

Chances are, one of these days you'll need to get a credit card, if you haven't already. And you probably should have one. Credit cards often are necessary, as mentioned earlier. Some banks won't even let you open an account if you don't have a credit card, and, as you learned in Chapter 4, it's important that you acquire credit in your name for use later on.

If you don't have a card, you can find applications at your local bank, if you use one. Or you can apply online for a card from a bank such as one of these:

- Bank of America (bankofamerica.com)

- Wells Fargo (wellsfargo.com)

- Citibank (citicards.com)

- Capital One (capitalone.com)

- Chase (chase.com)

If you're looking for a card, a site like NerdWallet (nerdwallet.com) or CreditCards.com (creditcards.com) can help you search for and find the card that best fits your needs. Criteria for "best card" varies depending on your circumstances, and these sites provide good information about fees, interest rates, and the like.

Normally, if you have no credit history but are at least 18 years old with a job and steady income, you'll be able to get a card with a limited credit amount, usually $500 to $1,000. Your chances of getting a credit card increase if you apply for a card through a bank with which you have an account. If you don't have a job, but you have a parent who is willing to be a cosigner or guarantor (see the next section), you can still get a credit card.

MONEY PIT

We know people who will spend hours, even days, shopping around for bargains. They'll never buy anything that's not on sale, yet they'll let their credit card debt accumulate and pay 13, 15, 18, or an even higher percent interest on it. Even if they find a bargain purchase, they'll still lose money by having to pay those high interest rates on their credit cards.

If you're diligent with your payments, you'll probably be able to have your credit limit upped after 6 to 12 months. The amount of the increase depends on your income or your ability to repay the line of credit.

Cosigners and Secured Cards

If you have no credit history and your earnings are low, or if you already have a bad credit history, you might not be able to get a card in your name alone. You might need to apply for a secured card or get someone to act as a *cosigner*. A cosigner, or a *guarantor*, is someone who agrees to assume responsibility if you can't, or don't, pay off your credit card debt.

If you need a guarantor to get a credit card, the person must be an adult with a good credit history. Usually, a parent takes this role, although it could be someone else, depending on the circumstances. Both you and the other person whose name appears on the card account are responsible for missed payments and overspending.

A secured card or credit account requires a deposit that serves as *collateral*. The deposit is equal to the amount of credit allowed on the card. For example, if you got a card with a $500 credit limit, you'd have to make a $500 deposit so the bank already has your money if you default on your debt. Other fees often are charged to open a secured account, although as more companies begin to offer these types of cards, some are dropping the fees to get an edge on the competition. Most do have an annual fee.

> **DEFINITION**
>
> A **cosigner** or **guarantor** is someone who assumes responsibility if you can't pay off credit card debt. **Collateral** is something of value put up as security for a loan to ensure that the lender won't lose the money loaned.

Some companies pay you a bit of interest on your deposit, but don't expect it to be very high. You, on the other hand, will pay up to 20 percent interest on unpaid balances because your credit risk is considered higher than someone's with a regular card. But if you want a card and want to begin a credit history, a secured card might be the way you'll need to go. If you have an account with a bank or credit union, that's a good place to start your search.

If you do get a secured card, be sure you find out when your account can be converted to a standard account. At that point, you should get your full deposit back, provided you've made timely payments and don't owe any money on your credit card.

Here are some secured cards with good reputations:

- Capital One Secured MasterCard (capitalone.com)
- Discover It Secured Credit Card (discover.com)
- OpenSky Secured Visa Credit Card (openskycc.com)
- Wells Fargo Secured Visa Card (wellsfargo.com)

A big word of warning here: be very wary of companies that offer credit cards, either secured or unsecured, at fabulous rates or to people who haven't been able to get a card. A rapidly growing number of unscrupulous companies are targeting people with poor or nonexistent credit ratings who can't get approved for credit cards through traditional issuers. The internet is full of offers for people who previously couldn't get cards. Some of these offers are pretty unbelievable and should be avoided.

> **MONEY PIT**
>
> The old saying, "If it sounds too good to be true, it probably is," definitely applies to credit card ads. You can get yourself into a lot of trouble if you make the mistake of dealing with a disreputable company. Many of the cards have "initial balances" (really substantial fees) on which you pay interest with very minimal monthly payments.

How Many Cards Should You Have?

After you get one credit card, it's easier to get more. In fact, you might find that you'll be getting offers from a number of credit card companies that would be happy to have your business. And some people do want and need a variety of cards, perhaps using one for business, one for personal expenses, one for internet purchases, etc. Unless there's a good reason that you need more than one or two credit cards, however, resist the temptation to open more, no matter how appealing the reward offers or rates might seem.

There's no reason to have a separate card for every department store, gas station, and electronics store in town. Having multiple cards in your wallet merely encourages you to use them and run up more debt. Nearly all retailers that accept credit cards take Visa and MasterCard. It's a lot easier to keep track of one credit limit (or two, if you really feel you need a backup) than a dozen cards from all over the place.

Types of Cards

You're likely to see many different kinds of credit cards. Let's look at some of the distinctions so you know what's what.

Charge Cards

These aren't really credit cards because you're required to pay off your balance at the end of each billing period. Charge cards are good because you have no interest charges, but they may come with an annual fee, and if you charge more than you can pay all at once when the bill comes, you'll be assessed a late fee.

Fixed-Rate Cards

These credit cards have a fixed interest rate, which is more comfortable for some people than a variable rate.

You should be aware, however, that all fixed-rate cards reserve the right to raise their rates from time to time, often with as little as a 15-day written notice. Rates on a fixed card won't vary as much as those on a variable-rate card, but they do fluctuate from time to time.

Variable-Rate Cards

The interest rate on these cards changes periodically based on the rate charged by the lending institution holding the card. The card is tied to an index—normally the Prime Rate. When the Prime Rate is raised, the interest rate on the card rises as well.

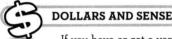

DOLLARS AND SENSE

If you have or get a variable-rate card, keep a close eye on your statements and any information you get from the credit card company so you're aware of when the rate changes.

Elite Cards

These status cards, often called Gold, Titanium, or Black cards, offer some advantages such as buyer protection plans or cash back after you spend a certain (high) amount. They also can offer perks like emergency roadside service, airport club access, hard-to-get reservations in popular restaurants, and insurance on newly purchased merchandise. These cards often have high credit limits, but they usually carry high annual fees.

Elite cards generally are available only to people with established credit reports and high credit scores.

Rewards Cards

An increasing number of credit card companies are offering rewards cards that give you something back. You might get cash back (as with a Discover Card), airline miles, a rebate on gas, rental car or hotel discounts, discounted shopping at particular stores, and more. Credit card companies do this to be competitive.

The more you charge to the credit card, the bigger your reward. However, there's usually a fee involved with getting one of these cards, so think carefully about whether it's a worthwhile venture.

DOLLARS AND SENSE

Some people use rewards cards to pay for almost every single thing they buy—from college tuitions to groceries. If you decide to go this route, be sure you're able to pay off your balance so you don't end up paying interest fees and cancel out the benefits of your rewards.

Prepaid Cards

Another way to avoid credit card debt, or to obtain a credit card if you're having trouble doing so for some reason, is to use a prepaid card. A *prepaid credit card* is just what its name implies—you pay up front and then use the card until you've spent the money. At that point, you need to put more money into your prepaid account or the card won't work.

The advantage of prepaid cards is that you never incur interest fees because you've already paid for your card purchases. Disadvantages, however, are that you often must pay a fee to set up an account and each time you "load" your card. And of course, you need to have money available to get a prepaid card.

Still, prepaid credit cards are useful for people who can't get a traditional card or are working hard to avoid high credit card interest fees. A site such as CreditCards.com can help you learn more about these cards and how to apply for them.

Understanding Annual Fees

There are as many credit cards deals as there are cards, and if you're going to be using one or more cards, it will be worth your while to shop around for the best deal you can find. Credit cards can cost you money, make no mistake about it. But there are ways to minimize those costs.

Intense competition among card companies has forced most of them to lower, or even drop, their *annual fees*. Only one in four credit cards came with an annual fee in 2015, and some credit card providers will waive the fee if you agree to make a certain number of purchases a month or other conditions.

DEFINITION

An **annual fee** is a charge you pay to the bank or credit card company for the privilege of holding its card.

Annual fees vary tremendously, so be sure to pay attention to what you're paying. CreditCards.com conducted a recent survey of 108 credit cards and found that 28 of them came with an annual fee. The median cost of the annual fee was $50, with fees ranging from $18 to $500 for a status card.

At your stage of life, it's unlikely that there's a good reason for you to have a status card, so you shouldn't incur a high cost for an annual fee. Ideally, get a card that does not require a yearly payment.

If your credit record is good and you're paying an annual fee on your credit card, it won't hurt to request that the fee be waived. It's better to ask and have your request denied than to be paying the fee unnecessarily.

Other Fees to Watch For

In addition to an annual fee, your credit card company probably has tacked on some additional costs. The average credit card comes with 6 fees, and some have as many as 12. Following are some other fees to look for on your own credit card, or when you're checking out an offer for a card.

Late Fees

You'll be charged a fee if your payment is late. That's in addition to the interest charges you'll incur for not paying off your balance by a specified time. Most but not all card companies charge a late fee, so be sure you find out when you apply for the card.

Cash Advance Fees

These are nasty fees, and because they are, you should try to never take a cash advance. When you borrow cash against your credit card, most cards forget about the grace period and start charging you interest right away.

About 50 percent of card companies charge you 2 to 6 percent more interest on a cash advance than on other charges not paid off by the end of the billing period. There's also usually a one-time fee of between 2 and 5 percent for each cash advance.

Discretionary Fees

These fees, imposed on you to pay for things such as credit life insurance or a shopping service you never ordered, are at the discretion of the card company, not you.

 **MONEY PIT**

Always read your bill carefully, and don't pay for anything you didn't order.

Credit Limit Increase Fees

It's not common, but some credit card companies charge you as much as $50 to increase your credit limit. Sometimes it's even more if the company increases your limit because you charged over your previous credit limit.

Copy Fees

In this age of digital everything, some credit card companies charge you for a paper copy of your statement. This is an easy cost to avoid if you opt for paperless billing and use the credit card company's website.

Account Reopening Fees

If you close your account and decide to reopen it, you could be charged for the privilege.

One-Time Processing Fees

These are fees you need to pay before you're allowed to use your card. They're not common, but some cards require you to pay nearly $100.

Be sure you read each bill carefully when you get it, and look for any charges you can't account for. If you feel you've been charged for something you didn't agree to in advance, by all means pick up the phone and talk with someone in customer service. The intense competition among credit card issuers is forcing them to be responsive to consumers' needs and complaints. Be sure you take advantage of it!

Making Sense of Interest

Credit card companies make money when you have to pay *interest* on your account balance. If you pay off your balance every month, you don't have to pay interest, which is a very good thing, especially if your interest rate is high. If you have a balance, however, you'll be charged a certain percentage of interest on it.

 DEFINITION

Interest is the fee the bank charges you to use its money to finance what you buy with your credit card.

When you get a credit card, it will come with an APR, or annual percentage rate of interest. The average APR on credit card interest at the end of 2015 was about 15 percent, but some rates can be as high as 29 percent. That can mean some hefty fees if you carry a balance.

Let's say you charge a new area rug for your living room for $300. The store where you got the rug collects its money from the bank that issued your credit card. The bank, in turn, gets its money back from you along with interest if you don't pay back the $300 within a specified time. You usually have a grace period, or a certain amount of time to pay off your purchases before you start getting charged interest. Be sure you know what the grace period on your card is. Card companies aren't required to provide a grace period, but nearly all do. The average grace period is about 21 days.

Even if you pay $200 of the $300 you owe for the rug, you still will be carrying a balance on your credit card bill. That wipes out your grace period, meaning you'll be paying interest on the balance.

This can get to be an expensive problem if you owe $1,000 on your credit card and you make only the minimum payment each month. It could take you months, or even *years,* to pay off the money you owe, and you'll end up paying nearly as much in interest as you owe on the loan. It's a really bad idea to let the interest keep building up your credit card debt. That rug could end up costing more than twice the amount you paid for it if you pay it off $10 a month, plus interest.

If you don't pay off your balance, your credit card provider is required to include information on your statement that tells you how long it will take to pay off your balance if you make only the minimum payment each month and how much more you'll end up paying. Take a look at your next statement. You might be surprised to see how easy it can be for a $1,000 bill to balloon into a $1,850 bill. With an average credit card interest of 15 percent, not paying off your bill every month can get very expensive, very quickly.

Use a website such as NerdWallet or CreditCards.com to compare interest rates and other features of credit cards. When you find a card with a good rate, go ahead and apply. If you've had a card for a while and you've maintained a good credit record, you should qualify for a better rate. If you've only had a card for a short time, it might be harder to get approved for a low interest rate. Still, it can't hurt to try. There's a lot of competition for cardholders, and some places are willing to give you a lower interest rate to keep your business. In some cases, all you have to do is ask.

If you haven't had much time to build up a credit record, and you're not approved for a lower interest rate, be diligent about keeping up with your payments, and try again in a year to get a better rate.

Paying Down Your Balance

If you pay off your credit card every month—which is the best way to do it—you won't incur any interest charges. Then your credit card is simply a convenient alternative to paying with cash.

If you have credit card debt, you need to make a plan for paying it down. One way to do this is with a balance transfer. A balance transfer doesn't mean you don't have to pay back your credit card debt, but it can help you to do so faster.

To do a balance transfer, you open a new credit card with a low interest rate and move the balance from your current card or cards onto it. Basically, you're paying off your old cards with the new one. Of course, you'll need to be able to qualify for and get a card with a low interest rate for this to work.

Some balance transfer cards offer a 0 percent interest rate for a specific time period, such as 15 months. If you owe a lot on your credit card and can reduce your interest rate from 15 to 0 percent, you should be able to pay off your debt a lot faster, ideally within the window of the no-interest rate offer. You'll be charged a balance transfer fee to move your balance onto the new card, but you still could end up saving a substantial amount of money. (Turn to Chapter 8 for more on balance transfers.)

 POCKET CHANGE

> NerdWallet recently released its 2016 list of best balance transfer and 0 percent interest credit cards. You can find it at nerdwallet.com/blog/top-credit-cards/ nerdwallets-best-balance-transfer-credit-cards.

If you can't get a low or no-interest balance transfer card, you'll need to figure out another way to pay down your debt. Think about possible sources of money. As difficult as it might be to go to a family member, confess your sins, and ask for a loan, it might be the healthiest thing for you to do, financially.

If you have any money in a savings account, break into it and use some to pay down your credit card debt. It's a sure bet that you're paying far more interest on your debt than you're earning on your savings account.

You'll learn a lot more about credit card debt in Chapter 6.

The Least You Need to Know

- Credit cards are available in all types, so do some homework to determine what card makes the most sense for you.

- If you're paying high fees and interest rates on your credit cards, it's time to look around for another, lower-rate card.

- Interest rates on credit card debit can add up quickly, so be sure you understand how it works and stay on top of it.

- Paying off your credit card bill in full and on time each month is the best way to go. If you can't, consider getting a balance transfer card or coming up with money from another source.

CHAPTER 6

The Truth About Credit Card Debt

Many Americans have a problem with spending too much. Nearly 1 million of us file for personal bankruptcy each year, and poor or excess use of credit is cited as the number-three reason, right after medical expenses and job loss. The difference, of course, is that although high medical bills and job loss might be unavoidable, excess spending, for most people, is not.

Many people, despite working extremely hard, just can't make ends meet because they don't earn enough money. Other people make plenty of money but still end up with credit card debt that gets them into trouble.

In This Chapter

- Avoiding credit card debt in the first place
- How credit card debt accumulates
- How long it can take to pay off credit card debt
- Understanding how debt settlement works
- Ensuring your card stays safe

In this chapter, we look at exactly how credit card debt works and steps that might help if you find yourself in trouble.

Resisting the Urge to Spend, Spend, Spend

An important thing to remember about credit cards is that just because you have them, doesn't mean you have to use them to rack up a lot of debt for stuff you don't need.

As gratifying as it might seem to throw a bunch of bags in the backseat as you leave the mall, your spending will catch up with you at the end of the billing period.

Knowing When to Use Your Card

Say you're driving 4 hours to visit some college friends for the weekend. You're about two thirds of the way there when you notice your car's temperature gauge is on the rise. The needle keeps nosing up, and pretty soon you notice little wisps of steam coming from under the hood. You pull over and call roadside travel assistance, which dispatches a tow truck that gets you and your car to a nearby service station.

It doesn't take the mechanic long to figure out that there's a hole in your radiator, and when he starts talking about replacing hoses, the dollar signs begin stacking up in your mind. You finally get the bill for the tow and the repairs—$347.93. You only have $40 in your wallet, and you're still hoping to get to your friend's house for the weekend.

This definitely is a situation in which you should use your credit card and be grateful you have it. Emergencies such as this are when credit cards are at their finest.

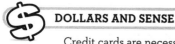 **DOLLARS AND SENSE**

> Credit cards are necessary if you run into an unexpected emergency expense, so don't leave home without one if you're traveling.

They're also great when you shop from a catalog or online or want to secure a hotel reservation, a car rental, or a plane ticket.

Sometimes Cash (or Debit) Is King

At other times and places, though, you should forget you even have a credit card. Many financial advisers will tell you to never use a credit card to buy anything that depreciates. This includes clothing, shoes, gas, restaurant meals, groceries, and so on. It's better to pay for these expenses with cash or a debit card to assure you won't run up a credit card bill you won't be able to pay off at the end of the billing period.

Of course, there are exceptions to this rule. For example, say you're on vacation and see a cool pair of sandals on sale you just love. If you pay cash for the sandals, you won't have enough cash for the rest of the vacation, so you buy the sandals and put the charge on your credit card. That's fine, as long as you'll be able to pay off the charge when the bill comes in.

As mentioned earlier, an increasing number of people are using cards to pay for nearly everything, either as a convenience or to rack up reward points. If you're not absolutely certain you can pay off your bill at the end of the month, however, that's not a good idea. No matter how disciplined you think you're going to be, it's just easier to spend with a credit card than when you're paying with a debit card or cash.

Here's a generally good rule to follow:

> Don't use a credit card to pay for something that will be gone or over when the bill comes.

When using a debit card instead of a credit card, remember to keep track of how much money is available in your account. If you have $500 in your checking account and just wrote checks totaling $450 to cover monthly bills, you'll still be able to access $500 with your debit card until the checks clear. The problem is, if you use your debit card to pay for $90 worth of groceries before those checks clear, you'll come up $40 short.

MONEY PIT

A debit card may not offer the protection a credit card does for items you purchase that are never delivered or are defective. If you pay for something with your debit card and you have a problem with the item, try to resolve it with the merchant. If you can't, contact your debit card issuer for advice.

The same is true with mobile wallets. Here, you carry your credit or debit card information in a digital form on your smartphone, smartwatch, or tablet and use the device instead of an actual card to pay for purchases. It's easy and convenient, but you still need to have funds available to pay for your purchases. If your mobile wallet app is linked to your debit card, you must have sufficient funds at time of purchase. If it's linked to your credit card, you'll get the bill at the end of your billing cycle.

DOLLARS AND SENSE

Using a mobile wallet is convenient, and many wallets offer rewards and discounts to encourage you to use them. If you switch to mobile pay, however, check out what security measures the wallet provides to protect your card information. Also, some varieties of mobile wallets only work with certain types of devices, so you'll need to find one that is compatible with the device(s) you have.

Understanding Credit Card Debt

As a nation, we owed a collective $721 billion in outstanding balances on credit cards in 2014, according to the Federal Reserve. The problem with credit card debt is that it often comes with high interest rates. The average rate is around 15 percent, but it's not uncommon to have a rate of 17 or 19 percent or even higher.

So if you owe a lot of money on credit cards and you don't have enough money to pay off your debt, the credit card company is going to charge you interest.

If you have a credit card, you get a monthly statement that tells you where you shopped and how much you spent. The dinner and drinks at that fun restaurant near the beach. The groceries you charged at Trader Joe's. The gas you bought at the corner station. The tuxedo you rented from Men's Wearhouse for your friend's wedding, and yep, the flowers you bought your mom for Mother's Day—it's all spelled out on your statement.

The statement also shows you your new balance and a minimum payment, which is the least amount you can pay on your next due date. You'll probably have between 21 and 25 days from the time you get the statement until the date by which you must make a payment.

If you don't pay off your entire balance, you'll accrue interest on your average daily balance. That interest is added to the amount you still owe on your balance. That amount actually ends up increasing daily because the balance of your account is multiplied by the daily periodic rate, and the interest calculated is added to your balance each day.

This daily interest accumulation adds up fast and can significantly increase your balance. When your next statement arrives, it will contain your latest purchases added to the balance from your last statement, along with the interest you've accrued.

Getting to a $0 Balance

It's pretty sobering to think about how long it can take to pay off credit card debt if you make only the minimum payment each month. Be aware that, as you are paying down your balance, the amount of your required minimum balance may go down. That might seem like a good thing, but it means you'll end up taking even more time to get rid of your debt.

If you look at your statement, you'll see that it contains that information because credit card companies are required to provide it. And payment calculators are available online to help you figure out how long it will take you to pay off a credit card bill.

Here are a couple examples:

- If you owe $10,000, have a 15 percent interest rate, and make just the minimum payments, it will take you almost *28 years* to pay off your debt and cost you almost *$21,000* in interest.

- If you owe $3,000, have a 15 percent interest rate, and make just the minimum payments, it will take you about *16 years* to pay off your debt and cost you *$3,641* in interest.

As you can see, paying off credit card debt can take a long time. The lesson, obviously, is to try to avoid making charges you can't pay for.

POCKET CHANGE

A company called Total Debt Relief has a video on YouTube that illustrates in a very entertaining manner how long it would take to pay off credit card debt. You can find it at youtube.com/watch?v=Vz05A6cP6Iw.

Credit Counseling, Debt Settlement, and Bankruptcy

Nobody wants to get into serious debt, but it happens all the time. We're assuming you won't need any of the options explained here, but it won't hurt to have an idea about how credit counseling, debt settlement, and bankruptcy work.

Credit Counseling

Credit counseling has been available for more than a half century to advise, serve as an intermediary with creditors, lower interest rates, and consolidate monthly bills. Many reputable, nonprofit companies provide these services, but be aware that numerous scam companies have surfaced over the past decade or so. If you get involved with one of the latter, you could end up with even bigger problems than you started with.

MONEY PIT

Beware of the credit counseling firm that advertises during late-night movies or uses telemarketers to promote its services.

If you're thinking of seeing a credit counselor or counseling firm, it's important that you keep a few things in mind. For example, ask what the total monthly fee will be. You should never have to pay more than $50 a month for the services of a credit counselor. Some predatory firms charge as much as 10 percent of their customer's payments, which ends up totaling a couple hundred dollars a month.

Check with your local Better Business Bureau or Consumer Protection Agency to see if any complaints have been filed or any current investigations are underway about the firms you're considering.

Never sign a contract at the first meeting. Be certain you have time to understand the agreement, the repayment schedule, and the fees. Never disclose your bank account number before you have signed a contract.

Be wary if a counseling service doesn't suggest other options besides its own debt management plan. Remember, it might be possible to sell some personal property or refinance your mortgage to lower your debt rather than embarking on a debt management plan.

Lack of affiliation with the National Foundation for Credit Counseling or the Association of Independent Consumer Credit Counseling Agencies may be a reason to avoid a firm. Such an affiliation doesn't guarantee you're getting the best firm, but it does mean the company obtains a majority of its income from grants and donations rather than from fees alone.

And remember, if it sounds too good to be true, it probably is.

MONEY PIT

Credit card companies have minimum-payment guidelines they use to lower their interest rates, so there's minimal negotiation for most folks. Beware of the firm that promises to remove your unsecured debt, offers to pay off debts with pennies on the dollar, or guarantees you'll avoid bankruptcy.

Debt Settlement

Debt settlement companies charge clients a fee to settle debt with a credit card company or other debt collectors. Typically, a debt settlement firm gets a credit card company to agree on a reduced balance that's considered payment in full and then charges the client for its services. Debt settlement also is known as *debt arbitration* or *debt negotiation.*

Although credit counselors typically get creditors to agree they won't continue to try to collect from a client when the client is in the credit counseling debt management program, debt settlement companies often don't provide that service. That can result in creditors charging late fees and penalty interest charges as well as continuing to pursue collection.

Seeking the services of a debt settlement company should definitely be a last resort.

POCKET CHANGE

Some credit card companies have standard policies for how much debt they'll forgive. If that's the case, you'll do as well negotiating with the company on your own as you would using a debt settlement company.

Bankruptcy

If you absolutely don't have enough money to pay what you owe, bankruptcy is a possible option. Achieving bankruptcy can give you a fresh financial start by erasing your debt. However, it definitely is not for everyone.

Basically, there are two types of bankruptcy:

- Chapter 7
- Chapter 13

To qualify for chapter 7 bankruptcy, your income has to be below a certain level. For chapter 13 bankruptcy, your debt must be below a specified amount.

Even if you qualify for bankruptcy, however, certain types of debt called *priority obligations* won't be eliminated. And filing for bankruptcy can have long-lasting financial consequences.

DEFINITION

Priority obligations are certain types of debt you'll still be responsible for when you file for bankruptcy. These can include child or spousal support and certain income taxes.

If you are ever at the point that you're thinking about filing bankruptcy, consult a bankruptcy attorney who can help you decide if it's the right move.

Credit Card Safety

For those who weren't already sensitive to the pressing need to protect credit card information, the Target data breach of 2014 probably came as a big wakeup call—40 million credit and debit card numbers were stolen from Target during the holiday shopping period, giving new meaning to shoplifting and rocking the card industry.

News of other major breaches followed, forcing both the industry and consumers to start asking how to keep their information safe. Although credit and debit card fraud and theft are common, you can take steps to ensure your cards are safe.

Safety Tips

Most trouble occurs with credit cards that have been lost or stolen, so you need to keep close tabs on your cards. This is especially important when you're traveling or in an area where pickpockets are common. Pickpockets in some cities, including Barcelona, Rome, Prague, Paris, Hanoi, and Buenos Aires, are notorious for their skill and frequency. It takes only seconds on a crowded street or train for a thief to grab your wallet and start racking up debt on all your credit cards.

 DOLLARS AND SENSE

> If you report a lost or stolen credit card before someone else uses it, your issuer can block the card and account number so they can't be used and also issue you a new card and number. If the card has already been used by the time you report it, U.S. law stipulates that you can't be charged more than $50 for those fraudulent purchases. Many issuers waive that charge if you report the card promptly. If your debit card is lost or stolen, the amount you might be charged depends on how quickly you report the loss, so speed is urgent.

Remember that someone looking to use your card doesn't need to have the actual piece of plastic to use it—only the account number and expiration date. Consider these tips to help avoid having someone steal your information:

- Don't ever share account numbers or personal information by email, even if requested in an email that looks like it's from your bank or other official institutions.

- Request for and pay your statements online to avoid having your information in the mail.

- Sign the back of your credit or debit card in ink as soon as you receive it, if applicable. Some new chip cards don't require a signature.

- Keep your credit and debit cards in a place where no one can see them, and be careful to keep your personal identification number private when using your debit card.

- Don't ever give your credit card number to someone over the phone unless you've initiated the transaction.

- Keep anything containing your card numbers in a safe place, and shred any papers before disposing of them.

- If you move, give your credit card company advance notice so your statements and other information don't end up in someone else's mailbox.

- Your credit card company will contact you if it suspects fraudulent charges to your card, so be sure it has your current contact information.

- Be sure you get your card back from the sales clerk after using it in a store.

- Hang on to receipts for credit and debit card purchases, and check your accounts frequently to ensure they match.

- When signing a receipt or check, draw a line through any extra spaces. For instance, if you're paying a restaurant check with a card but leaving a cash tip, cross out the tip line on the bill.

DOLLARS AND SENSE

Some people are reluctant to sign because of security concerns, but credit card companies claim it's the best and safest method of preventing someone else from using your card.

Most credit and debit card fraud is preventable, and you can avoid a lot of trouble by being diligent with your cards and using common sense. Credit and debit cards can quickly change from a convenience to a huge hassle if they're lost or stolen, so be aware of where you keep them and how you use them.

Electronic Safety Tips

Our electronic devices make it possible for us to bank, shop, and stay in touch from anywhere, but they also can make us vulnerable to security breaches. It's very important to safeguard your devices and networks as much as possible to avoid problems.

Here are some suggestions:

- See if your bank offers fraud protection software. Many banks offer this service for free.

- Download and install authorized software and operating system updates as they become available.

- Be sure your computer and internet have a firewall to prohibit unauthorized users.

- Install virus-protection software on your computer, and get updates as soon as they are available.

- Only make purchases from secure sites when shopping online. Look for web addresses that contain *https*.

- Secure electronic copies of receipts and confirmation numbers by printing or saving them to your desktop.

- Assign highly effective passwords to all accounts, and keep them secret. Change them periodically.

> **POCKET CHANGE**
>
> If you don't already have a credit card with an embedded microchip, chances are you soon will. A chip card looks like a standard credit card but contains both the traditional magnetic stripe and a new microchip. The chip provides enhanced security, and these cards will soon be standard, as liability for security breach is transferring onto merchants who do not employ chip card technology.

Credit card companies and retailers are working hard to improve security, but it continues to be a serious and well-publicized problem. You'll do well to remain vigilant with your credit cards and check your accounts often.

The Least You Need to Know

- Credit cards are great when used responsibly, but they can lead to financial nightmares when they're used to buy things you can't afford.

- It makes sense to use a credit card in certain situations, but not in *every* situation. Debit cards often are a good alternative to cash or credit cards.

- If you pay only the minimum fee on your credit card bill, interest will accrue, and it could take you a very long time to pay off your debt.
- If you get into trouble with your credit card bill, help is available.
- Regardless of how many or what types of credit cards you have, be sure to safeguard them to the greatest degree.

Paying Off Your Student Loans and Debt

Many millennials have a lot of student debt. In Part 3, we look at different types of student debt and explore some ways you can get your debt under control without sacrificing your financial future. If graduate school is in your future, keep reading because we also discuss how important it is that you have a sound plan for how you'll pay for it and help you determine whether an advanced degree is worth increasing your debt for.

When it's time to pay back your loans, we look at ways you may be able to consolidate your debt to get a better interest rate and make your payments more comfortable.

CHAPTER 7

Student Loan Debt and Costs of Education

You've probably heard the grim statistics regarding student debt: a recent study by NerdWallet found that the average for each household carrying student debt is $47,712, and collectively, Americans owe $1.2 trillion in student loans. The only thing we owe more money on than student debt as a nation are our mortgages. Of all that money, 70 percent of it is owed to the federal government.

Student loan debt has increased tremendously in the past decade as the cost of education has risen 6 percent higher than the rate of inflation.

In This Chapter

- The staggering cost of student loans
- Not all student loans are the same
- Getting a handle on exactly how much you owe
- Paying off your loans without sacrificing your future
- Weighing the costs and benefits of more education

Having to repay this debt has all kinds of implications for millennials. It can delay when you start saving for retirement and hamper your ability to save money for a down payment on a home. You might not start investing as soon as you would have otherwise because of student loan repayments, or you might not be able to start a college fund for your own children if you have them.

Student debt is a problem, there's no two ways about it. However, you can maximize your ability to pay it off and take control of your finances. We look at some of those strategies in this chapter and also examine the cost and value of furthering your education.

Types of Student Loans

Generally, there are two types of student loans: federal and nonfederal. Nonfederal loans are often called private loans. Both types are used to pay for educational expenses, but there are differences. Federal loans are issued through the U.S. Department of Education (DOE), while private loans are issued by banks or other lenders. Private loans may or may not be backed by the federal government.

POCKET CHANGE

According to the Institute for College Access and Success, 7 in 10 seniors who graduated from public and nonprofit colleges in 2014 had student loan debt, with an average of $28,950 per borrower.

Lending used to be more evenly split between private and federal sources, but private loans became less accessible during the recession and, therefore, the federal government began to play a bigger role. Federal loans have some protections that private loans probably would not provide, such as subsidized interest payments until the student graduates in some cases. Usually, the private loans require a cosigner or parents must sign directly for the loan.

Other advantages of federal loans, according to the U.S. Consumer Financial Protection Bureau, include the following:

- The interest rate is usually a fixed rate, whereas most private loans come with a variable rate that can rise and increase the amount of money you owe.

- You can limit the amount of money you repay every month based on your income.

- Loan forgiveness after 10 years might be an option for students who pursue a career in public service.

- Options for delaying payments may be available.

- The loan is forgiven if the borrower dies.

- The loan may be forgiven if the borrower becomes permanently disabled.

Private lenders probably will not offer flexible terms for repayment or the borrower protections you can get on federal loans. And private loans may still be harder to get than federal.

If you're thinking about borrowing money for higher education, shop around carefully and understand all the conditions of your loan—both while you're in school and after you graduate.

 **MONEY PIT**

> Uncle Sam might be willing to work with you on repayment of student loans, but defaulting is something the government takes seriously. If you don't repay your loans, your wages can be garnished or the money you owe can be taken from your tax refund.

Determining How Much You Owe

Take some time to calculate exactly how much you owe and what the interest rate is on your debt. Look at all your debt at this point, not just your student loans. If you have credit card debt with 19 percent interest, it doesn't make sense to double up on your student loan payments that carry 6 or 7 percent interest.

You can check how much you owe on federal loans on the DOE's National Student Loan Data System (NSLDS). This site can be invaluable for both obtaining student loans and helping you when it comes time to repay them, as it provides information gathered from schools, loan programs, guaranty agencies, and other sources. You'll need to create a profile and an ID to access the site. Once you've done so, you can check the original amount and remaining balance of your loan, your payment status, the business that services your loans, and the interest rate you'll pay.

If you have privately issued loans, you might have to work a little harder to figure out exactly how much they are. You might discover that the financial institution that originally gave you the loan has sold or "transferred" it to another institution or secondary market, making it challenging for you to access your information.

If you learn that your loan is being handled by an entity other than your original lender, contact the original lender and ask how you can access information about your loan. You also could check your credit report.

In addition to knowing how much you owe, pay attention to the terms of payment. Know when your grace period ends (if you have one), when you need to start making payments, and how much you'll need to pay in principle and interest. When you have that information in hand, you can figure out how you'll work the payments into your budget.

Paying Off Your Student Loans

If you've landed a job and are making enough money to easily handle your student loan payments, you're in good shape. If you are not working or have a low-paying job, things will be a little more difficult.

Let's say you fall into the former category and are earning enough money to comfortably make loan payments. If you have both federal and private loans, it's advisable to pay back the private loans first because they're likely to have variable interest rates, which will increase. Ask your lender if you can get reduced interest rates if you make automatic payments each month. Some lenders will slightly reduce your rate.

If you can, pay more than the minimum due, too. The sooner you pay back your loans, the less interest you'll pay overall.

If you're having trouble making your payments, it's imperative that you talk to your lender and see if any accommodations can be made. Most private lenders won't let you defer payments, but you might be able to negotiate a lower monthly rate.

You also could look into student loan refinancing, which enables you to consolidate your student loans and hopefully reduce your interest rate. To qualify for refinancing, you'll need to be employed, have a good credit score, and not have excessive debt in addition to your student loans.

Here are some reputable lenders that offer college loan refinancing:

- SoFi (sofi.com)
- Darien Rowayton Bank (DRB; drbank.com)
- LendKey (lendkey.com; uses community lenders to fund its loans)
- Citizens Bank (citizensbank.com)
- Common Bond (commonbond.co)

Be sure to compare the terms carefully before you apply.

If you have federal loans and are having trouble paying, the DOE offers several options to help you. You can change the date your payment is due each month so you get your paycheck before you have to pay your loan. Or you could apply for a Direct Consolidation Loan that lets you combine all your federal student loans into one payment.

If you're not earning much money, you can request to have an income-driven repayment plan, which determines how much you have to pay based on how much you're earning. The Revised Pay As You Earn (REPAYE) Plan was launched in December 2015 to make it easier for people to repay their loans. You can link to applications for Direct Consolidation Loans and the REPAY Plan at studentloans.gov/myDirectLoan/whatYouNeed.action?page=ibr.

MONEY PIT

Having your monthly payment based on your income can lower how much you owe, but be sure the amount you're paying covers both the principal and interest. If you're not, the balance of your loan will continue to grow and you'll end up paying more in the long term.

If it becomes necessary, you may be able to get a deferment or forbearance on your federal student loan payments that would let you temporarily stop making payments or lower the amount you have to pay. Learn more about that at studentaid.ed.gov/sa/repay-loans/deferment-forbearance.

Whatever you do, don't simply stop paying your loans if money gets tight. That will damage your credit and cause problems that can seriously affect your financial future.

If repaying your college loans is putting too big a dent in your wallet, consider finding additional work to earn extra money. You might be able to get a side job babysitting, tutoring, bartending, waiting tables, cleaning houses, assisting with events, or offering private lessons.

Does a Graduate Degree Makes Sense for You?

Some careers demand that you have more than an undergraduate degree. Many jobs in the medical and business fields require Master's degrees, with more moving in that direction. Earning a Master's in addition to a Bachelor's degree can make the difference between working as an assistant or a director. The problem, of course, is that although valuable, advanced degrees are expensive.

The fastest way to get a degree is to go back to school full-time. However, most people can't afford to do that. School has to be something that's done in addition to and around the schedule of your work and other responsibilities.

Colleges and universities eager to fill their graduate schools have gone to great lengths to make their graduate programs appealing to working men and women. Classes are often scheduled online, at night, and on weekends, catering to those with 9-to-5 commitments.

Spend some time comparing graduate programs before committing to one, and don't assume the school where you did your undergraduate work will have the best program for your postgraduate work. Find out if work-study programs are available to offset costs, and always ask if any scholarship money is available. Higher education is a competitive business, and schools often are willing to help out students to get them enrolled.

($) DOLLARS AND SENSE

Try to tailor your advanced degree to a particular career opportunity, if you can. For example, if you have a psychology degree and you're interested in working with industry, look for something such as a Master's program in industrial and organizational psychology.

Enrolling in graduate school and incurring debt, or additional debt, doesn't always make sense. Some jobs, such as customer service, public relations, communications, sales, and business development don't require advanced degrees, and you may not realize financial returns that justify the cost of earning a degree. Before enrolling in a graduate program, talk to someone at your work who is in a higher position than you about their education. You might be able to advance in your career without a Master's degree by obtaining certifications specific to your line of work, such as a Certified Financial Planner (CFP) for financial planners.

If, however, you're going to need an advanced degree to get ahead in your career, you might as well get it as early as possible to increase your chances of moving up earlier and earning more money before you retire. Overall, people with Master's degrees can expect to earn $400,000 more than those with Bachelor's degrees over the course of their careers. Earnings are even more for those who earn doctorates or professional degrees, such as law or medical.

Working in a job you love and find rewarding is priceless, and only you can decide what career is going to make you happy. The simple fact is that even with a Master's degree, some jobs are more financially rewarding than others.

Before you head back to school for a Master's degree, consider whether it will pay off for you. Monster.com ranked the five best-paying Master's degrees and the five worst-paying:

Best-paying Master's degrees:

- Master's in electrical engineering
- Master's in finance
- Master's in chemical engineering
- Master's in economics
- Master's in physics

Worst-paying Master's degrees:

- Master's in counseling
- Master's in social work
- Master's in music
- Master's in library and information science
- Master's in education

 POCKET CHANGE

Jobs requiring a Master's degree will grow the fastest over the next several years, according to the Bureau of Labor Statistics. Jobs requiring only a high school degree will have the slowest growth.

The Least You Need to Know

- High amounts of student debt have negative implications for millennials, but you can learn to manage your loans and pay them off.
- Be sure you know whether you have federal or private loans, or both, and take a close look at their terms of repayment.
- It's essential that you understand exactly how much you owe and the interest rates on your loans. Pay off the loans with higher interest rates first.
- Paying off your student loans enables you to start using your money for retirement savings.
- Earning a graduate degree can increase your lifetime earnings but isn't necessary for every job.

CHAPTER 8

Debt Consolidation and Payback Options

You read a little bit about consolidating and paying back debt in Chapter 6. In that chapter, we reviewed the basics of paying back credit card debt. And in Chapter 7, you learned some strategies for paying down your student loans without sacrificing your retirement accounts.

Credit card debt and student loan debt are the two largest categories of debt in the United States, aside from mortgages. And many people get into trouble when they borrow more money than they're able to pay back or charge too much on their credit cards.

In This Chapter

- Determining what you owe
- Strategies for paying off each bill
- Transferring credit card balances
- Refinancing your loans
- Consolidating your debt

In this chapter, we go a little deeper into what you can do to minimize your payments so you can get out of debt and look ahead to saving for other goals, like college for your kids and your own retirement.

How Much Debt Do You Have?

The first thing you need to do is determine exactly how much debt you have, and that can be a daunting task. If you use auto-pay for monthly payments and don't pay close attention to your account statements, it's likely you don't have a good handle on your *loan balance*.

 DEFINITION

Your **loan balance** is the total balance that remains on a loan you have. You need to know what your loan balances are to determine how to pay them off.

To begin, make a list of all your loans and credit card balances, noting the interest rates, monthly payment amounts, and due dates for each balance. This can be a very uncomfortable chore, but you must understand your situation before you can start to get it under control.

When you fully understand your debt, make a vow to not incur any more. Use cash or your debit card for all purchases, keeping a close record of what you're spending so you don't overdraw an account and incur fees. If you don't have the cash to pay for something, don't get it. This might require you to reexamine your lifestyle a bit and get back to living within your budget. If you don't have a budget, revisit Chapter 3 and make one.

Paying Off Bills, One at a Time

Now it's time to come up with a plan for getting rid of your credit card debt. Hopefully, it's not a lot and you don't have half a dozen cards on which you've incurred debt. If you do owe a lot on your cards, you have some options for paying it down.

Some people like to pay off as much as possible on balances that have the highest interest rates while making only the minimum payments on cards that carry lower rates. Starting with the card that has the highest interest rate, pay as much as you possibly can every month to reduce your balance. Once you get one high-interest card paid off, get rid of it and start working on the bill that carries the next highest rate of interest.

MONEY PIT

Remember that while you're focused on paying off the credit cards with the highest interest rate, you still have to make the minimum balance payments on your cards with lower rates. Ignoring the cards with smaller balances or lower interest rates means you'll be charged with fees and your balances will continue to rise.

Paying off your cards with the highest interest rates first is a good strategy, but other people prefer to get the smallest loans out of the way first. This can produce a sense of satisfaction as you pay off a loan and are able to apply the money to another card.

Either way, it's important to pay as much as you can and not miss any payments.

Transferring Credit Card Balances

You read a little bit about balance transfers in Chapter 5, but it's important to understand how they work and if a balance transfer might make sense for you.

Basically, a balance transfer allows you to open a new credit card that has a lower interest rate than the cards you have and transfer the balances from your old cards onto the new one. You're putting the debt from all your cards onto one card.

A credit card company might give you a 0 percent balance transfer card, but most require that you have a good to excellent credit score. If you've been scrambling to make minimum payments or missing payments, it's likely you would not qualify.

Even if you did qualify, there are some things to keep in mind. A balance transfer can save you money over the long haul if you use it correctly to pay back what you owe at a lower interest rate. You'll need to factor in costs though because many credit card companies charge a fee equal to 3 or 4 percent of the balance you're transferring. If you're transferring $10,000, your charge to do so could be $300 or $400.

Another thing to understand is that you'll need to make at least the minimum payment every month to maintain the 0 percent interest rate. If your payments lag, that great rate will disappear, so be sure you read all the fine print and understand the implications.

And remember that the 0 percent rate is only for a limited time. Would you be able to pay off your balance before higher rates kick in? If not, how will that affect you?

> **DOLLARS AND SENSE**
>
> Your credit score is negatively affected any time a credit card carries a balance that's above 30 percent of the credit limit on that card. If you transfer card balances, be sure your new card has a high enough credit limit so you don't end up hurting your credit score.

Continually transferring credit card balances can hurt your credit score, so don't plan on using a 0 percent card transfer until the interest rate rises and then looking for another one.

And remember that most of these cards charge you 0 percent only on the transferred balances. New charges will collect interest at the regular higher rate. Some cards will apply the introductory interest rate to new purchases, but only for a short time.

You need to read and understand all the rules before deciding if a balance transfer is the way to go. If it makes sense for you to be paying off debt you already owe at 0 percent interest, be sure you're not incurring additional credit card debt, either on the transfer card or a different one.

Alternatives to Balance Transfers

Another way to take charge of your credit card debt is to try to negotiate lower interest rates with the credit card company. If you've been a customer for a number of years and have always made payments on time, it's worth a try.

Ask to have your interest rate cut in half. Most of the time the credit card representative won't go that low, but it gives you a starting point.

Or look into peer-to-peer (P2P) lending with a company like Lending Club (lendingclub.com). Such online services match loaners with borrowers and often charge interest rates that are much lower than those of credit cards. If you apply for a loan and are approved, you'll be matched with a loaner. P2P lending is fairly new, so be sure to do some research before applying.

 POCKET CHANGE

> Nearly 70 percent of people who borrow money from Lending Club use the money to refinance loans or pay off credit cards.

If none of these alternatives seem like a solution, you might want to look at refinancing a loan or consolidating your debt through a credit counseling agency.

Refinancing Loans

You've probably heard of people refinancing a mortgage to get a better interest rate. The same can be done for other loans, such as money borrowed to pay for education.

In Chapter 7, we discussed consolidating federal student loans into one payment, so turn back there if you need to. If you have private student loans, or a mix of federal and private, you might want to think about trying to find a better interest rate than what you're currently paying.

If you have a steady income now and your credit score is good, a bank may be willing to work with you to refinance your loans at a lower interest rate. You'll need to pay attention to the terms of the loan, as refinancing options vary from bank to bank. Extending the length of your loan may lower your monthly payments, but you could end up paying more over the life of the loan.

 DOLLARS AND SENSE

> Refinancing your college loans through a private lender might enable to you to release the cosigner (a parent perhaps) on your original loans. This can be helpful if the cosigner is looking to pay off a mortgage or start a business.

More and more banks are getting into the student loan refinancing business, so be sure to take some time to see what kind of rates are available and to understand the terms of each contract you consider. Refinancing multiple student loans through a new lender can result in better interest rates and reduced stress by having all your loans at one place.

Considering Debt Consolidation

If you're at your wit's end trying to figure out interest rates, minimum payments, and payment dates on several credit cards, you might want to look into consolidating your loans. Just as explained with the refinancing of college debt, you may be able to consolidate and refinance credit card or other debt into one loan with a lower interest rate.

You read about credit counseling and debt settlement in Chapter 6, but there are some things you should understand about debt consolidation before you jump. When you consolidate your debt, you pay back everything you owe—unlike with bankruptcy, in which your obligations are lessened or released.

So although debt consolidation does less damage on your credit report than bankruptcy, it still can raise red flags to potential lenders because they'll see that you paid your debt through a third party. That third party is the credit counseling agency that collects your money and uses it to pay the credit card companies and other creditors you owe.

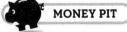

POCKET CHANGE

Online credit card payoff calculators can help you determine how long it will take you to become debt free. Find one from Bankrate at bankrate.com/calculators/credit-cards/credit-card-payoff-calculator.aspx.

If you're looking to consolidate your debt, pay close attention to the terms of the new loan. A debt consolidation loan usually carries a longer payback period, so expect that it may take you longer to get out of debt than usual.

MONEY PIT

Don't expect that you'll be able to pay off your debts in a few months—it could take years.

Also, know that debt consolidation is intended to repay unsecured debts, such as credit cards and personal loans. You can't use debt consolidation for expenses such as unpaid taxes or child support.

Your goal in consolidation should always be to get the lowest interest rate possible. When you find the option that's right for you, apply for the loan and use the proceeds to pay off your outstanding balances. Most lenders will repay your current debt for you instead of issuing you a check and having you pay. Be sure the loan has a fixed interest rate and a set repayment period, and use any extra cash you save each month to get closer to your savings goals.

Getting your debt under control and repaying credit cards, student loan debt, and any other money you owe is the only way you'll be able to move ahead financially. Once you're not worrying about paying high interest rates on your *debt*, you can start thinking about earning the highest interest rates possible on your *savings*.

The Least You Need to Know

- The first thing to do when dealing with debt is to calculate exactly how much money you owe.
- Options for repaying credit card debt include paying off the cards with the highest interest rates first, paying off the small balances first, or applying for a credit card balance transfer.
- Peer-to-peer (P2P) loans are a fairly new concept, but they might help you find a lower interest rate.

- Refinancing college loans can get you lower interest rates and lower your payments, but be sure you know exactly what you're getting into before deciding to refinance.

- Debt consolidation is good for certain financial situations, but it's definitely not a one-size-fits-all solution.

Your Money and Your Career

In Part 4, we offer some advice about stretching the money you have. We look at employee-sponsored benefits and discuss how to take best advantage of them.

And if you aren't working or if you're in a low-paying job, we provide strategies on how to get along financially without a regular paycheck or without as much money as you'd like.

Employed, Unemployed, Underemployed

Not everyone agreed, but at the start of 2016, many people felt jobs and the economy were moving in the right direction in the United States. That's good news because it's been a very long haul financially for a lot of people.

After the first quarter of 2016, the unemployment rate was down to 5 percent from 10 percent in October 2009. And reports from the U.S. Department of Labor showed that the number of jobs was on the rise and wages were increasing slightly—all factors that were encouraging people who have been out of work for a while to start applying for jobs again. That's good news for an economy and job market that has been shaky for years.

In This Chapter

- The cyclical job market
- Looking at employment, unemployment, and underemployment
- How to ask your boss for more money
- Feeling out the job market
- Sticking with the job you have

The Ups and Downs of the Job Market

The American economy is cyclical. It experiences highs, then lows, and then rebounds back again. The public's confidence in the economy—called *consumer confidence*—dips and rises along with the movement of the economy.

DEFINITION

Consumer confidence is a measure of how consumers feel at a given time about the current state of the economy.

The early 1980s and the early 1990s were periods of recession in the United States, and consumer confidence was very low. Then, with the booming stock market fueling the economy during the mid- and late 1990s and into the new century, consumer confidence rose sharply. It slipped again, however, after the first half of 2000, when the economy began to slow down and hundreds of thousands of jobs were eliminated.

The September 11 terrorist attacks caused the already-faltering U.S. economy to slow down even more, taking consumer confidence down along with it. Then we saw economic turnaround when the United States invaded Iraq in March 2003, expecting a short engagement from which we would emerge as victors, which, of course, didn't happen. Still, the stock market hit an all-time high in October 2007, but, as you know, that wouldn't last.

The Great Recession officially started in December 2007, wreaking havoc with the economy. The recession lasted for 18 months, although the effects were felt for much, much longer and linger even today.

All this economic uncertainty had—and still has many people, including those in their 20s and 30s—understandably nervous. Many baby boomers who were nearing or at retirement age during the recession delayed retirement, holding on to the higher-paying jobs that in better economic times would have been passed along to younger workers. Many people were out of jobs, and although the economy has improved significantly, many are still working jobs for which they're overqualified because of lingering economic uncertainty.

Maybe you graduated from college and didn't have any trouble landing a high-paying job as an engineer or computer systems analyst. But if you find yourself in a situation thinking that maybe you're lucky to have your job—even if it isn't that great—try not to be discouraged. Remember that the market is cyclical and has always rebounded from the dips it's taken in the past.

MONEY PIT

In 2015, the millennial generation represented about 40 percent of all unemployed people in the United States, with 13.8 percent of those between 18 and 29 out of work. Unemployment rates were much higher for those without college degrees than those who did have degrees. The good news, however, is that those rates are declining, and economists are hopeful that the trend will continue.

Are You Employed, Unemployed, or Underemployed?

If you've got a job you like that pays you enough money to cover your expenses, repay any debt you have, and put away some savings, you're off to a good start. If you are unemployed or severely underemployed, you'll need to adjust your lifestyle until you've found a job that pays you what you need. (You read more about that in Chapter 11.)

So what does it mean to be employed, unemployed, or underemployed? The first two are pretty easy to understand. Being employed means you have a job for which you are paid to do. If you don't have a job, you are unemployed and you don't work. But when you look a little more closely, the situation gets more complicated, and those terms may not mean what you think they do.

The U.S. Bureau of Labor Statistics (BLS) reported that 8 million Americans were unemployed after the first quarter of 2016. Of that number, 2.2 million—more than a quarter—were *long-term unemployed*.

In addition to those unemployed workers, more than 6 million Americans were *employed part-time for economic reasons*. This refers to workers who want to work full-time but are not because their hours were cut back or they can't find full-time jobs. So these people are working but not in the situation they'd prefer.

Another 1.7 million people were reported as *marginally attached to the labor force*. They're not working, but they're not considered unemployed because they hadn't looked for work in the 4 weeks before the government conducted the employment survey. Of that 1.7 million people who are not working but are not counted as unemployed, about a third had stopped looking for work because they believed there were no jobs available for them. Others weren't looking for work because of different reasons, like illness, school, or family responsibilities.

On top of all that, nearly 15 percent of all workers surveyed in a Gallup poll reported that they were *underemployed*, which means they're working in a job that does not pay much or does not require their skill level.

DEFINITION

Long-term unemployed refers to people who have been out of work for 27 weeks or more. **Employed part-time for economic reasons** refers to people who want to work full-time but can't find full-time jobs. **Marginally attached to the labor force** refers to people who aren't working but aren't considered unemployed because they haven't looked for work within 4 weeks. **Underemployed** refers to people who are skilled but working in low-paying or unskilled jobs.

When you break it down, employment and unemployment are a lot more complicated than they first appear. Let's take a look at where you may fall on the employment-unemployment-underemployment continuum.

Exploring Your Options

Let's say you graduated from college 3 years ago, and after a year and a half of freelancing, landed a job with a mid-size marketing firm. You're currently earning a yearly salary of about $33,000.

Although $33,000 sounds like a lot of money—and it is—we all know money goes fast, and there are a lot of things to spend it on. Hardly anyone who works thinks he or she makes enough money, even if you're grateful to have gotten a position in your field. It's no surprise that the most frequent complaints about jobs are not about bosses (although those probably run a close second) but about salaries.

If you have a job you like, but not the salary you'd like, you do have some options:

- You can (*gulp!*) ask for a raise.

- You can look for a higher-paying job.

- You can stay in the job you have and hope you'll advance or be able to move on as employment opportunities continue to improve.

Of these choices, the first two are definitely more proactive and require more courage than sticking it out and seeing what happens. It takes a fair amount of guts to march (or tiptoe) into your boss's office to ask for a raise, especially when many employers are still wary about the economy. And it takes a lot of energy to start a job hunt, especially if it hasn't been very long since you've been through one and you know competition for jobs is tough.

If there's an indication that there's room for advancement in your current job, the best thing to do might be to hang out, do your very best, and see what happens. But if your salary is so low you can't get by, or if you're forced to live paycheck to paycheck without being able to save a cent, you might have to take some action.

Asking for a Raise

If your plan is to ask for a raise, be sure you're in a position to do so. Obviously, if you've only been working for your company for a few weeks or months, you won't endear yourself to anyone by asking for more money. Or if the company is going through some lean times, which many firms still are, your boss isn't going to be at all happy when you saunter in and ask for more money.

Also consider your market value. Never go to your boss and complain that the guy in the next cubicle is making more than you are for doing the same job. Bosses hate knowing employees talk about their salaries, and opening that kind of conversation definitely won't put you in his or her good graces. Instead, if you know you're underpaid, point out what other people who are doing your job on the open market are making.

 DOLLARS AND SENSE

Trade publications and some professional associations do regular salary surveys and can be good sources of information. Or you can use Monster's salary tool to calculate what you make and see how that compares to others in similar jobs. Find it at career-advice.monster.com/salary-benefits/salary-information/salary-tools/article.aspx.

Looking for Another Job

If you're really unhappy with your job and your salary and know there's no chance for a raise anytime soon, you might be tempted to go out and look for another job. If that's the case, what kind of job should you look for?

Over the last decade or so, employers in some fields have become less likely to insist on a particular degree for a particular job. They're more likely to look for someone who is smart, versatile, willing to work, and able to work independently. If that sounds like you, it might give you a lot more flexibility if you decide to job hunt. Don't feel that you're stuck in a particular field just because that's what your degree or certification is in. You may be able to go from one career to another that interests you without much difficulty.

Whereas we once looked to big corporations for good jobs and job security, predictions are that small businesses, which can act quickly to implement new ideas and technology, will become increasingly important as employers. And guess who is starting many of these small businesses that are going to be so important? A survey released in 2015 by Bentley called millennials the true entrepreneur generation, with almost two thirds stating that their goals include starting their own business at some point.

The BLS reports that the number of self-employed young Americans is increasing and is expected to continue to grow. So don't neglect the small businesses when conducting your job search. Who knows? You may get inspired to create one of your own.

If you can't reconcile your salary problem, looking for another job might be the answer. Just be careful of inadvertently putting yourself into a worse situation than you are in now, either by jeopardizing your current position or rushing into another job that turns out to not be the position you expected.

 POCKET CHANGE

It's estimated that the average worker has about 11 jobs and 3 careers over his or her working life.

Staying Where You Are

If you can't get a raise in your current job and you're not inclined to go looking for a new one, your only choice is to stick it out. This might be your choice for several reasons.

Maybe you have a job you love that just doesn't happen to pay very much. Certain professions— social work and childcare, for instance—are notoriously low paying. Nobody going into these fields expects to get rich, but thankfully, dedicated people are willing to do these kinds of very important, but underpaid, jobs. If you have a low-paying job you love, you'll have to decide if you want to stay where you are. If you decide to keep it, you'll have to adjust your standard of living to mesh with your earnings.

Do keep in mind, however, that not all nonprofit or not-for-profit organizations offer only low-paying jobs. According to PayScale, Inc., the median salary for a development coordinator with between 5 and 9 years of experience who works for a nonprofit is $51,200. Could you make more than that in the private sector? Maybe. But some nonprofits offer generous benefits to make up for the lower pay.

If, on the other hand, you're staying in a low-paying job because you're too scared or unmotivated to go after a better one, you're dealing with a different issue. Reread the previous section about the job market, and give it a shot. You've got nothing to lose but a low-paying job.

The Least You Need to Know

- The job market tends to be cyclical, so be patient if you've been unable to find the job you want because of a current tight market.
- A low national employment rate doesn't tell the whole story about who's working and who's not.
- If you're dissatisfied with your salary, you need to decide what you're going to do about it.
- Asking for a salary increase isn't easy, but it could reap financial rewards.
- Sometimes it's smart to stay with the job you have, especially if there's room for advancement.

CHAPTER 10

Employer-Sponsored Benefits

If you've got a job that offers health insurance, a retirement savings plan, and other perks, consider yourself lucky. These benefits greatly increase the value of your earnings and give you an opportunity to save money for your future. The key, of course, is to take full advantage of savings opportunities. Research shows that most millenials who are offered savings plans through work take advantage of them, although many in this age group work in jobs that don't offer benefits.

There's a running debate in this country about the wisdom of linking jobs with health-care and retirement benefits, but the fact remains that more than half of Americans still get their health insurance through work, although that number has dropped during the past decade.

Let's take a look at what employer-sponsored benefits are and why they're so important.

In This Chapter

- Understanding employer-sponsored benefits
- How employer-sponsored benefits increase your compensation
- Finding the health-care plan for you
- Taking advantage of a 401(k) plan

What Are Employer-Sponsored Benefits?

An *employer-sponsored benefit plan* provides one or more types of benefits to employees at no or little cost. Typically, these benefits include health care and a retirement savings plan, although some employers also offer a life insurance policy, dental and vision care, education reimbursement, and other perks. Paid vacation is definitely a nice benefit.

> **DEFINITION**
>
> An **employer-sponsored benefit plan** is a benefit or package of benefits an employer provides for employees. These plans vary from company to company.

An often-overlooked benefit employers pay is half of your contribution to Social Security and Medicare. If you're self-employed, you have to pay both halves of those taxes.

Employee benefit programs are by no means a new concept in the American workplace. As early as 1875, the American Express Company offered a pension plan to employees. Montgomery Ward established a group health, life, and accident insurance plan for employees in 1910, and Baylor University Hospital offered a group hospitalization plan to its workers in 1929.

Employees benefit from these plans by getting discounted services, and employers get some tax advantages when they provide benefits. Providing benefits also plays a role in attracting and retaining good employees.

Benefits vary greatly, depending on the employer. An employee working for an insurance company in the Midwest might get basic health care for which she contributes part of the cost and 2 weeks of paid vacation, while someone who works for a tech company in Silicon Valley might get 4 weeks paid leave at the birth of a child, free meals every day, 100 percent paid health care, and the capability to bring his dog to work.

The Real Cost of Hiring You

At the end of 2015, the average pay for a civilian worker was $33.58 an hour, according to the U.S. Bureau of Labor Statistics. Of that amount, just under a third of the compensation resulted from benefits.

Wages and salaries averaged $23.06 per hour, and benefits contributed $10.52 an hour. So when you complain that your salary is too low, remember that you need to factor in your benefits as well.

POCKET CHANGE

Google is consistently ranked one of the best companies to work for, with employee perks cited as one of the reason. Fringe benefits include free massages, haircuts, gourmet food, and doctor visits, as well as nap pods.

Millennials recently became the largest group of working Americans, and many analysts feel that their influence will greatly affect the business community. As baby boomers retire and more and more millenials take their places, employers will need to find innovative ways of attracting and retaining them. Polls have found that these benefits—some traditional and some not-so-traditional—are important to many millennials:

- Comprehensive benefits package, including health care and a retirement savings plan such as a 401(k) plan.

- Flexibility, such as the ability to alter work hours and work from home.

- A positive social atmosphere at work, including things like snacks, open workplaces, a laid-back dress code, and community game areas.

- Work-life integration, which is a step beyond work-life balance. Work-life integration occurs in an environment that supports the blending of personal and professional lives.

- Family-friendly policies such as paid parental leave, lactation facilities, and onsite or subsidized child care.

- Concierge benefits such as dry-cleaning services and catering.

- Mentoring services that provide feedback and help millennials succeed quickly.

- Education and training such as tuition reimbursement.

- Competitive wages and financial incentives such as bonuses are important to all workers.

Depending on the number and type of benefits provided, the cost can add up for employers. As a result, some companies have reduced workers' hours to part-time to avoid paying benefits. Some industries, such as retail and hospitality, often don't provide any benefits for workers.

POCKET CHANGE

Sixty percent of millennials surveyed said they'd trade a higher salary for a great work atmosphere.

Employer-Provided Health Plans

Americans get health care in a variety of ways. For about 60 percent of us, our health care is provided through an employer. Employers with 50 or more full-time employees are required to sponsor plans. If you don't receive health care through your employer, you'll need to buy the Minimum Essential Coverage under the Affordable Care Act (ACA) or pay a penalty.

Many employers used to cover the full cost of their employees' health-care policies, but as the cost of coverage has risen, workers are increasingly being asked to contribute to the costs. In 2014, workers paid an average of just under $5,000 toward the cost of employer-sponsored health care for themselves and their families.

If the amount you have to pay toward your health exceeds 9.5 percent of your household income, you can opt out of that plan and buy it yourself from the Health Insurance Marketplace under the ACA (healthcare.gov). You'll be eligible for a tax credit if you do that.

If you don't pay more than 9.5 percent of your household income toward your employer-sponsored health care but want to opt out because you don't like the coverage or another reason, you won't be eligible for the tax credit. You can switch your plan if you like, but you won't receive the credit.

Some benefits consultants believe employer-sponsored health care is financially unsustainable and will soon cease to exist. Employers instead will shift to a defined-benefits plan, in which employees will be given money with which to buy their own health care.

 POCKET CHANGE

In their book, *The End of Employer-Provided Health Insurance: Why It's Good for You, Your Family, and Your Company*, Rick Lindquist and Paul Zane Pilzner, the president and founder respectively of Zane Benefits, make the case for the end of employer-sponsored health insurance plans. They argue that 90 percent of all businesses will stop offering health plans by 2025, switching instead to an employee health insurance stipend system.

That type of plan would get employers out of the insurance system but still enable them to provide a benefit to their employees. For now, however, if you're covered with health care provided by your employer, be sure you carefully read and understand the policy. Know what you're responsible for as far as co-pays, deductibles, prescription costs, and other costs.

You'll need to consider all those costs, plus any amount taken out of your check to help pay for the plan, when you're making a budget and figuring out your monthly expenses.

Employer-Sponsored Retirement Plans

If your employer offers a retirement savings plan, maximize that benefit by contributing as much as you can. This can be difficult when you're paying back college loans and have other expenses, but the sooner you start saving for retirement, the better off you'll be. You'll read a lot more about 401(k) plans and individual retirement accounts (IRAs) in Chapter 21.

For now, understand that pensions—plans employers set up to provide payments to employees when they retire at no cost to the employee—have become very rare. And Social Security payments are covering a declining share of earnings, meaning younger workers will need to rely on their own savings when they retire.

MONEY PIT

When regular monthly Social Security benefits payments started being made in 1940, the life expectancy of a 64-year-old was about another 14 years. Today it's 21 years. That and other factors are making it harder for Social Security to keep up and raises questions about the sustainability of the system.

Most millennials understand this and expect to self-fund their retirements. Fortunately, many employers are helping them by offering 401(k) plans with some level of matching contributions. Three quarters of millennials who have access to 401(k)s through work are making regular contributions to them.

The amount of employer-matched contribution varies from company to company. If you're lucky, your employer will match your contribution dollar for dollar up to a certain percentage of your paycheck. The most typical match is for every dollar an employee contributes up to 6 percent, the employer throws in 50 percent. By taking advantage of the match, you get an automatic 50 percent return on your money. Even with that incentive, however, it's estimated that one in every four employees does not contribute the maximum amount to get the full benefit of the employer's match.

Companies trying to attract new hires in competitive marketplaces may offer matches or partial matches to contributions up to 10 percent or even higher. Not taking advantage of those opportunities while they're available can have a real negative effect on your retirement.

Other Retirement Plan Options

If you're among the half of all American workers who doesn't have an employer-sponsored retirement fund, you can look into some other options.

About 17 states have addressed legislation that would create some type of state-sponsored retirement plan for workers who don't have plans through their employers. These kinds of plans, in which contributions are automatically deducted from workers' paychecks, are popular among younger people, according to a poll by Young Invincibles, a national advocacy group that works to educate young adults on issues relating to health care, finances, jobs, and higher education. Among all millennials who are registered to vote, 85 percent said they favored such a plan.

Another option for saving if you don't have an employer-sponsored plan is *my*RA, a starter retirement plan launched by the U.S. Department of the Treasury. You choose the amount of money you want deducted from your check, and you'll earn some interest on the savings. You can contribute up to $5,500 a year, and your investment is backed the U.S. Treasury. If you change jobs, your money moves with you. You can learn more about *my*RA at myra.gov.

If you don't have employer-sponsored benefits, you'll have to work harder to ensure you've got adequate health care and are starting to save some money for your retirement. If you do have these benefits, factor in their value to what you bring home in your paycheck. It's not advisable to take a job just because it offers good benefits, but it should be a factor the next time you're making a decision about accepting a position.

The Least You Need to Know

- Employer-sponsored benefit plans vary greatly from company to company but often include a health-care plan and a retirement savings plan.
- Just under one third of all compensation is paid in the form of employee benefits.
- If you need to contribute too much to your employer-sponsored health plan, you may be able to opt out and get a tax credit if you buy your own plan.
- Taking advantage of an employer-sponsored retirement savings plan can give you an early start on saving for your future.
- If you don't have access to an employer-sponsored savings plan, you'll need to look at other ways to save.

Surviving on Unemployment

If you're unemployed, you're in good company. Despite an improving job market, 8 million Americans were unemployed at the end of the first quarter of 2016.

As you read in Chapter 9, the job market, like many other aspects of the economy, is cyclical. If you're not working right now, don't assume you won't be able to find a good job in the future. The U.S. Bureau of Labor Statistics (BLS) estimates that 20.5 million new jobs will be added between 2010 and 2020 and that 657 out of 749 identified occupational groups would grow.

In This Chapter

- Determining if you're eligible for unemployment
- Making the most of your unemployment compensation
- Staying competitive while you're unemployed
- Landing a new position

In this chapter, we look at the importance of saving money and stretching your cash while you're unemployed. We also look at some job areas that are on the rise and share some tips for successful job hunting.

The History of Unemployment Compensation

Unemployed workers in the United States have been covered by the Federal-State Unemployment Insurance Program since 1935, when President Franklin D. Roosevelt signed the Social Security bill that contained provisions for *unemployment compensation*. Wisconsin had enacted a state unemployment insurance plan 3 years earlier in response to the Great Depression, during which 1 in 4 Americans were out of work.

DEFINITION

Unemployment compensation is temporary income support in the event that you lose your job due to circumstances that are not your fault. The income is meant to tide you over until you find a new job.

Prior to the depression, some industrial workers who belonged to trade unions were guaranteed unemployment compensation by their employers as part of their union contracts.

In Switzerland, unemployment insurance plans were put into place by trade unions as early as the late 1700s, and other parts of Europe followed suit in the 1800s and early 1900s.

Although some opposed the Unemployment Insurance (UI) program as part of the Social Security bill, it was recognized that people lose their jobs even in economically prosperous times and could be at risk for great economic hardship. The law has stood in place ever since.

POCKET CHANGE

For more on the history of unemployment insurance and compensation, go to the Social Welfare History Project website at socialwelfarehistory.com/social-security/social-security-unemployment-insurance.

Accessing Unemployment Compensation

If you have never had a job, you won't be eligible for unemployment benefits because they are intended for people who were working and lost their jobs through no fault of their own. If you were working and no longer are because you were laid off or the company that employed you closed, you might be eligible for compensation.

Unemployment compensation is a joint federal-state program. Every state offers unemployment benefits to qualified workers, but rules regarding compensation vary from state to state. You'll have to check on regulations that apply to your particular state if you're attempting to collect.

To be eligible for benefits, you must have worked in a qualifying position and for an employer who is covered by the UI program. You and your employer must have contributed to the unemployment compensation fund through payroll deductions.

If you lose your job, you'll need to file a claim with your state UI program. You can access your state's unemployment program and find out how you need to file your claim online. Some states require that you file in person, while others allow you to do so on the phone or online. Check your state unemployment office to find out for sure.

You'll need to provide some information such as the dates you worked and your employers' address(es). Your state's unemployment program will determine how much compensation you're eligible for, based on how much you earned during a specified time period. Once you're approved for unemployment compensation, you'll be required to file every week or every other week and report anything you earn while you're collecting.

MONEY PIT

In most states, it takes 2 or 3 weeks after you file for unemployment compensation to get your first check. If you lose your job and don't have an emergency fund, you'll need to figure out how you'll support yourself and pay your bills if your income is interrupted. Getting behind could set you up for financial problems in the future.

Regulations regarding working part-time while you're collecting unemployment benefits vary from state to state, so be sure you know what regulations apply to you. Many states let you work and still collect a portion of your benefits, and that may be beneficial because a part-time job could lead to networking opportunities and perhaps even a full-time job.

If you do get part-time work, you need to report how much you're earning when you file for your unemployment each week. If you earn more than your current benefits amount, you probably won't qualify for unemployment that week. Every state has a formula that determines how benefits are adjusted if you're earning money in a part-time job.

Also, your state might require you to register with your state employment center, which may be able to help you find employment. If you are instructed to register and fail to do so, you could lose your benefits.

MONEY PIT

If you're receiving unemployment compensation and you get a part-time job, do not be tempted to try to hide the fact when you file for benefits. That's unemployment fraud and can get you into a lot of trouble. Most employers notify states when they make a hire, so it's likely your employment status will be known. Many states encourage residents to report unemployment fraud, so don't take any chances. You're required to report income even if you're being paid "under the table."

If You're Denied Benefits or Your Benefits End

Your state unemployment office determines if you're eligible for benefits. If you are denied benefits, you have the right to appeal to try to get them started or reinstated. You'll find information on how to do that on your state's unemployment office website.

If you quit your job, you might still qualify for unemployment, but it varies by circumstance, and different states have different regulations.

Workers who leave a job simply because they don't like it or just don't feel like working any more are unlikely to qualify for benefits. In some cases and in some states, however, certain situations may qualify you for unemployment:

Illness or injury   If you need to stop working because you get sick or are injured, you can still qualify for unemployment in some states. This is particularly true if you were injured or became ill as a result of the job you were doing.

Family responsibilities   If you have a family member who is very ill and you quit your job to care for him or her, you may qualify for benefits. Rules vary from state to state regarding the relationship and severity of illness.

Intolerable conditions   If your employer constantly sexually harasses you or makes advances toward you, you probably will qualify for unemployment compensation if you quit. The same goes if you're being pressured to do something that's illegal as part of your job or being forced to work in dangerous conditions.

If you are fired from your job, you may or may not be eligible for unemployment benefits. In many states, an employee who is let go because he or she is simply not a good fit will be eligible for benefits. If you are fired for a more serious cause, however, it's likely you won't be able to get unemployment—at least not right away. Some examples of misconduct that are likely to disqualify you for benefits include the following:

Committing a crime   Stealing from your employer, intentionally injuring a coworker, or destroying company property will pretty much rule out any chance of receiving unemployment compensation.

Failing a drug test   Employees who fail a drug test are not eligible for unemployment in most states. Refusing to take the test also can be disqualifying.

Breaking the rules   If you get fired for violating safety rules or simply refuse to follow stated company policy, it's likely that your unemployment claim will be denied.

In most states, you can receive unemployment benefits for a maximum of 26 weeks. Hopefully, you'll find a job long before your benefits end, but if not, you may qualify for Extended Benefits (EB). You're more likely to get EB if your state has a high rate of unemployment. Be sure to ask about EB if you haven't found a job and your compensation is about to end.

Stretching Your Compensation Dollars

Your unemployment compensation will be less than your salary, so you'll have to figure out how to stretch the dollars you get. Hopefully, you have an emergency fund to help get you by until you're working again, but ideally, you'll use as little of that fund as possible.

DOLLARS AND SENSE

You can get a rough idea of how much weekly employment compensation you'll get by figuring out how much you earned during the yearly quarter when your income was highest. Divide that amount by 13, which is the number of weeks in a calendar quarter. Plan on getting about half of what your weekly income was while you were working. Not every state uses the high-quarter method to calculate what you get, but a majority does.

You can read all about trimming costs in Chapter 12. Remember that although some expenses are necessary, others are not. If you're living on your own, you need to keep coming up with rent money. You still have to pay for utilities, insurance, your car loan, food, and so forth. These are *nondiscretionary expenses.*

If you're paying back federal student loans, you might be able to adjust or delay your repayments, so be sure to inquire. You also can save money by cutting down on *discretionary expenses,* which are those such as vacations and entertainment.

> **DEFINITION**
>
> **Nondiscretionary expenses** are the ones you have to pay every month—they are necessary expenses. **Discretionary expenses,** on the other hand, are not necessary, such as vacation and dinners out.

It's easy to overspend when you're around people who have more money than you do. Resist spending more than you should to "keep up," and leave your credit card at home when you're out with your friends.

Take a little time to review Chapter 3, and try to think of areas in which you can cut back until you've found another job.

Staying in the Game While You're Unemployed

Different people approach unemployment in different ways. Some need time to get used to the idea and go into retreat mode, while others face their unemployment head-on and make finding a new position their "job."

If you lose your job and need a little time to lie on the couch and watch TV, that's not the worst thing in the world. Soon, however, you'll need to pick yourself up, dust yourself off, and get back in the game.

If you're looking for a job in the same field in which you were previously employed, start working any contacts you have. Let people know you're looking, and ask if you can submit a résumé. Get online, see what jobs are available, and apply.

If you're thinking of shifting into a different field, use some of the time you have to identify areas that are experiencing job growth. The U.S. Bureau of Labor Statistics (BLS) has identified the job areas that will be the fastest growing—both in terms of jobs added and salary increases—between the years of 2014 and 2024:

- Wind turbine service technicians
- Occupational therapy assistants
- Physical therapist assistants
- Physical therapist aides
- Home health aides
- Commercial drivers

- Nurse practitioners
- Physical therapists
- Statisticians
- Ambulance drivers and attendants
- Occupational therapy aides
- Physician assistants

- Operations research analysts

- Personal financial advisers

- Cartographers and photogrammetrists

- Genetic counselors

- Interpreters and translators

- Audiologists

- Hearing aid specialists

- Optometrists

- Forensic science technicians

- Web developers

- Occupational therapists

- Diagnostic medical sonographers

- Personal care aides

- Phlebotomists

- Ophthalmic medical technicians

- Nurse midwives

- Solar photovoltaic installers

- Emergency medical technicians and paramedics

Find more information about job growth, salaries, and other employment related issues at bls.gov.

 POCKET CHANGE

According to CareerCast (careercast.com), 10 jobs in which millennials are seeing the greatest gains are: advertising account executive, civil engineer, computer systems analyst, data scientist, financial planner, market research analyst, physical therapist, social media manager, software engineer, and statistician.

If you're thinking about changing jobs, Salary.com offers a list of apps and websites to help you. To maximize your chances of finding a job that's matched to your skills, experience, and interests, consider using it or one or more of the following resources.

Job Mo (jobmo.org)   Job Mo uses Google maps to let you search by location and find and apply for jobs on sites like Monster and The Ladders. You also can research companies and check out salary information.

SWITCH (switchapp.com)   SWITCH lets you search for jobs from your phone and notifies recruiters and employers if you're interested. If you're a candidate, the employer can contact you via the chat feature to set up an interview.

Jobr (jobapp.com)   Jobr lets you create a profile, post your résumé, and interact with a job concierge who can answer any questions.

LinkedIn (linkedin.com)   LinkedIn is a favorite website of employers, so you'll definitely want to get your profile on it. Then use the LinkedIn Jobs page to search for openings.

Jobcase (jobcase.com)   Jobcase is a website recommended for people who don't have a 4-year degree or a fancy résumé but have worked and have some job experience. It posts listings for hourly work and can connect you to mentors who can answer questions and provide direction.

Finding Job-Hunting Help

Even if your state unemployment office doesn't require you to register with your state employment center, you may be able to get some assistance there with your job hunt.

If you're not quite sure where you'd like to be headed, you might consider seeking the services of a *career counselor*. A career counselor does not go out and find you a job, but he or she can help you evaluate where you are, where you've been, and where you'd like to go.

You may be able to access the services of a career counselor for free at your college. If you don't live near your alma mater, a community college or other organization in your area may offer career counseling at no cost.

Another source of job-hunting help is a *headhunter*. If you seek the services of a headhunter, be aware that the headhunter's first loyalty is to the company seeking an employee, not to you. Normally, the company hires and pays the headhunter, although in some cases you'll be charged, so it's important to ask. If you decide to try a headhunter, be sure to check around and find one who is reliable and reputable.

> **DEFINITION**
>
> A **career counselor** is a certified individual who can help you clarify your career goals, assess your abilities and aptitudes, provide information about different careers, develop an individualized career plan, help you create a résumé, and teach you skills and strategies for job hunting. A **headhunter** matches you with a company that's looking for someone to fill a particular position. He or she also handles negotiations between a prospective employee and the company.

The Least You Need to Know

- Americans have been relying on unemployment compensation since the 1930s.
- To find out if you're eligible for unemployment benefits, contact your state's unemployment office.
- You have the right to appeal if you're denied unemployment benefits.

- Cutting back on discretionary expenses makes your unemployment benefits go further.

- Be sure you use every resource available to you when you're hunting for a new job.

- Multiple forms of job-hunting assistance are available if you need it.

Your Savings

Saving money is important for many reasons. When you have money saved, you have options. You can get things you want, help others, take vacations, and pay for education. Having savings also gives you a sense of security.

In Part 5, we discuss why saving money when you're young is important and how to grow your little savings now into big future savings. The more time your money has to grow, the better your chances you'll achieve a great financial future.

We also look at how you can cut costs to save more in these chapters as well as the best types of accounts for savings. We also explore investments and review some different options you have for investing your money.

CHAPTER 12

Cutting Costs

You read about the importance of making and sticking to a budget in Chapter 3. Hopefully, you're now working within a budget that makes sense for your financial framework.

If you've gotten a raise at work, it can be tempting to relax your budget. Maybe you're thinking you could afford a higher car payment and are considering trading in your older vehicle. Or perhaps you splurged on that fun cruise that seemed like a bargain.

In this part of the book, you learn about different ways to save. More importantly, though, you learn *why* saving money is so important and how even small savings can add up.

In This Chapter

- How we spend money
- Looking at where you live
- Trimming transportation costs
- Cutting back on food, clothing, and entertainment
- Saving on insurance

If you're living within a budget, good for you. But if your budget has gone by the wayside or you're having trouble sticking to it, it's time for a refresher course. Chances are you can find a lot of ways to cut costs and live more frugally. Making some sacrifices now can go a long way toward ensuring a successful financial future and can give you a lot more options and freedom in how you live.

Spending in America

Americans spend a lot of money on items and services most other people in the world live quite well without. For example, in 2014, we spent $2.8 billion on Halloween candy. Yes, Halloween candy. We hand over about $120 billion a year for fast food, and the average American spends $400 a year gambling on lottery tickets, on sporting events, in casinos, and so forth.

MONEY PIT

Smoking and excessive use of alcohol are not only bad for your health, they're also bad for your wallet. On average, Americans who earn $19,000 or less a year spend nearly $500 on alcohol and tobacco. Those in the $36,000 to $59,000 income group spend $733, and those earning more than $94,000 spend $1,260.

There are some things—taxes for instance—for which you must pay what you're required to pay. And you need a place to live, a way to get around, and food to eat every day. If you have debt, paying it down is an additional expense, which you read about in Chapter 8.

In America, our biggest chunks of income go to the following, in order:

- Housing
- Transportation
- Food
- Personal insurance and pension
- Health care
- Entertainment
- Clothing
- Charitable contributions

Let's take a look at some of these areas and ways you might save some money.

Housing Costs

The cost of housing includes more than your rent or mortgage. Energy expenses, property taxes, utility bills, maintenance fees, insurance, and other expenditures also count toward the cost of housing. All those dollars add up fast, which is why on average Americans spend one third of what they earn on housing.

If you're renting a house or apartment, you can cut costs by finding some roommates or moving to a place with a lower rent or mortgage. If you're thinking about buying a house, you learn a lot about that in Chapter 16. For now, let's look at some ways you can save on your housing costs.

Utilities

If you pay the utility bills where you live, you're probably already aware that keeping your house or apartment comfortable can be costly. Utilities are increasingly expensive, but you can reduce some of those costs:

Unplug   Electrical devices consume power even when they're not in use. Unplugging small appliances and devices when you're not using them can save you money.

Change your lightbulbs   If you haven't updated your lightbulbs to CFLs or LEDs yet, consider doing so. They're more expensive up front, but they begin to save you money quickly.

Check your water heater   Heating water accounts for more than 10 percent of energy costs in most homes. If the temperature on your water heater is set higher than 130°F, you're spending more than you need to. Turn down your heater to 125°F or 130°F, and wrap a water heater blanket around it to avoid losing heat. Your water will still be plenty warm, and you'll save money.

Air seal your home   Caulking and weather-stripping help reduce the amount of air that flows in and out of your home and can reduce your energy costs.

 POCKET CHANGE

The U.S. Department of Energy provides a do-it-yourself tutorial for air sealing your home at energy.gov/energysaver/air-sealing-your-home.

Go higher in summer and lower in winter   Turning up your air conditioner setting and turning down your heat setting just a couple degrees can lower your heating and cooling bills.

Think about your showers   According to the Environmental Protection Agency (EPA), Americans use more than 1 trillion gallons of water every year just for showers, with the average shower lasting 8 minutes. If you cut your shower time by 2 minutes and install an EPA-approved

WaterSense showerhead (available at home centers), you'll not only do your part for the environment but save money as well.

TV, Internet, and Phone

If it feels like you're spending too much on TV, internet, and phone services, you're not alone. Mintel, a market research firm, reported that the average household paid $165 a month for these services in 2015.

Millennials and some others have started finding ways around these high costs by giving up cable TV and using streaming boxes or a video service like Hulu. Others have purchased an antenna, which can be had for around $80. Cutting or drastically reducing your cable bill can save you serious money.

Phone service also is expensive, so it pays to shop around for the best plan you can find. And remember, you really can still live with your current smartphone after the new-and-improved version comes out.

Americans pay more for internet than their international peers and often get slower service in return. Compare plans before you agree to an internet provider, and look for bundling options that may save you some money, at least for an initial period.

Insurance and Taxes

If you own a home and think your taxes are too high, consider asking for a home reassessment. To get a reassessment, contact your county's tax collector's office, or the tax assessor's office, and request a reassessment.

Also ask the real estate agent who sold you your house to provide you with information about comparable sales in your area. If your house is assessed at higher than what other houses have sold for, you might stand a good chance of having your assessment lowered, which would mean your property taxes would be lowered, too.

A realtor with whom you've done business often will complete the form for you and even represent you if your county or state requires a hearing to consider the reassessment request. Don't be afraid to ask.

In addition, call your homeowner's insurance company and ask if there's a way you can lower your costs. If you don't have your home and car insurance with the same company, ask if bundling the coverages could lower your rate. Read your homeowner's policy carefully to see if you might be overinsured.

POCKET CHANGE

The Insurance Information Institute offers free information, including "Twelve Ways to Lower Your Homeowners Insurance Costs," at iii.org.

Refinancing Your Mortgage

Refinancing your mortgage essentially means you replace your current mortgage with one that has a lower rate. Lenders will tell you it makes sense to refinance your current mortgage when rates have fallen 1.5 percent or more below what you're currently paying. If that applies to your mortgage and you plan to stay in your home for a period of time, you might want to refinance.

Some lenders claim it makes sense to refinance when rates are less than 1 percent below your current rate, but depending on closing costs, the length of time you're planning to stay in your home, and other factors, that's questionable.

When you're thinking of refinancing, ask the lending agent to run the numbers for you, considering these factors:

- The interest rate to be charged on the loan

- Closing costs

- How long you will be in the house

The numbers should tell you what's best for your situation.

Transportation Costs

One thing is for certain: it's expensive to own and maintain a car. (You read much more about that in Chapter 15.) If you already own a car, you can save money by ensuring you take care of it properly to avoid big repair bills. If you don't own a car and are thinking about buying one, consider how much you'll need to drive it and why.

DOLLARS AND SENSE

Get in the habit of checking your tire pressure once a month and keeping your tires inflated to the maximum recommended pounds per square inch (PSI). Keeping your tires fully inflated can improve your gas mileage.

If you live in an area served by Uber or another car service, or that has a good public transportation system, you might be able to get away without a car. Could you walk or bike to work, or join a carpool and give the drivers some gas money in exchange for your ride? If you need a vehicle for a trip or another reason, you could always rent one.

Food Costs

The easiest way to save money on food is to buy and cook your own meals and eat at home instead of going out or getting takeout. This is generally healthier, too. You also can save money—a lot of money—by packing your lunch to take to work. Even spending $7 or $8 for lunch three times a week adds up to more than $1,000 a year. That's money that would be much better invested or saved.

Meal delivery plans like Blue Apron or Green Chef are fun and save you the trouble of running to the grocery store to shop for dinner, but the meals typically work out to between $10 and $13 for each person—far more than the U.S. Department of Agriculture's Cost of Food Analysis that set the cost of home-prepared meals at between $1.80 and $3.75 each.

Look for discount stores such as Aldi in your area, shop your local farmers' markets when they're in season, and use coupons to save more on your food bills.

 DOLLARS AND SENSE

Use an app such as SnipSnap (snipsnap.it) to scan coupons to your smartphone, eliminating the need to clip and carry paper ones with you. Stores such as Target and Giant Foods let you download a loyalty program app that gives you points for dollars spent to be used for discounts on gas, prizes, or other rewards.

Personal Insurance and Pension Costs

Personal insurance and pension costs are mostly the Social Security payments that are deducted from your paycheck. More than three quarters of all U.S. households contribute to Social Security, on average $5,275 a year. Remember that you only pay half of your Social Security contribution—your employer pays the other half.

There's nothing you can do about your Social Security contribution; it's got to be paid.

If, however, you have life insurance or other personal insurance, you might be able to lower your premiums. Look over your policy carefully, and talk to your insurance provider.

MONEY PIT

If you are self-employed, you'll need to pay the entire Social Security contribution yourself via the self-employment tax. This takes a big bite out of your income and is something to consider if you're thinking about starting a business.

Health-Care Costs

You read a lot about health-care costs in Chapter 10, so we'll just remind you to be thankful if you have a job that provides health-care benefits. If your job doesn't provide benefits or you're not working, you'll need to do some research on how to get the policy you need at the best rate.

If you haven't turned 26 yet, you can be covered on your parents' health-care plan—thank you, President Obama. If you have to buy your own insurance, check out the federal marketplace at HealthCare.gov and compare what you can get there with some private plans. A high-deductible plan may make sense if you're young and don't have any medical conditions.

Entertainment Costs

Nobody is going to argue that relaxation is important or that entertainment costs are not a legitimate spending item in your budget. What we will argue is that cutting costs on entertainment that isn't all that great is smart because you save money and have funds for the things you really want to do.

Sure, you can go to happy hour three nights a week after work, but maybe it would be better to save that money for a spring vacation in a couple years. Making a few snacks and asking your friends to bring their favorite beverages to your apartment after work instead could save you a lot of money you'll have later for something you really want or need.

If you're paying a lot for a gym membership, consider whether you're using it to its full value. Exercising outdoors when it's feasible is fun and a lot less expensive.

If you enjoy travel, look into getting credit cards that reward you with free flights or hotel stays, and join a travel website that sends you reduced rate deals on trips, such as these:

- Travelzoo (travelzoo.com)
- Travelocity (travelocity.com)
- Kayak (kayak.com)

Also check out some apps designed to save you money on travel. Here are a few to look at:

- LoungeBuddy (loungebuddy.com)
- ExpertFlyer (expertflyer.com)
- Priority Pass (prioritypass.com)

Clothing Costs

Most of us have clothes in our closets we haven't worn for months—maybe longer. And yet we keep buying more. The average American spends almost $1,500 a year on clothes—some of which never make it out of the house.

If you think you're spending too much on clothing, consider the following suggestions.

Buy used   Look for an upscale secondhand shop in your area, and check it out. You may be able to find designer clothing at a fraction of the cost you'd pay for it new.

Buy off-season   The best time to buy a winter coat or a pair of boots is in late February. A swimsuit or sundress? Late August. Consider what you'll need for the next season, and take advantage of low prices.

Beware of outlet shopping   Outlet shopping might be cheap, but brand-name clothing sometimes is made specifically for outlets and is of a lower quality than what you'd get in a department store. You're probably better off to shop department store sales for clothes you'll wear often and save the outlet shopping for an occasional trendy item you'll wear occasionally.

Stick with the basics   Buy basic items you can change up with accessories, limiting the amount of trendy clothing you'll only wear a couple times.

 POCKET CHANGE

A fun way to mix up your wardrobe is to do a clothing swap with friends. Turn your living room into an indoor yard sale by inviting friends to bring gently used clothing and accessories they no longer want and exchanging them for something "new."

Charitable Contributions

Most people agree that supporting causes you believe in is a good thing to do. But how much should you give? Many churches urge members to tithe—or contribute 10 percent of their income. On average, according to the Charities Review Council, American households contribute 3.2 percent of incomes to charities, or about $1,620 a year.

If you're just getting started financially and trying to save some money, consider donating your time and talents instead of your money to causes you support. That might mean volunteering at a shelter for the homeless or painting for Habitat for Humanity.

There's no shortage of need and many ways you can help.

The Least You Need to Know

- Some expenses you must pay, but there are many ways to cut back on your spending.
- Americans spend the largest percentages of their incomes on housing, transportation, food, personal insurance and pension, health care, entertainment, clothing, and charitable giving.
- An effective way to cut household spending is to get control of your utility bills.
- Cutting spending at this stage of your life gives you more money to save and more options for your future.

CHAPTER 13

Your Savings Options

Saving money isn't always easy, but it's necessary to secure your financial future. And once you get the hang of putting away money, it's not as hard as it might seem.

People who have some money saved tend to be less anxious than those who live paycheck to paycheck. Nearly everyone worries from time to time about how to pay the rent, or the taxes, or the cable bill. Having some money in your savings gives you a cushion if you run short of cash.

Saved money also gives you more options. That trip to Spain with some friends is possible if you've been careful with your spending and have some money tucked away in savings.

In This Chapter

- The benefits of saving
- Types of accounts for saving
- The pros and cons of various accounts
- Growing your money with interest

As your savings grow, your money can work for your future and, if applicable, the future of your family. Sending a child to college or retiring might seem like a long way off when you're in your 20s and 30s, but years pass quickly, and saving enough for the future takes time and effort. Saving money now can ensure you'll be able to reach your future goals.

Hopefully, you're convinced that saving money is smart. Even a small amount every week adds up, if you know the best ways to save.

Where to Save Your Money

You have some choices about where to save your money. Sure, you can stash it in a box under your bed, but there are better options. It's important that you find the savings account that matches your needs.

When deciding where to park your funds, consider the following:

- When will you need the money you're saving?

- How accessible does your money need to be?

- How much interest will you earn?

- Will the account give you the services you might need?

- What kind of penalties might you incur if you need to get your money?

The goal is to save money in an account where you'll earn some interest but still have access to it when you need it. Let's look at some types of available accounts and consider some of their advantages and disadvantages.

Savings Accounts

Putting your money in a savings account at a bank or credit union is reliable and safe, but you won't get much reward for parking your hard-earned cash there. Back in the day, banks were required to pay 5 percent interest on savings accounts, but that required interest ended with banking deregulation in 1986. At the beginning of 2016, the national average for interest banks pay on savings accounts was 0.26 percent, according to MyBankTracker (mybanktracker.com), an independent resource that lets consumers compare banks.

That being said, however, it pays to shop around because the amount of interest paid varies significantly from bank to bank, and some high-yield savings accounts are available. For example, some banks were offering 0.01 percent interest on savings in February 2016, but others—mostly online banks—came in as high as 1.0 percent, with no minimum deposit. Check out MyBankTracker for a comparison of rates.

Savings accounts are safe because the money they hold is insured by the Federal Deposit Insurance Commission (FDIC). Before you open an account, though, get all the details. Ask if there are fees, such as a service fee for transactions over a certain limit. Do you have to keep a specific amount in the account to avoid fees? How will you access the money in the event that you need it? Does the bank use a tiered account system?

POCKET CHANGE

It's usually a good idea to have a checking account in addition to a savings account because a checking account is set up for transactions. Checking accounts also are insured by the FDIC.

Many different savings accounts are available, so take some time to look around and find one that offers some interest and has low fees. GOBankingRates (gobankingrates.com) recommends savings accounts with these institutions for 2016, considering fees, deposit rules, minimum balances, and interest rates:

- Ally Bank (ally.com)

- American Express (americanexpress.com)

- Bank5 Connect (bank5connect.com)

- Barclays (banking.barclaysus.com)

- Capital One (capitalone.com)

- CIT Bank (bankoncit.com)

- FNBO Direct (fnbodirect.com)

- iGObanking.com (igobanking.com)

- MySavingsDirect (mysavingsdirect.com)

- Synchrony Bank (synchronybank.com)

Of the 10 recommended, MySavingsDirect's MySavings Account was ranked first.

Money Market Accounts

Money market accounts (MMAs) are a type of savings account that generally pay higher interest than regular savings accounts. Most MMAs allow you to write a minimum number of checks on the account each month, usually between three and six. With some accounts, you can transfer money or access it through an ATM. As with checking accounts, some online banks offer relatively high interest rates on MMAs. Because these accounts are offered by banks, your money is insured by the FDIC.

If you write only a couple checks a month, a money market account might be worth considering. But there's usually a hefty fee if you write more than the number of checks permitted, and the bank may require a higher minimum balance than what's required with a savings account. And you'll need to remember to move money from your MMA to your checking account before you need it to pay a bill. Also, some money market accounts only allow you to write a check over a certain amount. Remember that any additional interest you might earn is quickly chewed up if you have to pay for extra checks or a low-balance fee.

 POCKET CHANGE

According to Bankrate, almost half of all American bank deposits are invested in MMAs. That's about $5 trillion sitting in these accounts.

The national average annual percentage yield (APY) for money market accounts was only 0.08 percent at the beginning of 2016, but some higher rates can be found. Learn who's paying the best interest rates at NerdWallet's list of best MMAs at nerdwallet.com/blog/banking/best-money-market-accounts.

Money Market Funds

Money market funds (MMFs) are different from MMAs in that they're not offered by banks but by mutual fund families and brokerages. They're actually a type of mutual fund, an investment vehicle you'll learn more about in Chapter 14. MMFs are not FDIC insured or guaranteed, but most mutual fund companies try to keep them safe enough so the fund value is never a problem.

MMFs are invested only in short-term debt obligations such as certificates of deposit (CDs) and Treasury bills. A share of a money market fund usually costs $1, but the interest rates earned go up and down. Unfortunately, interest rates currently are very low, but at their height, money market funds yielded up to 12 percent. These funds are designed to keep your principal safe, so they can be a good place to park your money until you need it for something else.

Money market funds are safe choices for short-term investments. Your original investment is fairly secure while you earn a bit of interest. For example, if you invest $500 in a money market fund, you'll get $500 back at the due date, plus a little interest. They're not the most exciting investment vehicles, but if you have money you need to keep at a constant value, you might want to give them a look.

> **POCKET CHANGE**
>
> Money market funds have been increasing in popularity, with more than $2.6 trillion invested in them in the United States.

Certificates of Deposit

CDs aren't as widely used as they used to be because interest rates have plummeted, but they're still worth a look for funds you know you'll need sooner rather than later. CDs require that you deposit your money for a certain amount of time—days, months, or years, depending on the type of CD you choose. The financial institution that holds the CD agrees to pay you a certain interest rate and yield for the time it has your money.

CDs are investments for security. If you pick an insured bank or credit union, for example, your money is guaranteed to be there when the CD matures, or comes due, because it's guaranteed by the FDIC.

The most popular CDs are the ones for 6 months or 1, 2, 3, 4, or 5 years. Normally, the longer you keep your money in a CD, the more interest you get. This increased interest rate is the financial institution's way of rewarding you for allowing it to keep your money for that period of time.

If you don't hold up your end of the bargain and you take your money out of the account before the specified amount of time has expired, you'll be charged a penalty. The amount of the penalty varies by each institution, but it can be pretty hefty. If you pull out your money early, you could even end up with less money than you started with if the circumstances are right. You'd lose not only whatever interest you'd earned but part of your principal as well.

Interest rates vary, but most CDs pay a little more than savings accounts or money market accounts. Most pay fixed rates, but some offer variable rates, meaning the interest rate can change. The interest rates on CDs vary not only from bank to bank, but they also change within a bank. Rates are contingent on many factors (watch for CD specials), but they tend to mirror the interest rates in the general market. If you buy CDs with low interest rates, purchase short-term CDs and wait for rates to rise. This eliminates you tying up your funds for long periods of time.

Some banks might allow you to add money to a CD account at the interest rate of that particular day. That way, if you opened the account on a day when the rate was low, you can boost your earnings by adding money at a higher interest rate later.

Banks also may have a "bump-up" provision, which is a one-time chance to increase the interest rate on the CD.

And in today's world of banks competing for your deposits, some banks won't even charge a penalty for early withdrawal.

MONEY PIT

Some CDs advertise no penalties, but they probably have many stipulations. By law, CDs are required to charge a penalty if the money is withdrawn within the first 7 days, so there really can be no such thing as a no-penalty CD. A CD that's advertised as having no penalty is probably a money market account in disguise.

If you're going CD shopping, don't just start and stop at your local bank. Check out the rates at credit unions and online at Bankrate (bankrate.com). Credit unions typically pay up to half a percentage point higher interest on CDs than banks do.

A CD isn't the most exciting investment you'll ever make. But if you have some money you can afford to be without for a specified period yet can't afford to lose, it might be worth your consideration. Many different kinds of CDs exist, so do your homework before investing your money.

Treasury Bills and Treasury Notes

Treasury bills and Treasury notes, often just called *treasuries,* are safe savings vehicles because they're backed by the U.S. government. The good news is that you don't have to pay state or local taxes on treasuries, and they come in different maturity lengths.

With a Treasury bill, you buy at a discount and get the full value of the bill when it reaches maturity. You might buy a $500 treasury for $450, for instance, but when the bill matures, it will be worth the face value of $500.

Treasury notes come with maturity periods of 2, 3, 5, 7, and 10 years. You earn a certain amount of interest every 6 months you hold them. And like a Treasury bill, if you buy the note at a discount, it will be worth the face value at maturity.

You only need a minimum of $100 to buy a Treasury bill or note, so they're an easy way to begin saving in a safe vehicle.

The Magic of Interest

It's hard to imagine that saving small amounts of money can make a difference in your financial future, but it does. Interest, especially compound interest, can give you big returns on small investments. That's why, regardless of how much you save, consider the interest you'll be getting on your money.

Simple interest, which is what we normally just refer to as interest, is a method of calculating what you earn on the money you deposited or invested by applying the stated interest rate to your deposit or investment for the period of deposit. For example, if you invest $2,000 in an account for 1 year at 5 percent interest, the bank would pay you $100 at the end of the year (5% of $2,000 = $100). Not bad, huh? You get $100 just for letting your money sit there. But if you were earning *compound interest* on your $2,000, you'd be in even better shape.

Compound interest is paid on an initial deposit plus any accumulated interest from period to period. Compound interest gives you interest on your interest. It's definitely the way to invest. Compounding interest at 5 percent over 1 year wouldn't make a great difference on a $2,000 deposit, but it still would give you a couple more dollars for your money. When you get into big investments at higher interest rates, compounding interest really becomes significant.

DEFINITION

Simple interest enables you to earn extra money on your deposit by applying the stated interest rate on only what you deposited for the exact period of deposit. **Compound interest** is paid on an initial deposit plus any accumulated interest from period to period.

Interest is generally compounded in one of several ways: continuously, daily, weekly, monthly, quarterly, and annually. The more often it's compounded, the better off you'll be.

They're getting harder and harder to find, but look for banks that compound interest continuously or daily. When your money starts growing, you'll be pleasantly surprised.

Sounds pretty amazing, doesn't it? This is the power of compound interest and why a penny saved is a lot more than a penny earned.

The Least You Need to Know

- Saving money can give you peace of mind, security for the future, and options for what you do.
- Consider the pros and cons of various savings vehicles before you hand over money to a bank or other institution.
- Interest rates on savings accounts, money market accounts, and CDs aren't much to talk about these days, but it's important to find the best rates you can, which may be from online banks.
- When you understand interest, you can appreciate how saving even small amounts of money adds up.

CHAPTER 14

Your Investing Options

When you're a little more established financially, you might start thinking about investing some of your money. Many millennials have expressed distrust in traditional investment opportunities, and many people in their 20s and 30s have an uneasy relationship with Wall Street. And yet, despite some traumatic ups and downs of the stock market during the past decade, most experts still insist that in the long term, investing in the market is the best way to ensure your money will grow. History has shown that markets are cyclical and conditions will improve.

In This Chapter

- Knowing when it's time to start investing
- Why are you investing?
- Assessing your risk tolerance
- Mutual funds and exchange traded funds
- Navigating the stock market
- Lending your money by buying bonds

Having money to invest means you have savings you want to put to work for you. Everybody should have some investments so their funds grow. Even with fluctuating markets, good investments grow over time, which helps you keep up with inflation and helps ensure your financial security when you retire.

In this chapter, we take a look at some of the basics of investing. We think the subject will seem less intimidating after you finish reading it.

When to Start Investing

Before you even think about investing money in stocks, mutual funds, or exchange traded funds (ETFs), take a close look at where you stand financially. How are you doing paying back your student loans? Are your credit cards under control? Do you have some money stashed in a safe place for your emergency fund? Are you making regular contributions to your 401(k) or another retirement savings plan? If all those things are taken care of and in good shape, you probably should think about putting some money in other investment vehicles.

You don't need a ton of money to start investing, and you don't necessarily need a financial adviser or a salesperson to tell you where to put your money. You can purchase many investments without a salesperson, and if you do your homework carefully, you'll be able to figure out on your own the best places to put your money at this time in your life.

Almost everyone who begins investing starts small and builds up their investments over time. If you work carefully and patiently, you'll do the same. It's fun to watch the growth, particularly when you remember that you started small.

MONEY PIT

Don't even think about investing yet if you still have credit card debt. Making 6 or 7 percent off an investment pales in comparison to paying out 18 or 22 percent or more on your Visa. Pay off the plastic first. You can't get ahead while you're carrying a load of debt.

Your Investment Goals Matter

Before you begin the investment process, sit down and identify just why you're investing. Do you want to make money for a down payment on your first house? A beach house in 20 or 25 years? College money for your kids? Additional funds for your retirement years?

Each investor has different goals he or she needs to consider before beginning the investment process. If you're investing in hopes of sending your child off to Princeton in 10 years, for example, you'll invest differently than you would for your retirement 35 years down the road. What you're investing for should largely determine the type of investments you make.

If you're young and investing money you won't need for a long time, you can afford to put your funds in higher-risk investments than you would if you were nearing retirement age and would soon need money from your investments.

If you're investing so you'll have money for a down payment on a house in 5 years, you'd be smart to consider an investment vehicle that's more like a savings account—a certificate of deposit or money market account that pays you interest.

 POCKET CHANGE

> If you're investing money you'll need within 2 years or less, you're generally considered a short-term investor. Investing your money for 2 to 7 years puts you in the midterm range. If you won't need your money for more than 7 years, you're considered a long-range investor.

People invest for all kinds of reasons. They might want to build wealth to pass on to their children or to fund the trip of their dreams in 20 years. Many people invest for their kids' educations, and everyone should be looking toward retirement funds.

As you learn more about investment vehicles, you'll find out which ones are good for short-term investments and which ones to go with for the long haul. That's important because you don't want to tie up money for 20 years might need in 2. How you invest your money depends largely on how long it can remain out of your reach. It also depends on how much of it you can afford to lose.

Some investments are a lot riskier than others, and you need to know what you're getting into before you throw your money into the pot.

What Kind of Risk Are You Willing to Take?

Some people are just naturally more risk averse or risk tolerant than others. You probably know people who like to play it safe in most everything they do and others who love the thrill of an adrenaline rush.

Those qualities extend to making investments. Everyone who invests money hopes the value of his or her investment will increase, of course. But some investors are willing to take a lot more risk than others to make that happen.

High-Risk Investors

People can be high-risk investors by choice, or they can be high-risk investors because they don't know enough about what they're doing. (The latter is more often the case.) A high-risk investor is generally classified as someone who can live with losing about a quarter of his or her *investment portfolio* in a year.

If you have $10,000 to invest, and the thought of losing $2,500 of it doesn't give you chills, you might qualify as high risk. But even if you're a high-risk investor, you still have to do your homework and find out where your money has the best chance of earning you more.

Suppose an investor chooses to be high risk. He jumps into the stock market and buys only investments with potential for very high returns. He got a hot tip from a buddy of his that a certain industry is about to take off, so he loads most of his money into that industry's stock. Even if this guy knows what he's doing, he's a daredevil. But if he's making high-risk investments because he hasn't done his homework and doesn't understand the importance of diversification or that his money should be spread around, he's risking catastrophe—he's *speculating*.

Speculating, like gambling, is taking chances and rolling the dice to try to make a killing in the market quickly. Getting a hot tip at a cocktail party and acting on it by putting down $5,000 is speculating. Investing, on the other hand, is buying 100 shares of IBM stock after you've investigated exactly what the company does, the fundamentals (explained later in the chapter), and the company's outlook for the future.

> **DEFINITION**
>
> Your **investment portfolio** is the listing and value of all your investments at a given point in time. **Speculating** is taking above-average risks to achieve above-average returns, generally during a relatively short period of time. Speculation involves buying something on the basis of its potential selling price rather than on the basis of its actual value.

Moderate-Risk Investors

If you're a moderate-risk investor, you won't bet the farm on a tip you overhear while you're getting your hair cut or taking a yoga class. You're generally classified as a moderate-risk investor if you determine you can stand to lose up to 15 percent of that $10,000 in your portfolio. The thought of being out $1,500 doesn't make you jump up and down, but it won't keep you up every night either.

Conservative Investors

Conservative investors are the meat-and-potatoes people of the investment world. Keep your fancy appetizers, your cream sauces, and your puff pastry desserts; just give these folks something they can depend on, something that won't give them any surprises, and something they don't have to worry about. They don't want to take any chances with their investments and will gladly give up even the possibility of high returns to know their money will be there when they want it.

Conservative investors generally start having nightmares at the thought of losing even 5 or 6 percent of their portfolios over 1 year's time. The thought of losing $600 of that $10,000 investment makes them very nervous.

Mutual Funds

Mutual funds are a very popular investment vehicle for individuals because they don't require a lot of money to get started. They carry some other advantages as well.

 DEFINITION

Mutual funds are an aggregate of stocks, bonds, and assets purchased with money from many investors and typically managed by a portfolio manager and investment experts who research the market and recommend which investments to add to the fund.

Mutual funds are investments that pool many people's money and place it into stocks, bonds, and/or other holdings according to the investment policy of the fund that's stated in the fund's prospectus, or plan. When you put your money into a mutual fund, you're throwing it into a pot with another couple hundred million dollars or so. Most mutual funds contain more than $1 billion.

The money in the mutual fund is managed by a portfolio manager and a team of researchers who are responsible for finding the best places to invest the money. A portfolio is a group of investments selected and assembled to meet a financial goal. A portfolio manager is paid to supervise the investment decisions of others and handle the management of a portfolio, be it for individuals or for a mutual fund.

Types of Mutual Funds

Most mutual funds fall into one of five categories:

- Money market funds
- Stock funds
- Bond funds
- Balanced funds
- Target date funds

Features of each type vary, as do the risks and rewards:

Money market funds   These are low risk because your investment can only be placed in short-term, dependable investments issued by the U.S. government or corporations.

Stock funds   These funds invest in corporate stock and come in different types. Your money might be invested in a growth fund, which aims for above-average gains, or an income fund that pays regular dividends. A sector fund concentrates on a particular area, such as health care, biotech, or technology. An index fund is concentrated on a particular market index, such as the Standard & Poor's 500.

Bond funds   As the name implies, these are invested in bonds. They usually pay periodic dividends to investors.

Balanced funds   Often called *hybrid funds*, balanced funds own both stocks and bonds. They usually contain about 60 percent stocks and 40 percent bonds—a reasonably balanced mix of assets.

Target date funds   These hold a variety of stocks, bonds, and other investments, selected depending on the age of the investor. If you invest in a target date fund when you're 24, your mix will be more high risk than that of someone who invests when they're 54. As you get nearer to retirement age, your investments will be shifted so they incur less risk. The mutual fund company manages your portfolio to minimize risk as you get older so you don't have to.

Advantages of Mutual Funds

Mutual funds are popular because they can offer some great advantages. For example, money can be taken directly from your bank account each month and transferred into a mutual fund. This makes investing nearly painless.

Mutual funds also can offer *diversification*. If you are diversified and one or more of your investments hits a slump, you can rely on your other investments to boost your total portfolio. For instance, you could divide your money among three or four different types of stock funds so you'd always have some money invested in a profitable area of the market.

DEFINITION

Diversification means investing your money in various securities in different industries, hoping to protect your investment against one or more companies undergoing financial disaster.

Part of diversification is investing in bonds or fixed income as well as different types of stocks. It can be difficult for you to plan that diversification on your own, which is why people look to mutual funds to diversify their portfolios. Diversification is very important, particularly in uncertain economic times such as those we've experienced in the past decade.

It doesn't cost much out of pocket to buy mutual fund shares. You can purchase a *no-load fund,* which is a type of mutual fund in which shares are sold without a sales charge or commission. You do not pay a sales charge to buy the fund. If a sales charge or commission is charged, the mutual fund is called a *load fund*.

Brokerage for the investments within the mutual fund, or the cost of buying or selling shares of the stocks or bonds, are generally far lower than standard brokerage because the fund managers buy or sell so many shares of a security at one time and buy and sell frequently. Having this power enables them to negotiate trades for a lot less money than you could on your own.

You can direct almost any amount of money to where you want it. If you're into a mutual fund for the long haul, you can direct your money to funds that invest more heavily in stocks instead of more-conservative bond funds. A balanced mutual fund is a good initial investment.

Plenty of information is available about reliable mutual funds, including funds that don't require a lot of money to start and have the most reasonable fees. Check out the following to learn more:

- "MONEY 50: The World's Best Mutual Funds and ETFs" (time.com/money/3648639/money-50-best-mutual-funds-and-etfs)

- Kiplinger's "Great Mutual Funds for Young Investors" (kiplinger.com/article/investing/T041-C009-S001-great-mutual-funds-for-young-investors.html)

- TheStreet Ratings's "Top Rated Mutual Funds" (thestreet.com/stock-market-news/10571219/top-rated-mutual-funds/top-rated-mutual-funds.html)

One final advantage of mutual funds is that they carry almost no risk of going bankrupt. Due to diversification within a fund, a mutual fund is very unlikely to lose its entire value. You can invest $5,000 into XYZ Computer Company, for example, and within 5 years, the value could drop to $0, but if you invest $5,000 in a diversified general mutual fund, your money should follow the ups and downs of the stock market, not just one stock.

Look carefully at mutual funds as you begin to think about investing your money. They're a great place to start investing and are an excellent vehicle in which your money can grow. Don't just pick the fund by the name; read the information online about what the fund is actually invested in.

Exchange Traded Funds

ETFs are a more recent investment alternative. ETFs combine the diversification advantages of mutual funds with the trading flexibility and continual pricing of stocks and bonds. Mutual funds are sold only at the end of the day, but ETFs can be sold any time during the trading day. Index ETFs are available as well as managed ETFs.

ETFs were introduced in Canada in 1989 and started catching on in the United States soon thereafter. ETFs are as varied as mutual funds and have steadily increased in popularity, although Americans still have much more money invested in mutual funds than ETFs.

ETFs often have lower expenses and operating costs than mutual funds because they initially were mostly index funds, which do not require as much active management as some other types of funds; less active management results in lower costs. Many people like the idea of less active management and lower costs, while others prefer the active strategy work that goes into managing mutual funds.

Much debate and speculation surround mutual funds and ETFs and which is better. Most experts feel one is not better than the other and that both mutual funds and ETFs can be good fits in a portfolio. Be sure to read about whatever fund you're considering before deciding where to put your money.

The Stock Market

For many reasons, the stock market is not a simple topic. Before you start investing your hard-earned money there, be sure to do some additional research and get a good understanding of how it works. For now, let's have a look at what the stock market is and how you can get started.

Simply speaking, the *stock market* is the arena in which shares of publicly held companies, or *securities,* are released and traded. Trades occur within organized markets called *exchanges.*

> **DEFINITION**
>
> The **stock market** is the organized securities exchange for stock and bond transactions. **Securities** are investments that represent evidence of debt, ownership of a business, or the legal right to acquire or sell an ownership interest in a business. **Exchanges** are marketplaces where stocks, bonds, indexes, and commodities are traded.

The Major U.S. Stock Exchanges

The United States is home to three major stock exchanges:

- New York Stock Exchange (NYSE)

- American Stock Exchange (AMEX)

- National Association of Securities Dealers Automated Quotation System (NASDAQ)

The NYSE, formed in 1792, is the largest organized stock exchange in the United States.

The AMEX was known as the American Curb Exchange prior to 1951 because trading was conducted on the curb of Wall and Broad Streets in New York City. The AMEX has less-stringent listing requirements than the NYSE, so it attracts many smaller companies, ETFs, and derivatives.

Unlike the NYSE, there's no physical location for the NASDAQ; trading is done by computer. The AMEX and NASDAQ have merged but maintain their own names and identities.

The overall performance of the stock market is evaluated in many different ways. The Dow Jones Industrial Average (DJIA) is one measure of the stock market, and the standard we hear nearly every day. It consists of three indices that include averages for utilities, industrial, and transportation stocks as well as the composite averages. Each average reflects the simple mathematical average of the closing prices (the prices at the end of the day) and indicates the day-to-day changes in the market prices of stocks in the designated index.

Okay, what does that mean? The DJIA is a composite (group) of 30 stocks with a daily average. Tomorrow, if the stocks go up in price as an average, the DJIA goes up. If the average value of these selected stocks goes down, the DJIA goes down. If market trends are moving increasingly upward, it's called a *bull market*. Market trends that are moving continuously downward are called a *bear market*.

> **DEFINITION**
>
> When market trends move upward, it's called a **bull market.** It's a **bear market** when trends move continuously downward.

Knowing What Stocks to Buy

The stock market can seem confusing, but the basic concept of investing isn't all that complicated. When you buy a company's stock, you're really buying a little piece of the company represented by its stock. The more pieces, or *shares,* of stock in one company you have, the bigger a piece of the company you own. Owning stock makes you a *shareholder* in the company.

Stocks come in different kinds, such as *blue-chip stock,* which refers to stock of well-established companies like IBM and Exxon, and *growth stock,* which is that of companies on their way up.

> **DEFINITION**
>
> **Shares** are what you own when you buy stock in a particular company. A **shareholder** is the person who owns the shares of stock. **Blue-chip stock** is the stock of established companies and considered less risky than **growth stock,** which is the stock of less-established companies.

Obviously, when you buy a company's stock, you want that company to succeed and grow. For that reason, you should never buy stock—either on your own or with the help of a broker—without first thoroughly researching the company. You need to gain a good understanding of the goods or services the company provides, who its customers are, its market share, the size of the company, its history, the management team, and so forth. You also want to learn about the industry the company is in and check out financial aspects such as the company's earnings, debt ratios, and trends.

You can use a variety of sources to learn all this information, but a good place to start is with market reports, available both in print and online. Compilations of news affecting either a particular market or the general stock market, market reports give you lots of information about the overall market and economy. This is valuable information when you're trying to figure out what stocks to buy. After you've purchased some stock, market reports keep you up to date with information relating to your particular holdings.

Once you own stock, you can keep up with how it's doing on a major financial site like the following:

- CBS MarketWatch (marketwatch.com)

- MSN MoneyCentral (msn.com/en-us/money)

- Yahoo! Finance (finance.yahoo.com)

Every publicly traded security has a ticker symbol that identifies and represents it. The ticket symbol for Microsoft, for instance, is MSFT. You simply enter the ticket symbol into the quote box on any of these sites to instantly learn how your stock is faring.

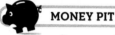
MONEY PIT

Some people are attracted to the stock market because they think it's exciting, even glamorous. We're not discouraging you from Wall Street, but remember to put your financial house in order first. If you don't consider all the advantages—and disadvantages (including taxes)—before you invest, you could be putting your personal financial situation at risk.

Enlisting the Help of a Broker

Some people spend their days online buying and selling stocks. When you're first starting out, however, it's a good idea to work with a broker. Basically, there are four types of stockbrokers that range greatly in services and price:

Online discount brokers   These brokers work with you on the phone or internet. You normally pay on a per-transaction or per-share basis, so you can open an account with an online broker with relatively little money and start buying and selling stock immediately. The downside is that discount online brokers don't provide any kind of financial advice, although most provide links to information and resources for you to access.

Discount brokers with assistance   Similar to online discount brokers, discount brokers with assistance provide some extra help by giving you tips on how to invest or directing you to reports and other information. They don't, however, give you suggestions or advice about what to buy, and they generally charge a small fee for their assistance.

Full-service brokers   These brokers charge between 1 and 2 percent of the value of your investment, but presumably they possess knowledge and information concerning your particular investment, and you would benefit from his or her expertise. A full-service broker should take time to get to know you and gain an understanding of your financial goals and factors that relate to you. A good full-service broker can be well worth the fees charged.

Money managers   Finally, these brokers do what the title implies—they manage your investment account. People who hire money managers normally have hefty portfolios and are willing to pay someone to handle them while they're doing other things. At this stage of life, it's highly unlikely that you need a money manager.

> **$ DOLLARS AND SENSE**
>
> A broker can be your best friend when it comes to buying and selling stock. Remember, however, that ultimately you are responsible for what your money buys, meaning it's important that you do your homework and don't rely solely on your broker.

Some analysts say you can save 50 percent or more by buying stock from a big discount broker such as Charles Schwab or TD Waterhouse rather than from the traditional brokerage firms such as Merrill Lynch or Morgan Stanley. Full-service or discount broker? The choice is yours. If you feel you need advice and direction, look for a full-service broker. If you know what you want, or if you have another type of financial adviser, a discount broker should be fine.

Understanding the Risks of the Stock Market

Every investment you make, including buying stock, involves a certain level of investment risk, with the chance that you'll lose the money you invest or the investment won't perform as well as you thought. Investments with the chance for higher returns carry greater risk than those without the return potential.

Stocks can make money in two ways. As a shareholder, you may get annual dividends. Hopefully, the price of the stock also will increase so if you wanted to, you could sell your stock for more than what you bought it for and make a profit.

> **DEFINITION**
>
> A **dividend** is a share of a company's net profits, distributed by the company to a class of its stockholders, and paid in a fixed amount for each share of stock held. Dividends are usually fixed in preferred stock, which is a special class of securities; dividends from common stock vary as the company's performance shifts.

The amount of dividends a corporation pays out is a reflection of the type of company it is. The stock of a growing company won't pay out as many dividends as, say, an established utility company. It's important to remember this difference if you're planning to buy shares of a company. Will you receive a good annual income from your stocks, or are you banking on profits that will occur a few years or more down the road? At this stage of your life, it's likely you'd buy stock with potential for growth, hang on to it for a while, and sell at a profit in the future.

What happens, though, if the stock you purchase takes a nosedive and loses much of its value? First, don't panic. One thing you can count on it that the stock market will rise and fall, and rushing to sell stock that's lost value is not a wise move.

The goal of investing in the stock market is to buy when the stock price is low—or at least relatively low—and sell when the price is high. If the value of your stock decreases, consider the state of the overall market. It may be that the whole market is down due to an event such as lower-than-expected job creation numbers. If that's the case, it makes no sense to sell your stock.

If the value has declined due to a reason specific to the company in which you own stock, you need to take a close look at the underlying fundamentals of the company and try to figure out what's happening. Has there been a change in management? A trade problem? Do some investigative work, and think carefully about whether it makes sense for you to hang on to the stock or to sell. A full-service broker can advise you.

 DOLLARS AND SENSE

Check out your local newspaper's business page for a "stocks of local interest" column. Read these stock reports daily for a week or two to get a feeling for how local companies are doing in the market. It's sometimes easier to understand the stock market if you look at how it pertains to something you're familiar with.

Bonds

When you buy a company's stock, you're buying a little piece of the company. That makes you an owner. Another way to invest is lend your money to an organization and have it agree to pay you back, with interest, over a specified time. When it comes to investing, you can own or you can loan.

When you loan money with the understanding that it will be repaid to you with interest, you're participating in a *lending investment*. We most commonly think of *bonds* as lending investments, and they are the most widely used. Bonds come in many varieties, including municipal bonds, general obligation bonds, revenue bonds, corporate bonds, high-yield bonds, savings bonds, and government agency bonds. Other investments in which you lend money are certificates of deposit (CDs), Treasury bills, and Treasury notes.

> **DEFINITION**
>
> With a **lending investment,** you loan your money with the understanding that you'll get it back—with interest—after a specified time. Think of a **bond** as an IOU. When you buy a bond, you're lending your money to the company or government for a specified period of time.

All these are investments in which you give your money to a particular entity with the goal of getting it back at a certain time with an agreed-upon amount of interest added. The entity borrowing your money varies from a bank, which generally administers CDs; to a corporation such as AutoZone, for example; to the U.S. government, which offers bonds. Corporations also offer bonds; they borrow funds from you in the form of a bond and pay you back with interest, which generates income for you.

The conditions, such as the length of time the money will be invested, the amount of interest paid, and so forth, are different for each of these types of lending investments. In most cases, bonds offer a fixed interest rate. That is, the rate remains steady throughout the life of the loan. Some bonds offer variable interest rates, for which the changes are defined in the fine print. Be sure you know what you're buying.

When interest rates go up, the value of your bond goes down. When interest rates go down, the value of your bond goes up. When your bond matures, you get your money back. Let's look at an example: if you're holding a bond that pays 5 percent interest and the interest rate jumps to 7 percent, you lose on the value of your bond if you sell it. But if you're earning 7 percent interest on your bond and the interest rate drops to 5 percent, you're still entitled to 7 percent, the agreed-upon rate. In that case, your bond would have increased in value (known as a *premium bond*) compared to new bonds being issued. Either way, you'll get your initial investment back when the investment matures.

Always be sure the bonds you buy have a clear *maturity date* so you'll know exactly when you can get your money back.

> **DEFINITION**
>
> A **premium bond** is a bond for which the value has increased. The **maturity date** of a bond is the agreed-upon time at which you stop loaning your money to the government. You get back your investment and the specified interest when the bond reaches its maturity date.

The Least You Need to Know

- Start thinking about investing after you've repaid your college loans, built up an emergency fund, gotten control of credit card debt, and are funding a retirement account.

- Being clear about your investing goals helps you determine what types of investments make sense for you.

- Assess your tolerance for financial risk before deciding where to invest your money.

- Mutual funds and exchange traded funds are popular investments because they offer diversification and you don't need a lot of money to purchase them.

- Stocks are investments you buy. Bonds are investments for which you loan money and get interest in return.

Big-Ticket Purchases

While you're saving money, you're also going to need to be spending some. In Part 6, we discuss the big-ticket purchases you'll be faced with. Not everybody needs a car, but if you do, you need to determine the best way to pay for one, whether it's leasing or buying.

In addition, it might be time to start thinking about buying a house. We explore the advantages and disadvantages of owning versus renting a home, share tips on applying for a mortgage, go over the costs associated with home ownership, and offer guidance on protecting what you own with insurance.

CHAPTER 15

Buying Versus Leasing a Car

The rumor that millennials are turning their backs on owning cars and even driving may be just that—a rumor. There's been a lot of talk in the past couple years about millennials giving up cars to use public transportation, Uber, or car-sharing services. Recent studies, however, reveal some very different information regarding millennials' attitudes about owning and driving cars.

In April 2015, global marketing information services firm J.D. Power and Associates reported that millennials accounted for 27 percent of new car sales—more than any group other than baby boomers. And a recent study by MTV found that three quarters of millennials reported they would rather give up social media for a day than their cars. About the same number said they would give up texting for a week rather than their cars for the same amount of time.

In This Chapter

- Deciding what kind of car to buy
- Buying versus leasing
- Buying new versus used
- The added expenses of car ownership

So although millennials might be getting driver's licenses and purchasing vehicles later than their Gen X or baby boomer counterparts, most are, indeed, getting their licenses and driving, and many are buying or leasing cars. By doing so, they join the long-lived American love affair with automobiles.

Car, Truck, or Something Else?

We've always taken our cars pretty seriously in this country. For teenagers, getting a car has been a rite of passage—a symbol of emerging adulthood. Many adults, both young and old, need cars to get around.

What vehicles we buy depends on many factors. When oil prices are high and gas rises to $4 a gallon at the pumps, sales of gas-guzzling trucks and SUVs tend to fall off. When gas gets below $2 a gallon, we kind of forget about the pain of expensive fuel and shift back to larger vehicles. An increasing number of environmentally minded drivers are turning to hybrid or electric cars in an effort to reduce their carbon footprint, regardless of the price of fossil fuel.

A car provides you the freedom to go where you want, when you want to, but it might just be that not everybody needs to have one. After all, vehicles are expensive to buy and to maintain. They break down occasionally, and you've got to find a place to park them—in some cases paying a lot of money to do so. They require time and attention, and by the time you pay for them, they're hardly worth the metal they're made of. Based on the fact that 88 percent of American households own at least one vehicle, however, it seems that most of us still can't imagine life without our wheels.

 DOLLARS AND SENSE

If you use public transportation regularly, be sure you check out commuter passes, which enable you to buy quantities of bus, train, or subway tickets at reduced prices.

The majority of Americans have cars, but plenty of people still get along perfectly fine without a vehicle of their own, especially if they live in a city or a small, walkable town. Some of these folks hitch a ride when they need one, or they walk or ride a bike or scooter. Others use public transportation, including the buses, trains, subways, and trolleys that carry people across town and across the country every day. Others call a cab or a car service like Uber or Lyft, rent a car, or subscribe to a car-sharing service like Zipcar.

Let's take quick look at some alternatives to having your own vehicle.

Renting a Car

Renting a car makes a lot of sense if you live in a city and want to travel to another city. Sure, you could take a bus from New York City to visit your college roommate in Washington, D.C., but that can be a hassle. Depending on how many stops you make along the way, it can turn a 225-mile, less-than-4-hour car trip into an all-day adventure. And sometimes you're just not in the mood to chat with the person in the next seat, who is going home to her mother because she just found out her husband is having an affair.

If you use a site like Kayak and are resourceful, you probably can find a rental car for about $20 a day. Sure, you have to pay for gas and maybe some other additional fees, but after you deduct the cost of the bus and consider your time, it probably won't be a budget-buster.

Sharing a Car

Car-share programs, which started in European cities, are gaining popularity in the United States and achieving an almost cultlike following in some cities, where users love the convenience of having cars available without the hassles and expenses of owning them. These services don't make economic sense for someone who drives long distances back and forth to work every day, but car sharing can be a great option for someone who needs a car only occasionally.

Car-share programs vary from city to city, so spend a little time researching to see what's available near you.

 POCKET CHANGE

> Ford Motor Company recently announced an innovative car-sharing program called Ford Credit Link that lets up to six people lease the same vehicle and share it. The pilot program launched in Austin, Texas, in 2016 and is designed to attract people who want part-time access to a vehicle. Learn more at fordcreditlink.com.

Bike-sharing programs are available in some U.S. cities and gaining in popularity.

Owning a Car Costs More Than You Think

The initial purchase of a car is a big expense. Americans paid an average of $33,560 for a new car in 2015 and $15,900 for a used vehicle. Those costs, however, are just the beginning. A car continues to cost money for as long as you own it.

You'll need to think about maintenance costs—both routine and nonroutine. You also must have insurance on your car and pay for fuel to keep it running.

MONEY PIT

Don't feel obligated to have your car maintained by the dealer from whom you bought it. An independent mechanic might be cheaper. Ask some people who have the same kind of car as you where they go for maintenance. A good mechanic you can trust might not be the easiest thing to find, but it's worth it to try.

Then there are tolls, parking fees, finance charges, inspections, and cleanings. When you add it all up, the average yearly cost of owning and operating a car is $8,698, according to AAA's 2015 Your Driving Costs study. That comes out to almost $725 a month.

The accepted rule of thumb is that you should spend no more than 20 percent of your monthly income (take home—not gross) on a car payment. Because a car consistently loses value, it's not a good investment. You can find all sorts of things to do with your money that will result in far greater benefits than car payments.

Bankrate provides a calculator to help you determine how much you should plan to spend on a car. You can access it at bankrate.com/calculators/auto/auto-loan-calculator.aspx.

Buying a Car

Although it might not be necessary for everyone to own a car, most of us do. Buying a car means paying out a lot of money to get one, followed by more money to keep it running.

If you're in the market for a new car, take your time and consider all the angles before you buy. Maybe you've had a good job for a few years and have put some money aside for a down payment on a new car. Or maybe a used car makes more sense for you. And then there's the big question: should you buy a vehicle or lease it?

One fact is indisputable: cars are expensive. Even if you're not looking for anything fancy, you'll pay a lot of money for a new car, despite any manufacturer and dealer specials you get. If you're going to buy a car, there are a few ways of doing it. You can walk into the dealership, plunk down $33,000, and drive off in your new wheels. Or if you're like most people, you can finance your car.

Financing Your Car

Most dealerships offer car financing. And it's tempting to get your loan through the dealer because it's easy. You can sign up, be approved, and drive your new car off the lot all in the same day. However, unless you can get a special deal like 0 percent financing, be sure to check out the rates on a loan from your bank or credit union before committing to the dealer's offer.

Dealer financing sometimes is cheaper than a bank, but not always. You should contact your local bank, see what it can do for you, and compare its rates with what the dealer is offering. One thing to remember: if the car dealer controls your loan, a salesman could try to talk you into buying a more expensive car than you intended to by assuring you they'll give you the extra money you need to cover it.

Even if a dealer offers what sounds like a terrific financing deal, be sure you consider all the facts and know what the actual cost of the car will be when the financing kicks in. And don't let a dealer persuade you that it's okay to drive the car off the lot before the financing is approved. Car dealers are out to make money one way or another, whether it's from the cost of the car or through finance charges.

If you can find a bank-financed car loan that has a lower interest rate than what you can get through the dealer and get preapproved before buying your car, you'll be in a great position to negotiate on your price. Here's why: you know how much money you have, and you buy within that amount; the car salesperson knows you're serious about buying, and he'll do everything he can to be sure you buy from him; and you're not at the mercy of the dealership to get your loan. Instead, the dealership has to work on your terms.

 MONEY PIT

Stay away from finance companies that offer guaranteed, same-day loans and other ploys to get your business. The rates such companies give you are virtually always higher than what you'd get from a bank or credit union. Most of these companies cater to people with bad credit, who would have trouble getting a bank loan.

Consider the following when looking for and getting a car loan:

Compare interest rates   Shop around for interest rates. Often, credit unions offer the best rates on car loans, so be sure you look there as well as at banks and the dealership.

Go for simple   Instead of an installment loan, go for a simple interest loan, which lets you pay interest only on the remaining amount of your loan. The bank will figure out the total interest on your loan and set up a plan where you'll pay the same amount each month for the life of your loan. That's better than a front-end installment loan, which requires you to pay interest each month on the full amount of the loan.

Make a large down payment   Put down as much money as you can. The more you put down toward your car, the lower your interest rate will probably be. Plus, you'll be financing less, thereby paying less interest overall.

Boost your down payment with rebates   Use rebates (money the car manufacturer offers you as an incentive to buy its cars) to make your down payment bigger. If you're offered a rebate on a new car, by all means take advantage of it. But don't buy a more expensive car just because you get a rebate.

Keep your loan short Take the shortest loan term you can manage. Don't pay back a loan over 5 years if you can do it in 3. Even though your monthly payment will be smaller on the 5-year loan, you'll be paying interest for a longer time and end up paying more in the long run.

Pay off your loan early If you can, it's beneficial to pay off your loan early. Some lenders let you pay off a loan early, but others will penalize you if you do so. Be sure to find out about that before you sign for the loan. Don't take out a loan that won't permit you to pay it off early.

Consider a home-equity loan The interest you pay on a car loan is not tax-deductible, but the interest on a home equity loan is. If you own a home and need to borrow money for a car, look into getting a home-equity loan to use instead of a car loan.

Pay off any credit cards first Finally, don't put extra money toward a 7 percent car loan if you have an 18 percent credit card bill outstanding. The extra money will go a lot farther if you use it to pay off the credit card bill.

Cash Back Versus 0 Percent Financing

Auto manufacturers want to sell you their cars, and many will make tempting offers to lure you onto the lot. At the beginning of 2016, for example, Mazda was offering 0 percent financing on the popular Mazda3, and Ford would sell you a brand-new Fusion with 0 percent financing for 5 years or more than $2,000 cash back.

If you can't get an offer for 0 percent interest, it's likely that you'd be able to find a deal for low financing. Some dealers combine low financing with cash-back offers or deals that start with 0 percent financing and increase over time depending on the length of the loan and other factors.

MONEY PIT

Some dealers offer new cars for no money down. Be careful though, because if for some reason you end up keeping the car for only a short time, you could find yourself in big trouble when you go to sell it. The value of a car depreciates dramatically in its first year. If you made no down payment, you actually could end up owing more than the car is worth at the end of a year or so.

If you're offered a choice between free financing and cash back, which should you take? Which option will save you more over the life of your loan?

Cash rebates and 0 percent financing deals will both reduce the monthly payments on your loan. Using the rebate as part or all of your down payment means that you'll owe less over the life of the loan. Free financing means you'll pay less because interest charges won't be added to your monthly bill. You'll have to make your monthly payments, of course, but they'll be less than they would be with interest added.

POCKET CHANGE

Just because an auto manufacturer offers cash rebates and/or 0 percent financing doesn't guarantee that you'll qualify for it. You'll need to have a solid credit history and good credit score for the finance company to approve a 0 percent interest deal. And, it's likely that you'll need to come up with a sizeable down payment in exchange for no interest.

If you do qualify for 0 percent financing and/or a cash rebate, you can find online calculators to help you figure out and compare which will help you to save more. For free, easy-to-use calculators, check out edmunds.com/calculators/incentives-rebates.html or bankrate.com/calculators/auto/car-rebates-calculator.aspx. To use the calculators, you'll need to know information such as your state's vehicle sales tax rate, the total cost of the vehicle you're buying before tax, the amount of the car manufacturer's rebate, and the amount of your down payment.

Having to choose between 0 percent financing and cash back is a good problem to have. Just take your time to figure out which makes more sense for you.

Leasing a Car

Leasing has been gaining in popularity, and many people—including millennials—are embracing it. In 2015, leasing accounted for 29 percent of all new car purchases among millennials, according to an Edmunds analysis. That's a 46 percent increase since 2010.

Leasing certainly is an option, but you should take some time to consider whether it makes more sense to lease or to purchase. Basically, when you lease a car, you pay for the estimated depreciation that's occurring to the car while you're driving it. You pay only for the part of the car's value you use, plus interest. However, leasing often can enable you to drive a more expensive car than buying.

When you begin a lease agreement, the dealer estimates what the car's *residual value* will be at the end of your lease.

DEFINITION

Leasing is the practice of paying a specified amount of money over a specified time for the use of a product. **Residual value** is what your car is worth at the end of the lease. It's what it would cost you to buy the car, used, at that time.

If you have a closed-end lease, you simply come to the end of your lease agreement, turn in your car, and walk away.

If you have an open-end lease, you may not be able to walk away free and clear at the end of the lease; you may owe the difference between the residual value of the car and the actual market value at the end of the lease. This might be the way to go, as long as the street value of the car has remained above the residual value determined by the dealer. You would then be buying the car for less than you could anywhere else. If the dealer overestimated the car's residual value, however, you'd be paying more for it than you would somewhere else.

See what we mean about leasing being a tricky business?

There are some good reasons to lease a car, but there are some good reasons not to as well. One major consideration is that you'll never pay less overall for leasing than you do for buying because you'll always be paying for but never actually own the car. It's sort of like renting a car for an extended period of time.

Still, many people like leasing for one reason or another. Those who have a special need for a particular vehicle for a limited amount of time, for example, might consider a lease.

Before you decide to lease, consider some of the following pros and cons.

Pros of Leasing

There are some good reasons why people like leasing vehicles:

- Many leases don't require a down payment, or at least not a very high down payment.

- You probably can lease a more expensive car than you'd be able to buy. The majority of millennial car shoppers surveyed said they would put down no more than $3,000 and pay no more than $300 a month for a new car. That would limit your purchase to a car priced at less than $20,000. For the same money, however, you could lease a car priced as high as $35,000.

- When your lease ends, you don't have to worry about getting rid of your car; you simply give it back.

Cons of Leasing

There are, however, some not-so-good aspects of leasing a car:

- The total cost of leasing is almost always more expensive than buying a car with cash and can be more expensive than financing a car.

- When your lease ends, you're out of a car.

- If you decide to buy the car at the end of the lease, you will owe sales tax.

- Most lease agreements impose mileage limits. If you go over the number of miles allowed, you'll have to pay a penalty.

- Leasing doesn't cover insurance or maintenance, so you don't save these costs.

- You might have to pay for the dealer's cost of auctioning the car when your lease expires. These fees are called *disposition charges*.

DEFINITION

Disposition charges are just a fancy name for the dealer's costs to auction your car when your lease is over.

Before You Lease

If, after considering the pros and cons, you decide to lease a car, do your homework before you sign anything. There are as many lease deals as there are kinds of cars. Check out websites such as Edmunds.com (edmunds.com) or Bankrate (bankrate.com) for more information about leasing.

When you feel you're sufficiently prepared to negotiate a lease, keep the following tips in mind:

Opt for a closed-end agreement   Always get a closed-end agreement. This enables you to turn in your car and say adios. If you fall in love with your leased vehicle, you can negotiate for it, but you won't be obligated to buy it.

Understand repair requirements   You're still responsible for repairs when you lease a car. Be sure you know in what condition you're expected to return the car.

Also check out the manufacturer's *warranty* on the car. This is a good guide as to how long your lease should be. You don't want to end up paying for costly repairs.

DEFINITION

A **warranty** is a written guarantee for the condition and performance of the car. It makes the manufacturer responsible for the repair or replacement of defective parts. **Gap insurance** can be included in your lease agreement and pays the difference between the value your insurance will pay if your leased car is stolen or wrecked and the amount you owe when you terminate the lease.

Find out what happens if you lease a lemon. Cars you buy are covered by lemon laws. Be sure there's a similar provision if you lease.

Push for a higher residual value   Negotiate the highest residual value on the vehicle you can. If you decide to buy it, you can renegotiate. If you don't buy it, you'll end up paying less for the part of the car's value you've used.

Talk about mileage   Be up front with the dealer about how many miles you plan to put on the car each year. If you exceed the dealer's limit (usually around 15,000 miles a year), you'll be fined.

If you drive 10,000 miles a year or less, ask whether you qualify for a low-mileage discount. Be persistent if the dealer is reluctant to give it to you.

Get gap insurance   Be sure the lease has *gap insurance.* Ask to have it included in the agreement with no additional charge.

Consider the length of the lease   Don't sign a lease for longer than you'll want the car. For instance, if there's a possibility you'll be transferred to Singapore for work in 2 years, don't sign a 3-year lease. You'll be penalized for breaking it.

Finally, don't let a dealer talk you into a lease agreement that's shorter than what you want. The dealer is eager to get you back into the showroom to look at another car, and some dealers push for very short leases for that reason. However, it could end up costing you more than necessary.

Lease agreements are notorious for being complicated pieces of confusing legalese, decipherable only by a Harvard Business School PhD. But if you know what to look out for, you can approach the whole process with a lot less aggravation.

The more you know about leasing and lease agreements going into the showroom, the less likely a salesperson will be to take advantage of you and give you something you don't need or want that will cost extra money. Remember these definitions:

Capitalized cost   The price you pay for the car.

Finance charge   The interest you pay on the car.

Residual value   According to the dealer, the amount the car is worth when the lease is over.

Compare these numbers in every agreement you look at.

Also read up on leasing, be prepared with questions, and don't be pressured into getting something you don't want. If you decide to lease and follow those guidelines, you'll do just fine.

New or Used?

Regardless of whether you decide to buy or lease a car, you need to consider the value of the car you're getting and what you can realistically afford. Sure, you might be able to borrow $30,000 to buy a new car, but why would you? If you want a new car, look at everything available.

To get a better idea of how much specific cars cost, check out IntelliChoice (intellichoice.com). This site lists the best overall values for cars of various sizes, and its categories are divided into price ranges.

In addition to saving money on your purchase now, you also can save for your future. After all, you're probably going to buy several cars before you hang up the keys for the last time. Money you save now and invest will buy you more cars and other extras you might want later on.

So who says you need a *new* car? Yeah, you're taking a chance if you buy a used car out of some guy's front yard, but many reputable car dealerships offer a good selection of used cars—known these days as *certified preowned vehicles*—complete with extended warranties and other perks. These cars can be had for a fraction of what they'd cost new, and if you take good care of yours, it should give you years of service.

> **MONEY PIT**
>
> If for some reason you must have a new car instead of one that's been used, consider that the minute you drive the new car off the lot, it's lost a percentage of its value. It's already a used car, and you haven't even gotten it home yet!

If you buy a used car for half or two thirds of what a new one costs, you can afford to pay a greater percentage of the cost up front and have to borrow less. Your monthly payments will be less as well, giving you more money for other things.

Sure, you'll have to factor in some repair and maintenance costs, but if you're diligent about checking out the quality of the car before you buy it and insist on a good warranty, you're still likely to come out ahead.

Safety Counts

Regardless of the type or size of car you buy, remember that some vehicles are safer than others. Sure, any car can be safe or unsafe depending on how it's driven, but some cars hold up better in crashes than others, giving you and your passengers a better chance of surviving. You also can get better insurance rates if you drive a car that's rated as safe.

How can you find out which cars are safer? One source is *Consumer Reports*. Each year, it publishes a list of the 25 safest vehicles, based on how well they're designed to avoid a crash and how they hold up in the event that a crash can't be avoided. Another place to look is Kelley Blue Book, at kbb.com/best-safety-rated-cars.

Remember, though, that no vehicle is safe if you're trying to talk on your cell phone, eat your lunch, and fumble for your favorite CD while you're driving. And that goes double when you start hauling kids with you.

Best Places—Online and Off—to Shop for a Car

Car shopping is a big deal because it involves spending a lot of money, so it's important to know the best places to shop. The face of car-buying has changed over the past decade or so, due to internet car sales. Cars once were primarily sold at car dealerships, on used car lots, or even on somebody's front lawn, but you now can buy a car on eBay or craigslist.

At a Dealership

The most traditional way to buy a car is still to go to a car dealership, haggle with the salesperson, and strike a deal on the vehicle you want.

If you're contemplating buying a car from a dealer, be sure to get online at Edmunds.com (edmunds.com) or Kelley Blue Book (kbb.com) to get all the information you need about the car you're thinking about. At either site, you can compare dealer costs and incentives, contact dealers to determine inventory and bargaining potential, and contrast transaction prices.

 **DOLLARS AND SENSE**

Don't forget about classified ads and car-shopper publications that list cars for sale in your area.

Online

Or you can buy your car online, without ever having to leave your home. Check out a site such as CarsDirect (carsdirect.com), where you can order the car you want for a price the site has already negotiated with a dealer. You order the car online, specifying exactly what options you want, the color you like, and other preferences, and the site finds a dealer near you that has it.

If you're willing to go the extra mile, you might be able to get a great deal on a car that's for sale on the internet at a site like eBay Motors (ebay.com/motors). But you'll need to do your homework here and find out the value of the car, whether there are any complaints posted on the site about the person selling the car, and so forth. If the car happens to be located near where you live, it's easier than if you need to travel to see the car. If you have to buy a plane ticket to check out the car, add the cost of your ticket to the cost of the car.

Helpful Apps

Some car-related apps can give you information so you'll know exactly what you're talking about when you begin the process of negotiating a price on a new or used car. Here are a few of them:

Edmunds App (edmunds.com)   Edmunds is an authority in the car world and now offers an app. You can look up the fair price of a new or used vehicle, check vehicle reviews, and see what's available in your area. The app even gives you estimates on what it costs to maintain a particular vehicle.

CarMax (carmax.com)   CarMax is the largest seller of used cars in the United States, and its app, tied directly into its website, lets you locate and check the stock of the CarMax closest to you. You get multiple photos of each vehicle along with information about its history, features, warranty, and cost. Price calculators are available to help you figure out how much you'll pay over time, and the app enables you to contact the CarMax dealership about vehicles you like by email or with your phone.

Kelley Blue Book (kbb.com)   Car buyers have depended on the Kelley Blue Book for generations. Its app puts the information you need on your phone or tablet and gives you the specific value of new and used cars, even if the model has been discontinued. It also lets you know about incentives available on new cars and contains video reviews of the latest vehicles.

Regardless of how and where you decide to shop for a car, be sure to do your homework. The more informed you are, the better.

The Least You Need to Know

- Despite the rumors that millennials have not embraced driving and cars, recent studies indicate otherwise.
- For some people, owning a car is not essential; other modes of transportation can get you where you want to go.
- Buying the car is the first expense, but they don't end there. It costs a lot to operate a vehicle.
- There are advantages and disadvantages to both buying and leasing vehicles. Be sure to do your homework before doing either one.
- Buying a less-expensive car can yield big savings for your future.

CHAPTER 16

Owning Versus Renting a Home

There's speculation that millennials simply are not interested in home ownership, that they want to live in cities, rent apartments that require minimal upkeep, and just enjoy life.

Not so, claims the online real estate site Trulia. A recent survey revealed that 93 percent of millennials someday plan to buy a home. While millennials are delaying both marriage and buying their first homes—factors attributed to the Great Recession, a job market many claim has not fully recovered from said recession, credit problems, and alarming amounts of student debt—statistics indicate that most will eventually embrace both institutions.

In This Chapter

- Deciding whether to rent or buy
- The good and bad about taxes
- Qualifying for a mortgage
- Understanding different types of mortgages
- House hunting
- Insuring your home

The Mystique of Owning a Home

People aspire to own their own home for many reasons. They get tired of paying rent every month, or they outgrow an apartment and decide to get a house instead. Maybe they think a house would be a good financial move, or maybe they just like the *idea* of having a house. They imagine having friends over for summer deck parties or picture the family gathered around the Thanksgiving table. For whatever reason, each year, many people buy homes for the first time, and many more people plan to buy in the future. If you're among either of those groups, you're considering a move that will affect your life, and your finances, for a very long time.

Only you can decide whether owning a home is right for you. The implications of home ownership extend well past the financial ones, so you'll have to examine the whole picture and then make a decision. If it's not the right time to consider home ownership, don't feel bad. You can revisit the topic when it makes more sense.

Advantages of Renting

The first thing to remember is that having a home requires a great deal of responsibility. There are always things to be done, sometimes at considerable expense, and houses require constant attention and upkeep. If you think you don't want to deal with the never-ending concerns that come with owning a house and you live in an area where rents are affordable, consider renting.

Rental agreements vary widely, but many usually stipulate that the homeowner is responsible for most repairs. You might be responsible for routine upkeep like cutting grass and shoveling the sidewalks, if that; but if the heater breaks down or the garbage disposal goes, you'll just need to contact the homeowner or leasing company about the problem.

Another reason to think about renting is if you know—or suspect—your life situation will be changing soon. None of us can know what will happen in our future, but if you think you'll be transferred in 6 months to a year, it's not a good time to think about buying a home. The same thing applies if your marriage is on shaky ground, or if your job security is threatened, or if you've just learned you'll need an advanced degree to keep your job.

Renting instead of buying may provide financial advantages at this point of your life. Assuming you'd be paying less to rent a place than you'd have to pay on your mortgage each month, you could use the difference to contribute to a specific financial goal, such as paying off student loans, investing, saving for future travel, or building an education fund. Renting also means you won't face the burden of property taxes, which can be significant.

If you live in an area where rents are sky high and affordable rental homes are at a premium, you'll have to work harder to find something you can afford. The cost of renting a home has increased dramatically during the past decade, and salaries have not kept up.

Economists are worried about this trend, as it doesn't seem to be about to change. Ideally, you should spend no more than 30 percent of your income on rent. Increasingly, however, renters are paying 35, 40, or even 50 percent or more for rent. This not only makes it more difficult to live, it also limits your chances of being able to save money to use for a down payment so you can buy your own home.

 DOLLARS AND SENSE

Landlords are sometimes willing to reduce rental prices for a tenant who stays with them long term. If you're looking to rent for a period of time, discuss this possibility with your prospective landlord before you sign your lease.

In Washington, D.C., for instance, more than a quarter of all median-wage earners—those earning more than low-income workers but not as much as high-paid workers—spend more than 50 percent of their total incomes for rent each month, according to a recent study by New York University's Furman Center for Real Estate and Urban Policy.

For many people, renting a home is the way to go. If you live in an area where rental prices are very high and you're spending a disproportionate amount of your salary to live there, you might need to get creative and consider looking for roommates, moving to where rents are less expensive, or looking for a smaller place.

Advantages of Buying

If rents are affordable in your area, renting definitely has advantages, but there also are some very good reasons why you should consider buying a house.

There are all of those intangible things, like becoming a part of a community and having a stake in its well-being. Then, there are some important financial reasons why buying instead of renting can be a good thing. Instead of handing over money to someone else, you build up *equity* in your house as you pay off your mortgage. You have something that's yours, not simply a place where you pay to live.

 DEFINITION

Equity in a home is the difference between the current market value of the home and the money you still owe on the mortgage, plus any equity or lines of credit loans.

Owning a home also gives you good tax advantages. When you buy a house, Uncle Sam gives you a little housewarming gift and lets you deduct three of the biggest owning-a-home expenses from your federal income tax: the interest on your mortgage, your property taxes, and your primary mortgage insurance. Other, one-time deductions also are available to you, such as the points you pay at closing, but interest and property taxes and primary mortgage insurance (PMI), which protects the lender in the event that you default on your mortgage, are the long-term biggies.

These deductions are great news for homeowners. When paying the mortgage bill every month starts to seem like more than you can bear, remember that, come April, you'll be happily filling out Schedule A (Form 1040), "Itemized Deductions," which is a part of your federal income tax return. If you itemize deductions, the interest you pay on your loan, the property taxes you pay on your home, and your PMI all lower your tax liability. That's a good thing!

 DOLLARS AND SENSE

In 2015, Congress passed a law allowing homeowners to deduct primary mortgage insurance (PMI). You'll probably be required to buy PMI if you cannot come up with at least 20 percent for a down payment. Once you've begun paying back your mortgage and have paid enough to cover 20 percent of the cost of the home, ask your mortgage holder to have the PMI payment removed.

Tax deductions can be itemized and subtracted from your adjusted gross income if they're greater than the standard deduction the tax laws allow. The deductions and personal exemptions are subtracted from your income before you figure out how much tax you have to pay on it. If your total income is $45,200 but you have $8,500 in deductions and personal exemptions totaling $4,050, you'll pay tax on only $32,650 ($45,200 − $8,500 − $4,050 = $32,650).

When you become a homeowner, you get the privilege of taking some pretty hefty deductions. If you haven't itemized your deductions before buying the house, be sure you find out all the deductions you're entitled to before you pay this year's taxes. Deducting your mortgage interest, property taxes, and PMI can take quite a large chunk out of your income.

Points usually are the responsibility of the buyer, but a seller who really wants to sell can sometimes be convinced to assume responsibility for paying some or all of the cost of the points. If you can convince the seller to pay the points, you win in two ways: you don't have to pay the points, and you can still deduct them from your income tax. If you and the seller split the points, you still get to deduct the total amount.

 DEFINITION

Points are prepaid interest paid as a fee to a mortgage lender to cover the cost of applying for the loan; 1 point is 1 percent of the loan's value.

In addition to deducting mortgage interest and points, you can deduct some of the property taxes and other expenses that are finalized at settlement. Some of the expenses you pay at settlement can be deducted from your income tax, and some of the other expenses are considered capital expenses when you sell your home.

DOLLARS AND SENSE

To get a quick idea of how much you'll save on taxes as a homeowner, add up the amounts of your property taxes, your mortgage interest, and your PMI, if applicable. Multiply that amount by your marginal federal tax rate, which you can figure out with Bankrate's tax calculator at bankrate.com/finance/taxes/tax-brackets.aspx. It's not an exact formula, but it can give you a good idea of the savings you can expect.

The Downside to Taxes

Sure, there are tax advantages to home ownership, but there also are taxes you'll need to pay, and they can be quite expensive. *Property taxes* can be especially hard on the wallet.

Property tax rates vary significantly but usually run somewhere about 1.5 percent of the value of your property. Because paying property taxes can be prohibitive, many lenders require that homeowners pay money into an *escrow account* to cover the cost of the taxes when they come due. An escrow account is a special account used to hold money designated for a particular purpose, such as property taxes.

In most areas, you pay local property taxes (also known as your school tax), county taxes, and sometimes some oddball taxes from your *municipality*. Taxes can vary, depending on the quirks, wishes, and wealth of the municipal boards that impose them.

DEFINITION

Property taxes are taxes levied by the municipality and/or school district where you live. They're based on the value of your property. An **escrow account** is a separate account that holds money designated for a specific purpose. A **municipality** is a zoned area such as a city, borough, or township that has an incorporated government.

The majority of property taxes you pay go toward funding your local school district. A portion also goes to the borough or township where you live, and some goes to your county. You normally pay your taxes to a local tax collector, who distributes them to the proper places.

You can be assessed for your taxes once a year, twice a year, or even more often. Property taxes have gotten so high in some areas that officials are allowing residents to pay their taxes quarterly to relieve the burden of huge lump sums.

Many property owners and legislators agree that property taxes are not an equitable means of raising money to support public education and other services. Elderly people whose children graduated from high school 40 or 50 years ago still pay property taxes if they own homes. And people who don't own property enjoy the same services without having to pay the high taxes. Property tax is an issue in almost every state, and movements are underway in many states to reform the tax.

The really annoying thing about property taxes is that the municipality imposing them can raise them by reassessing your home. Every now and then, municipal governments declare a major property reassessment. When that happens, look out. At that point, the municipality probably has reached its upper allowable tax limit and is looking for a way to make more revenue. If it can't increase your tax rate, it can reassess the value of your home. You can challenge your assessment by filing an appeal, which can be approved or denied.

MONEY PIT

The average American household pays $2,089 a year in property taxes. In some states though, the taxes are much higher. Residents of New Jersey, the state with the highest property taxes, pay nearly $5,000 a year. Illinois, New Hampshire, Wisconsin, and Texas also have much higher than average property taxes.

Obviously, other expenses besides taxes are involved with owning a home, and you can expect to pay various taxes in addition to your property tax. You might be charged additional taxes for streetlights, fire hydrants, trash collection, sewage, water, and the like. Unfortunately, these taxes are not tax-deductible.

All this means you have to be careful when breaking down your expenses for your tax return. The bank might pay $2,000 to your municipality for your taxes, but only $1,550 of the $2,000 is deductible on your taxes. It's a good idea to keep copies of all bills and the payments you make so you have them handy when tax time comes around.

Enlisting Help

Buying your first house—or any house—is a big decision, and you're going to need some help. Some people insist on doing it themselves, but that's not advisable, especially for first-time buyers.

First, you should secure the services of a good, reputable real estate agent who can walk you through the process of finding and purchasing a home. A good agent can be your best friend when you're searching for the home of your dreams.

You also might want to identify a mortgage broker to help you locate and obtain the mortgage that makes the most sense for you. You have to pay for a broker's services, but if you don't have time to shop around for the best mortgage, or if you feel intimidated by it all, it might be worth your while to hire one. If you apply for a mortgage and are turned down, you should call a broker.

Be sure to check the qualifications of anyone you hire to help you in the process of buying a home.

Qualifying for a Mortgage

Because hardly anybody has a couple hundred thousand dollars available to hand over for a home, we rely heavily on *mortgages* when purchasing homes.

POCKET CHANGE

The median sales price of an existing home at the end of February 2016 was $210,800, according to the Federal Reserve Bank. Trulia has an interactive map that lets you see median prices for every county in the country. Find it at trulia.com/home_prices.

A mortgage is a loan you get from a bank or other lender. You borrow the difference between the cost of the house and the money you have for a down payment and agree to pay it back over a specified period of time and at a specified rate of interest.

On one hand, mortgages are great because they provide a means for buying a house. On the other hand, they can be financially crippling if they're not managed properly.

To get a mortgage, you have to meet certain criteria. During the financial crisis and recession, we saw what happens when people get loans for houses and are unable to pay them back. About 5.5 million U.S. homes were lost to *foreclosure* between the end of 2007 and the end of 2015.

DEFINITION

A **mortgage** is a loan for the purpose of property. The loan is secured by a lien on the property and comes with conditions regarding the length of time over which it will be repaid, the amount of interest you'll pay on the loan, and other factors. **Foreclosure** is the legal process in which ownership of a home transfers from the homeowner to the mortgage lender. This occurs when the homeowner does not make the agreed-upon payments on the mortgage.

The lending industry pulled back tremendously in response, and for a while, getting money loaned to do anything was extremely difficult. New rules to ensure borrowers will be able to repay their mortgages went into effect in January 2014. Hopefully, this will even out the lending field by assuring banks their money will be returned and making it easier for qualified buyers to get mortgages.

To determine how much you'd be able to get for a mortgage, you need to consider a few things. First, think about how much money you have available to put down. Then consider how much you earn and what your expenses are. These factors will help you figure out how much you can afford to borrow.

The Down Payment

Generally, a lender such as a bank or a mortgage company requires that you have about 20 percent of the selling price of the home you want to buy to use as a down payment. This makes it difficult for many younger people today because wage growth has been slow, the cost of renting is high, and the average student loan debt is $30,000.

The real estate research firm RealtyTrac estimated that a typical millennial would need 12½ years to save enough money for a 20 percent down payment on a home.

There's good news, however. In 2015, the federal government reduced the cost of mortgage insurance and the minimum amount of money needed for a down payment for first-time homeowners who qualify for a government-backed mortgage such as through the Federal Housing Administration or from the Federal National Mortgage Association (*Fannie Mae*) or the Federal Home Loan Mortgage Corporation (*Freddie Mac*).

 DEFINITION

Fannie Mae and **Freddie Mac** are publicly chartered corporations that buy mortgage loans from lenders. This ensures that mortgage money is available at all times, everywhere across the country. In September 2008, the federal government took over both of these corporations as they teetered on the brink of failure. The takeover was meant to keep the companies afloat and mortgage money available.

If you qualify for a Fannie Mae or Freddie Mac mortgage, you may be able to get a minimum down payment of only 3 percent, down from 5 percent previously. Not everyone supports these home-buying incentives, but they are the government's response to the lowest rate of home ownership in the United States in 20 years. Only about 65 percent of all Americans owned homes in 2015, and only about 36 percent of people under 35 owned.

If you don't qualify for a government-backed mortgage, you'll probably need a larger down payment. The bigger the down payment you make, the less your monthly mortgage payment will be. This can work in your favor in two ways: you can lower your monthly payments and have more money to invest or for other purposes, or you could afford a more expensive house with a bigger down payment because you'll be financing less of the cost of the home. For example, if you buy a $175,000 home and make a $10,000 down payment, you have to finance $165,000. But if you have $35,000 for a down payment, you could buy a $200,000 home and only have to finance the same amount as you would have on the less-expensive home with a smaller down payment.

Your Income and Expenses

To determine how big a mortgage you probably can get, look at how much money you make before taxes. This amount is your *gross income.* The recommended guideline is that you should spend no more than 28 percent of your gross monthly income on your mortgage payment.

 MONEY PIT

> Some financial advisers, and many mortgage lenders, will tell you that it's okay to spend more than 28 percent of your monthly income on your mortgage. Many recommend not going higher than 33 percent—some may even go 1 or 2 points higher. Remember, however, that many people have made themselves "house poor" by buying a more expensive home than they reasonably could afford.

The mortgage payment includes the *principal,* interest, real estate taxes, homeowner's insurance, and PMI if applicable. The principal of a mortgage is the amount loaned. If you borrow $200,000, that amount is the principal, and you are obligated to repay a portion of that mortgage amount each month. You pay principal every month based on the unpaid balance of the mortgage. The interest is the fee the lender charges you to use its money.

 DEFINITION

> Your **gross income** is your income before taxes are deducted. The **principal** of a mortgage is the amount of money loaned to you. The **interest** is the fee you are charged to use the principal.

When you're thinking about applying for a mortgage, you must pay close attention to all your expenses as they relate to your income. Although the recommended maximum for your mortgage payment is 28 percent of your gross monthly income, the historical maximum for your total monthly debt is 36 percent of your income. That means all your debt other than a mortgage—such as your car payment, credit card bills, student loans, child support payments, and other bills—should total no more than 8 percent of your gross income.

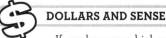

> **DOLLARS AND SENSE**
>
> If you have very high monthly expenses because of high credit card or other debt, reduce the debt as much as you can before you apply for a mortgage. Those expenses will work against you on your mortgage application.

You need to take a realistic look at your gross income and all the expenses you'll be faced with once you've bought a house. Then consider your down payment, and you'll be able to determine how much you can afford to borrow. Many good mortgage calculators are available online, or you can get an app such as Quicken Loans' Mortgage Calculator to help you.

Getting the Right Mortgage

You'll find many different kinds of mortgages. They vary tremendously in time needed to pay them back, the frequency of payments, and other factors. Much good information about mortgages is out there, and it's important that you take time to research.

The two most common types of mortgages are *fixed-rate mortgages* (*FRMs*) and *adjustable-rate mortgages* (*ARMs*).

> **DEFINITION**
>
> With a **fixed-rate mortgage (FRM)**, the interest rate remains constant over the life of the loan. With an **adjustable-rate mortgage (ARM)**, the interest rate usually stays the same for a specified amount of time but then may fluctuate.

Fixed-Rate Mortgages

With more than three quarters of the people who get mortgages choosing FRMs, they're the most common type. They're also the easiest to understand: you agree to pay a certain amount of interest on your mortgage for as long as you have it. If you pay 4 percent interest the first month, you'll pay 4 percent interest the last month as well. The rate doesn't change, and neither does your monthly payment. You receive a schedule of payments, and you know exactly how much you must pay each month. So if you like to know precisely how to plan your long-term budget, you'll probably like FRMs. It removes the guesswork.

The interest rates a lender charges on a mortgage or another type of loan depend on inflation and the state of the general economy. Interest rates are controlled by the Federal Reserve, through the interest rates this federal agency charges to banks. If the Fed charges banks high interest, your mortgage rate will be high; if rates are low, a mortgage you take out should have a low rate.

The problem with FRMs is that if the interest rates drop dramatically, you're still stuck paying the higher rate. You can *refinance* your mortgage to take advantage of low rates, but this process requires time and involves significant expense.

DEFINITION

Refinancing your mortgage is trading in your old mortgage for a new one. People refinance to get better interest rates and, thus, lower their monthly payment, shorten the term of the loan, and/or change their mortgage from one type to another.

Still, there are reasons why more people have FRMs than any other kind. They're easy to keep track of, for example, and you can count on making a specific payment each month.

Let's have a look at how a FRM compares with one that has an adjustable rate.

Adjustable-Rate Mortgages

ARMs are different from FRMs because the interest rate doesn't stay the same for the entire term of the loan. Because of that, your monthly mortgage payment varies as well. Homebuyers generally are attracted to ARMs because they offer some initial savings like no points and a lower beginning interest rate.

With ARMs, you generally agree to pay a fixed interest rate for a certain amount of time, after which your rate and monthly payment may start to fluctuate. The interest rates for ARMs are tied into various indexes that determine how they'll rise or fall. The indexes used for the interest adjustment are based on the current interest rate scenario evident at the time the ARM rate is adjusted. Your lender will specify what index is used to determine your rate.

Most ARMs also include annual caps, so your interest rate can't keep increasing forever. However, you could end up paying hundreds of dollars more on your monthly payment down the road than you do initially if the interest rates rise dramatically. On the other hand, if interest rates stay low, an ARM can be a good deal.

The initial savings of an ARM over a FRM can be tempting. But don't get sucked into an adjustable-rate deal, especially when interest rates are low, unless you fully understand how it works and are willing to take the risks. Get all the information you can about different types of mortgages before you decide what type is best for you.

Finding Your Dream Home

An important rule to remember when you're house hunting is to keep an open mind. Don't refuse to look at homes anywhere outside of the three-block area you have your heart set on because you're sure to miss out on some good properties. The house of your dreams might be just on the other side of the street you've set as your boundary, or on the other side of town, or the county.

Real estate prices vary tremendously, based in large part on the location of the home. You might be able to afford a townhouse in the "in" neighborhood or a much larger single home in another area. It's a matter of getting your priorities and your finances straight.

MONEY PIT

> Hunting for a house can become nearly an obsession if you're not careful. Determine ahead of time just how many hours a week you can spend house hunting, and stick to it.

You'll find many different kinds of homes, and you should think about what makes sense for you at this point of your life. Don't be pressured into thinking you must have the house of your dreams at this age. You'll have time to upgrade later.

Types of Homes

Let's consider some different styles of homes.

Single home   This is a freestanding home. It can be a one-story ranch or a three-story mansion, and it often has more land than some of the other options.

Double house   In this structure, two homes are side by side and share a common wall. Each dwelling in a double home can be quite large, and each half often includes some property. Double homes generally are less expensive than single homes and can be a good value.

Townhouse   Townhomes, sometimes called row houses, are attached to the homes on either side. They are generally less expensive than singles, unless they're in an extremely trendy area. Townhouses offer advantages such as security, community, and financial value. As with double homes, only you know how you feel about living in close proximity with your neighbors.

Duplex   Another example of non-single-family housing, a duplex holds one complete living unit above another complete living unit. Duplexes are popular investment properties, and the owner often lives either upstairs or downstairs and rents the other unit.

Condominium   When you buy a condominium, you own everything from the walls in and part of everything else in the community. That means you normally have shared costs for maintenance and other expenses. Condos are great for people who have no time, skill, or interest in the upkeep involved with the exterior of a single home and property.

Apartment   We normally think about renting apartments, but they also can be purchased, particularly if you live in a large city. An apartment is a living unit contained within a larger building with other living units.

Location, Location, Location

In addition to thinking about what type of home you want, you need to consider its location. People choose the neighborhoods they live in for many different reasons, such as the quality of the schools, proximity to shopping or work, safety, and property size.

Regardless of why you choose the neighborhood you do, be sure to check it out thoroughly before buying a home there.

 DOLLARS AND SENSE

> Always ask the person who's selling his home why he's moving. If he gives you a reason but you suspect there's something he's not telling you, press a little bit harder for a more honest answer. There could be a problem about the neighborhood he's not initially forthcoming about.

Protecting Your Investment

Your home is probably the biggest investment you'll ever make. And it holds the people and things most important to you. To protect your home, you must buy homeowner's insurance. You'll probably need to show proof of insurance before obtaining a mortgage as well. Homeowner's insurance includes personal property coverage for the contents of your home and liability insurance for the damage that could occur to other people who visit and to their property.

In the event of a fire or other catastrophe, homeowner's insurance can't replace your wedding videos and the coffee table that belonged to your great-grandmother, but it can at least enable you to rebuild your home and make a new start. It can't protect your emotional investment in your home, but it can protect your financial one.

Homeowner's insurance is designed to repair or replace your primary residence if it's damaged or destroyed. Coverage usually is based on the sale price of the home when purchased, but remember that the sale price includes the value of the land. If your entire property is valued at, say, $275,000, but your house would cost only $200,000 to rebuild, you don't need homeowner's insurance based on the entire value.

The part of your homeowner's insurance that covers your house (the structure, that is) is called *dwelling coverage.* Dwelling coverage isn't based on how much you paid for your house or how much money you borrowed to buy it. It's based on how much it would cost you to rebuild your house if it were completely destroyed, known as the replacement value.

DEFINITION

The part of your homeowner's insurance that covers the structure in which you live is called **dwelling coverage.**

The cost to rebuild is normally based on the square footage of your home, the type of home you have, and when it was built. If you have an older home with lots of details, such as a wooden staircase, stained glass above the doors, or ornate plaster work, your insurer is likely to tell you that sort of detail could not be matched if your house had to be replaced. You can expect to pay more for your homeowner's insurance if you have a lot of extras in your home, such as ceiling fans, spas, French doors, propane fireplaces, and so forth.

We can't stress enough how important it is for you to closely examine your insurance policies and know exactly what coverages you have and don't have. It can be financially devastating to assume you're covered for something, only to find out after a catastrophe that you're not.

The Least You Need to Know

- Buying and renting each come with advantages and disadvantages.
- It's important to get a real estate agent you trust professionally, as well as one you like and can work with effectively, when you're house hunting.
- If you want to buy a house, you need to figure out how much you'll be able to pay by calculating how much you have for a down payment, how much you earn, and what your expenses are.
- Mortgages come in a variety of flavors, but the main decision you'll need to make is whether to get a fixed- or adjustable-rate mortgage.
- When you start looking for a house, remain open-minded on the type of structure and location.
- Insuring your home and its contents is crucial. Do your homework, and be sure you have adequate protection for your home and your possessions.

CHAPTER 17

Insuring Yourself and Your Property

Insurance has been a big topic of discussion in recent years, due largely to health-care legislation known as the Affordable Care Act (ACA), or Obamacare. If you're under 26 and don't have a job that offers health insurance, chances are you like the ACA because it allows you to remain on your parent's policy until you reach that age. The same goes if you have a preexisting condition like asthma or diabetes and were having trouble finding an insurer who would cover you. If you've been thrown into the marketplace and can't find a plan at a price you like, chances are you're not such a fan of the ACA. Whether or not you care for this particular breed of insurance, it certainly has ignited conversation.

In This Chapter

- Understanding how insurance works
- Insurance you need and don't need
- Shopping around for the best rates
- Fighting back for fair treatment

Many of us have a kind of love-hate relationship with insurance, including health insurance. You know you should have it, but you don't like that it takes a bite out of your budget, especially when you might not even need it. Still, it's better to have insurance than not to—and better yet to have it and never need it.

Insurance is a method of sharing risk among a large group of people. Everybody pays for it, whether you use it or not. Hopefully, you make your payments on time, never need to make a claim, and recognize how lucky you are. If you do need it, however, paying into that pot of money will have been well worth it.

If you learn one thing about insurance from this chapter, let it be this: insurance is meant to protect the important things in your life—your life itself, your health, the health of your family, your home, etc.—against big losses. If you get sick and can't work, you'd better have insurance to cover your lost income, even if you're supporting only yourself. If you have a house and it burns down, you'd better have insurance to rebuild and replace the stuff you lost. Whenever you walk outside and get into your car, there's the potential for an accident, and you need to be insured just in case.

Insurance 101

More kinds of insurance policies are available than you probably can imagine, and we Americans buy tons of it. Most people, though, don't really understand the insurance industry and how it works. Many aren't even sure about what kinds of insurance they should have, or how to go about finding out that information.

The insurance industry is huge, and it commands a large chunk of our nation's economy—and its attention. Hardly a day goes by when you don't read or hear some news related to the insurance industry. Tens of thousands of insurance companies are at work in this country, and nearly 2.4 million people are employed in the industry, making it one of the country's largest employers.

Insurance is a powerful industry as well. It has an extremely strong lobby that exerts tremendous pressure on the government agencies that are supposed to oversee it. As a result, it has become a formidable force in our society.

Insurance is an issue we all need to think about because we need to have it.

DOLLARS AND SENSE

Think of insurance as a tool that helps you deal with trouble, should trouble arise. That way it seems less like a necessary evil and more like, well, insurance.

Although some insurance companies, including GEICO and United Services Automobile Association (USAA) sell directly to the public, most insurance is sold through agents or brokers who work for insurance companies like Allstate, State Farm, Nationwide, Liberty Mutual, and thousands of others. The agents earn commissions from the insurance companies, based on how much and what type of insurance they sell. Insurance agents aren't the only people out there who work on commission (real estate agents and many other types of salespeople do as well), and there's nothing wrong with a commission system, but be aware that that's how the insurance industry works.

If an agent is going to get a big commission for selling a certain type of policy or a policy for a specific company, you can be sure he's going to knock himself out trying to sell it. That's how he makes his living, and some agents are really good at convincing you you need something that's completely unnecessary. In fact, some analysts say nearly 50 percent of insurance agents and brokers try to sell you policies that generate the highest commissions for them. If you don't know what you want or need, you could be suckered into buying unnecessary coverage while lining the agent's pockets.

After you read this chapter, you'll have a better understanding of what you need and don't need. Don't let an agent talk you into buying something you don't need, for which you'll end up paying a large *premium*. Be sure he or she understands your situation so you get the kind of coverage you really should have.

DEFINITION

A **premium** is the amount of money you pay, at regular predetermined intervals, for a certain insurance policy.

If you don't know anyone who sells insurance, you'll have to take your chances with a referral or someone you find on your own. Choose someone with a CLU (Chartered Life Underwriter), ChFC (Chartered Financial Consultant), or CFP (Certified Financial Planner) designation, which demonstrates that the agent has taken courses to further educate him- or herself about the industry. It also implies that the agent has affirmed to practice ethically.

You also could use a service such as Angie's List when searching for an insurance agent or look for an established insurance company within your community and ask to see a list of agents and their qualifications.

You can buy insurance online, but if you're purchasing for the first time, it's probably a good idea to work with a reputable agent who can help you figure out exactly what you need and explain the ins and outs of various policies. If you end up paying a bit more, it's probably worth it.

Insurance Must-Haves

You should think big when it concerns insurance. Forget the little stuff, even if it's tempting because it doesn't seem to cost very much. In many cases, the same coverage offered with "specialty" policies, such as mortgage life insurance or flight insurance, is already provided for in your regular life insurance policy.

If you buy a lot of little insurance policies hoping to cover every possibility for loss, you'll end up spending a lot more on the policies than you would fixing the things that go wrong. If your computer or cellphone breaks, by the time you pay the deductible, spend an hour or two filling out the claim, and try to cut through the inevitable red tape, you're probably better off having it fixed on your own.

Make no mistake about it: you can buy as much insurance as you want. You can insure all your electronics, your road bike, your drum set, your toaster oven, and your snowboard if you want to. You can pay $44 a month to buy health insurance on your 5-year-old golden retriever and still be out a $500 deductible and 20 percent of costs for care in the event she needs it. You can insure your lawn mower, your microwave, and the locket you wore when you were a baby. Before you start buying insurance on everything you own, however, consider what you really need.

POCKET CHANGE

Among the "15 Insurance Policies You Don't Need," according to Investopedia, are rental car insurance, flight insurance, credit card loss insurance, and extended warranties.

Types of Policies You Might Need

The types of insurance you do need depend on where you are in your life. Let's review the types of policies you may need broken down by various stages of your life:

Single with no dependents   At this point in your life, you need health insurance; auto insurance; homeowner's insurance if you own a place; and enough life insurance to cover your burial, final expenses, and any outstanding loans. If you rent, you also should have renter's insurance. Disability insurance also makes sense for you now.

Married with no kids   Now you need some life insurance, especially if your spouse doesn't work or if you own a home. Auto and homeowner's or renter's insurance are necessary, as are health and disability insurance.

Married with kids   Kids bump up the amount and types of insurance you need. If you don't have life insurance yet, you definitely need it now. Term life insurance, for which you pay a certain amount per year and your survivors receive a certain amount if you die (more about this in Chapter 19), is probably your best bet. You still need health and disability insurance, too, along with auto (pay special attention to that one after the babies get to be teenagers and start driving!) and homeowner's insurance. It's a good idea at this point to reexamine all your policies to be sure you're adequately covered. Having kids makes you responsible for them, and you want to be sure they'd have plenty to get by on if you suddenly became disabled.

Let's concentrate on the types of insurance necessary for people in the first two categories, single with no dependents and married with no kids. We also touch briefly on what you need if you're in the third category, married with kids.

Health Insurance

You need to be covered for hospitalization, physician costs, and charges for procedures such as x-rays, lab tests, and diagnostic tests. Maternity benefits, mammograms, and annual physicals are all required coverages under the ACA.

As mentioned earlier, health-care insurance has become a hot political issue due to the ACA being passed into law. As Congress plans to tweak (or repeal) the coverage, it remains an upfront topic of conversation. Many politicians and citizens claim to not like the ACA, but it has reduced the number of Americans who are without health insurance. According to the Centers for Disease Control and Prevention, after the first half of 2015, for the first time in more than a half-century, more than 90 percent of all Americans had health insurance.

 POCKET CHANGE

One of the most popular aspects of the ACA is the requirement that insurers offer dependent care coverage for an adult child until age 26. This has been a huge relief for many young people (and their parents) who came out of college into a depressed job market and have had a difficult time finding a full-time job with benefits.

More people insured is good news, but it does raise questions about how we'll pay for our growing cost of health care. And many people are still underinsured or have policies with deductibles and other high out-of-pocket costs. The United States spends more of its gross domestic product on health care than any other major industrialized nation, with many patients facing increasing out-of-pocket costs.

If you're lucky enough to have health care provided through your employer, chances are you're contributing more toward it than you would have been a decade ago. On average, a family health insurance plan in 2015 cost an employer about $16,000, with employees paying about a quarter of that cost. For a single worker, the tab to an employer was almost $6,000, with employees contributing about $1,000. The cost of health care for American workers has risen dramatically more than wages or inflation.

If your employer doesn't provide coverage, or if you are self-employed, you need to buy your own health insurance. You can either get private insurance on our own or check out what the ACA has to offer by calling 800-410-9538 or going to HealthCare.gov. Regardless of which route you take, be sure to research thoroughly, as options and conditions change.

If you're leaving a job where you have an insurance plan, look into the possibility of extending your coverage when you leave. COBRA (Consolidated Omnibus Budget Reconciliation Act) requires your employer to continue your health coverage after a job loss, death of an employee, divorce, or attaining a certain age (as when a child reaches an age and is no longer covered under the plan). Your employer is required to offer COBRA coverage for 18 months after you quit your job or 36 months for other situations (such as divorce). You have to pay for the insurance, but at least you'll be covered and your insurance won't lapse.

Compare the benefits of coverage under COBRA and through the Affordable Care Act Marketplace (healthcare.gov). COBRA is expensive (105 percent of the cost of the coverage), but you continue with your current *deductibles, co-pays,* and pharmaceutical coverages. Your premiums may be less expensive if you buy through the ACA Marketplace, but you may face larger deductibles and other out-of-pocket costs.

It used to be the general rule of thumb—and still is, in some states—that you could get a better rate with a *health maintenance organization* (*HMO*) or *preferred provider organization* (*PPO*) plan, both of which limit your choice of health-care providers, than with a plan that allows you to see whatever provider you choose. The health insurance arena is changing, however, and HMOs and PPOs aren't always available in all areas, nor are they always the most economical types of plans.

 DEFINITION

A **deductible** is the amount of money you have to pay before your insurance coverage picks up the cost. A **co-pay** is the amount you're expected to pay for a medical expense at the time of the visit or service. It also can refer to the difference between what your doctor charges and what your insurance company covers for a particular service. **Health maintenance organizations (HMOs)** and **preferred provider organizations (PPOs)** are health plans that restrict your choice of health-care providers. As a result, these plans often, but not always, cost less than those that don't restrict providers.

If you can get an HMO or PPO plan in your area, do check them out because they may still be your best deal. Don't reject HMOs and PPOs outright because you think you'll have to find a new doctor. Many HMOs and PPOs probably include your current physicians, so ask to see a list of which doctors are included as providers before you make your decision.

Check out a big health-care insurer such as Blue Cross Blue Shield if you're shopping for a policy. They normally can get better rates from health-care providers and are more stable than many smaller companies. Look for a plan that has the highest lifetime maximum benefits you can find and is guaranteed to be renewable.

Because health-care insurance changes so often and so quickly, and the regulations vary greatly from state to state, shopping for a policy can be extremely challenging. If you need to find your own insurance, consider these suggestions:

Go to the ACA website at healthcare.gov. It is imperative to carefully compare the policies you'll find there. You'll need to consider not only the cost of a policy, but also the deductibles and whether or not you qualify for a subsidy. One of the key provisions of the ACA is the availability of subsidies to offset the cost of coverage. If you qualify for a subsidy, you'll have to file a federal income tax return to confirm that your income is what you stated on the application.

Another option is to find a health insurance agent to help you identify a viable insurance plan. An agent should be able to guide you not only on price, but also on the ins and outs of various companies, deductibles, co-pays, and so forth. The National Association of Health Underwriters (nahu.org) can point you to an agent in your area. Remember, however, that the only way to qualify for the government subsidy is to obtain your insurance through the ACA Marketplace.

Also check out your state's insurance department website. Most sites include the names of companies that offer policies within your state through the ACA Marketplace, along with some information about them. State sites also may include a record of complaints against various companies. One of the popular provisions of the ACA is that no one is disqualified from coverage due to a prior medical condition.

A medical savings account is another option for certain people. As the name implies, this is a savings account created for the purpose of paying for medical expenses, attempting to make medical insurance more affordable. It works in conjunction with qualified major medical insurance and can be used to help pay deductibles and expenses insurance doesn't cover. Generally, these plans are options for people who are self-employed, who work for a company with 50 or fewer employees, or who themselves employ 50 or fewer workers. The Internal Revenue Service (IRS) offers a form on medical savings accounts, 969, "Health Savings Accounts and Other Tax-Favored Health Plans." Access it at the IRS website, irs.gov.

> ### $ DOLLARS AND SENSE
>
> If you're buying your own health insurance, take the largest deductible (the amount you're required to pay before the insurance company will pay a claim) you can afford to keep the cost down. Also consider a co-payment option, where you'd pay a percentage of your health costs. Be sure the co-payment option includes a maximum out-of-pocket limit, though.

Auto Insurance

You must have car insurance because the liability risk if you're in an accident is too great to ignore. Auto insurance is expensive, but it's required by law in nearly every state (except New Hampshire). Even if it wasn't legally required, you couldn't afford to be without it.

Liability coverage   Different types of coverage are associated with car insurance, but the one required by almost all states is liability. Liability coverage is twofold: bodily injury and property damage.

Bodily injury liability coverage protects you against lawsuits in the event someone is injured in an accident in which you're involved. Although it varies from state to state, most states impose a minimum amount of bodily injury coverage, between $25,000 and $50,000 per person and up to $100,000 per accident. If you lend your car to someone else to drive, remember that the insurance follows the car. That means your coverage is the primary insurance in the event of an accident, counting as an accident on your record and increasing your policy costs.

> ### 🐷 MONEY PIT
>
> Although $100,000 sounds like a lot of bodily injury coverage, experts say that to protect your assets in case you're sued, you should have up to $300,000 in coverage. If you buy only the minimum amount, it might not cover all your liability in the event of a lawsuit.

Property damage liability covers damage to other cars and property that's caused by your car. It would cover not only the cost of fixing a car you hit, but also pay to repair or replace the fence you ran over, too. Most states require a minimum of $10,000 in property coverage, although many require significantly more.

Collision and comprehensive coverage   If you have a loan on your car, you'll need collision and comprehensive coverage as well. Collision coverage pays for damage to your car if you're in an accident or pays to replace a car that's totaled. Comprehensive coverage protects you from car theft or weird things that could happen to your car, such as a tree falling on it or it being damaged during a riot, fire, or flood.

Uninsured motorist coverage   If you get hit by someone who doesn't have insurance (not as unusual as you might think), you'll need uninsured motorist coverage. This insurance covers your medical expenses and lost wages in the event that you're injured by an uninsured motorist.

When you rent a car, your policy provides coverage unless it states otherwise. Read your policy, and always call before you go on a trip. If your deductibles are high, you should purchase coverage from the rental company.

> **POCKET CHANGE**
>
> Here's something to think about the next time your insurance premium is due. In 2013, insurance provider GEICO spent $1.8 billion for advertising. Allstate and State Farm were second and third in spending, according to SNL Financial. That's a lot of advertising!

There's a big difference in auto insurance rates, so shop around. Be aware that a poor driving record will dramatically increase your insurance rates.

Look for cars with good safety records (the Insurance Institute for Highway Safety's Highway Loss Data Institute provides a list of these at iihs.org/iihs/ratings/TSP-List), and stay away from hot sports cars or convertibles if you're interested in keeping your rates down. If you're shopping for a new or used car, learn how rates vary from model to model before making your purchase.

If you're over 25, you'll generally get a better rate than someone who is younger. Also, being married, living in what is considered a safe neighborhood, and having a relatively short work commute (driving less than 7,500 miles per year or not using your car for work) also will lower your insurance rates.

Property Insurance

You're required to buy property insurance before you can get a mortgage, so if you own a home, you already have homeowner's insurance.

If you're renting an apartment, you need renter's insurance if you have a lot of stuff you want to protect. Damage to the building is not your responsibility, but if your TV or laptop is stolen or damaged, you need insurance if you want to replace it without paying out of pocket. If you have a bunch of good computer equipment or a rare-coin collection, you definitely should look into renter's insurance.

Your best bet is to get a policy that provides replacement value. It will cost a little more, but it will pay you what it would cost to replace your TV or computer at the current purchase price—not the price you paid 5 years ago.

Disability Insurance

What would happen if you had a serious accident while skiing that resulted in a head injury? Pretty gruesome to think about, right? Still, nobody is immune to accidents or injury. You have a greater chance of being disabled by age 65 than dying, and if you were hurt and unable to work for a long period of time, you'd be out of luck.

You'd be a little less out of luck, though, if you had *disability* insurance, which would provide you with an income to live on until you could work again. Most large companies provide disability insurance to employees who are unable to work because of a physical or mental disability.

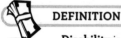 **DEFINITION**

> **Disability** is the inability to work because of a physical or mental condition. More than one third of all disabilities are reported among people who are under 45 years old.

There are two types of disability insurance coverage: short term (usually for up to 3 or 6 months) and long term (beginning after 6 months). But if you work for a small company or are self-employed, you might have to buy it on your own. If you can't afford to be without a paycheck for an extended period of time, you'd better have disability insurance. By the way, if you don't work, you can't get disability insurance.

How much disability insurance you need depends on how much money you have. If you've been living paycheck to paycheck and have no money saved, you'd better have insurance to cover as much of your income as you can purchase. This is usually 60 percent of your income. If you have enough money in the bank to live off of for 6 months or a year, you can skimp a little.

Disability insurance becomes increasingly important as you gain dependents. If you're married and your spouse doesn't work or doesn't earn enough to support both of you, you can't be without it. If your spouse is making enough to support both of you, it's not as important. If you have kids, however, you've got to have disability insurance, unless your spouse makes enough money to support the entire family for an extended period of time.

Be sure you know what's included in your disability coverage if you get it through work. Many people don't take the time to find out, and you can't depend on the benefits department to seek you out and tell you you're eligible for coverage. Most companies have short-term and long-term provisions, so if you find out you need an operation and will be out of work for a couple weeks, you'll want to know whether you're eligible for benefits.

Also be sure the short-term and long-term disability provisions "match," so that once you are on disability, you continue to receive benefits without having to incur another elimination period, or the number of days you must be disabled before the insurance kicks in.

If you need to buy your own disability insurance, go for the longest elimination period you think you could handle. This will result in a significantly lower rate. A 90-day elimination period often is recommended, but you'd need to be able to support yourself (and your family, if applicable) for that period of time.

Also, be sure you understand how the policy defines "disabled." Some policies require that you be hospitalized to receive benefits. You should look for a policy that will keep paying you as long as you're unable to perform your job duties.

Don't depend on government programs such as Social Security (you must be off work for at least 6 months to qualify for Social Security benefits) or workers' compensation to provide you with benefits in the event of a disability. If you're eligible for coverage, your benefits won't be as much as you need. Also, your chances of being injured off the job are probably as good, or better, as those of being injured at work. You need coverage in the event of any disability.

 DOLLARS AND SENSE

If you don't have disability insurance through your employer, you might be able to purchase it through a professional organization in which you're eligible for membership. Groups are often able to buy insurance for less than individuals, so you should be able to get a better rate. The American Medical Association (ama-assn.org), National Education Association (nea.org), Writers Guild of America (wga.org), and Society of Financial Service Professionals (financialpro.org) are all professional organizations. If you need coverage, find out if you can qualify under such a group.

Insurance You Don't Need

In addition to extended warranties for your computer, washer, and hair dryer, there are some other insurance goodies you can live without. If an agent tries to get you to buy the following sorts of policies, just say no.

Dental Insurance

If your employer offers dental insurance, by all means, go ahead and use it. If not, though, don't bother getting it on your own. It usually doesn't pay for extensive work, and it's not worth buying to cover having your teeth cleaned a few times a year.

Flight Insurance

This novelty insurance plays on the fears of people who don't like to fly. If your life is worth a lot of money, you'll have your life insurance up to date anyway.

Credit Life and Disability Insurance

Sold by credit card companies, these policies pay a small amount to your beneficiaries if you die with a credit card balance. The policy only covers the debt on that one card. Don't bother. Your term life insurance policy should be large enough to cover all your debts.

Life Insurance for Your Kids

Life insurance is to protect income, and children generally don't have income. If your child dies, a small amount of insurance money isn't going to make things better for you. You may purchase a child rider on your life insurance policy to cover a funeral and final expenses if you wouldn't be able to afford these if your child were to die.

Shop Around and Save

Insurance costs can vary greatly, so to limit the costs of your insurance policies, you must comparison shop.

We mentioned earlier that you should take the highest deductibles you can afford on your insurance. Of course, you'll pay more in the event that something happens, but you'll pay less on your premiums. Chances are, you'll end up paying more in premiums than you will on a higher deductible for an occasional claim. If you have a very low deductible, you'll end up filing claims a lot more often than if your deductible is higher.

Say your roof leaked during that last nasty thunderstorm. It's nothing too bad, but the estimate to repair the damage was $175. If your deductible is $100, you're going to spend a lot of time filling out claim forms and hassling with the insurance company for the sake of $75. Also, if you report every minor claim, you can bet the insurance company will soon be hiking up your rates. If you have a $500 deductible, though, you'll save significant money on your premiums—a savings you can use to make minor repairs. Comparison shop the premium savings and the deductible limits and then determine what you can afford to pay out if you have a claim.

Also mentioned earlier was the advantage of getting a group rate on an insurance policy rather than buying it on your own. Whenever possible, check out group rates through your employer or an organization you belong to. You often can save significant money by doing so. A benefit of having an individual policy is that you can retain the coverage if you change jobs.

Finally, when you're shopping around, check out the rating of the insurance company you're thinking of doing business with. Various organizations evaluate and rate insurance companies, judging them on their financial stability and health. Look to A.M. Best (ambest.com), Standard and Poor's (standardandpoors.com), Weiss Research (weissinc.com), or Moody's (moodys.com) rating services.

MONEY PIT

Insurance agents are paid to sell certain products and policies, and in some cases, they may focus on their own needs before yours. Before meeting with an agent, read buying guides on the website of your state's insurance department. These can give you an idea of what different insurances should cost and cover. Write down questions you want to ask the agent, and insist they are specific about what policies cover.

When You're Not Covered

Coming from your insurance agent, "You're not covered" can strike fear in even the staunchest hearts. If you've filed a claim and your insurer doesn't want to pay it, or wants to pay only part of what you believe it should, don't roll over. There are things you can do to assure your best shot at getting what you deserve.

Document Your Losses

If you're in a car accident, get the names and addresses of all possible witnesses. If your property was damaged, take photos or videos of the damage. File police reports when necessary, and get several estimates for what it will cost to repair or replace whatever was damaged. If you aren't at fault in the accident, be certain that's noted on your policy. Whether or not your premium increases at your next renewal depends largely on who is at fault for the accident. Some companies now offer a one-accident forgiveness feature, which is something to consider when you are shopping around.

Don't Give Up

If you file a claim for $2,286 for repairs to your car after a wreck and the insurance company says it will give you $1,500, find out why. If you don't get any satisfaction from the *adjuster*, ask to talk to the supervisors and managers. Ask your agent to help you, too.

DEFINITION

An insurance **adjuster** is a person who inspects damage and determines the amount the insurance company should pay for repairs or replacement.

Prepare Your Claim Carefully

Be sure your policy covers the claim you're about to make, and write out your claim report carefully and clearly. By all means, keep a copy of the report, and document all conversations you have with anyone concerning your claim.

Get Help

If you've been denied coverage for a major claim you feel you're entitled to, call your state insurance department and discuss the situation with a representative. If you're still not satisfied, you might want to review the matter with a lawyer who specializes in insurance concerns. Hiring an attorney can be expensive, but if there's a significant amount of money at stake, it might be worth it.

Insurance is a big, powerful industry, and it's in the business of making money. Don't expect your insurer to go out of its way to please you and make you happy. Although you shouldn't assume an adversarial position with your insurance company, you should remain alert to the possibility that you'll have to do a little haggling to get what you deserve. Good companies do, and all companies are expected to, honor their commitments and promises to their customers.

The Least You Need to Know

- Purchase insurance to cover major losses, not to protect you against every little thing that could go wrong.
- Some types of policies are recommended for almost everyone, and some hardly anyone should buy.
- You can save money when buying insurance, so it pays to know what you need and look around before you buy.
- If your insurer hassles you about paying a claim, be prepared to fight.

Relationships and Money

Life keeps changing, and those life changes can affect your finances in a very big way. In Part 7, we discuss how relationships can affect your finances as far as the types of accounts you'll have and the way you'll pay taxes, among other factors.

As your life responsibilities increase, you also need to learn about things like life insurance, setting up a will, and getting a power-of-attorney in place in the event that you would become incapacitated.

It's a lot to ponder, but we offer lots of advice and tips to get you started.

CHAPTER 18

Life, Love, and Money

Life, in many ways, is not a game of chance. It moves along at its own pace. Days pass; seasons change; and all of a sudden, you're another year older.

Your life is changing, too. You're probably better established in your career than you were a year or so ago, and it might seem like a lifetime ago that you left college and started working. Hopefully, your personal finances are on track, and you're enjoying having a little extra money—not only for things you want to buy, but for investing in your future as well.

Let's have a look at how different stages of life can affect your personal finances and how you can make the most of each of those stages.

In This Chapter

- How your life affects your finances
- Being single and earning a paycheck
- Living together and your finances
- Marriage and money
- The financial implications of divorce
- Borrowing money from people you know

Footloose and Fancy-Free

Your single years can be some of the best of your life. You're getting your career off the ground and starting to be recognized for your accomplishments. You're meeting lots of new people and enjoying an active social life. You're not broke like you were in college and the first couple years when you started working, so you can afford to do some things now you couldn't do before. You're also learning a little about investments, putting some money away in your 401(k) plan, and maybe even thinking about buying a place of your own.

If you're still living with your parents, you're by no means alone. Many millennials are staying at home longer, and among other reasons, they say it's so they can repay college loans and save some money.

 POCKET CHANGE

Many millennials count on financial help from parents or other relatives, according to a *USA Today*/Bank of America Better Money Habits poll of millennials. More than half of all 18- to 25-year-olds were getting some help with groceries and cell phone bills in 2014. The number dipped to 20 percent for those between the ages of 26 and 34.

However, not all single people are financially responsible. Some not-so-young-anymore singles haven't saved a dime, and they aren't looking into the future past their next paycheck.

In earlier chapters, we talked about investments, taxes, and other topics that can affect your finances and your future. Hopefully, you've learned something and are doing what you need to both enjoy your single years and ensure your future. At the very least, you should by now be paying back college loans, working to reduce (and hopefully eliminate) credit card debt, saving money in an emergency fund, and putting some money into your employer's 401(k) plan or another type of tax-deferred retirement plan.

We'd never suggest you miss out on the opportunity to enjoy your great single years because you're saving every penny you make and never have any money to do anything with. Just don't lose sight of the fact that you have a lot of life ahead of you, and all the fun you have when you're footloose and fancy-free won't finance your retirement.

Living Together

So you've met somebody you really, really like. Okay, you're in love. You're spending a lot of time together. Actually, you're together almost all the time. You talk about a future together, but neither of you feels like you're quite ready to start shopping for an engagement ring. And then one day you're just hanging out when it happens: your significant other asks you to move in.

This scenario is becoming increasingly common, as more than 6.4 million unmarried couples are living together in the United States, according to U.S. Census figures. That's a change from 35 years ago, when fewer than 1 million unmarried couples cohabitated.

Couples live together for a variety of reasons. Some do it because it's convenient; it eliminates running back and forth between two apartments and shuffling belongings all over town. Some couples use living together as a sort of "trial run" for marriage; they reason it makes more sense to see whether it will work out before they get married than risk a divorce later.

POCKET CHANGE

Americans are waiting longer and longer to get married, and fewer are getting married at all. The average age for first marriages in America is 27 for women and 29 for men, according to a report from the University of Virginia's National Marriage Project. That compares with 23 for women and 26 for men in 1990, and 20 for women and 22 for men in 1960.

Financial considerations also can factor into a couple's decision to live together rather than get married. Many couples set a goal of saving a specific amount of money, paying off student loans, or getting enough for a down payment on a house before taking the plunge. Some want to establish their careers before getting married and live together while they do.

Whatever the reasons, plenty of couples choose to live together. Although cohabitation is common and widely accepted, it can still be a sticky arrangement. There are financial and legal ramifications as well as the less-tangible emotional aspects to consider.

You're on your own to figure out the emotional particulars of living together, but we can tell you some things you should know about the legal and financial aspects.

Financial Pros of Living Together

Living together definitely comes with some financial advantages:

Reduced costs   If you each had an apartment before you moved in together, you'll cut your housing costs by about 50 percent by sharing your space. That makes more sense than paying rent on an apartment that was empty most of the time, anyway. You'll also be sharing costs for utilities, so you'll see some savings there. If you were living a considerable distance apart, you'll save money on transportation, too.

Tax advantages   You'll also realize some tax advantages by living together instead of opting for marriage. Although you're living together, you'll continue filing your tax returns as singles. That can save you some money, especially if you and your significant other earn above-average salaries. Even with changes to tax laws that lessen tax-rate disparities, many married couples still pay more combined income tax than two singles filing separately.

POCKET CHANGE

Unmarried couples are staying together longer than they used to, according to recent study from the National Center for Health Statistics, but more than a quarter of all unmarried couples still break up within 3 years of cohabitating.

Financial Cons of Living Together

Although living together does have some financial benefits, it's not all a bed of roses. In some instances, you'd be better off financially if you were married. Consider the following:

Health benefits   Some employers offer health and dental benefits to spouses of employees but not to unmarried partners.

Life insurance   If an employer offers life insurance and the employee dies, benefits automatically go to the spouse of the deceased. An unmarried partner must be named as a beneficiary to receive the benefits.

Property   If you live together in a house or condo that's in only one of your names, the significant other may have no claim on the property, despite having invested $30,000 in the new kitchen.

Social Security   If a person dies while employed, the spouse might be eligible for some Social Security benefits upon reaching age 60. An unmarried partner isn't eligible for these benefits.

Memberships   Unmarried couples may not be eligible for money-saving "family" memberships in clubs and organizations.

We're not trying to turn marriage into a business transaction, but as you can see, there are financial advantages and disadvantages to living together instead of getting married you should consider.

One thing to remember, though, is that marriage implies love and commitment that extend far past the savings account. If you're putting off marriage because you might be taxed at a higher rate, you might have to ask yourself whether you're looking for an excuse to stay single.

DOLLARS AND SENSE

If you are in a committed relationship but not married, you might be able to sign an affidavit declaring your relationship. A domestic partnership affidavit may enable you to receive benefits and considerations normally intended for a spouse.

Getting Married

You're tying the knot! Hearty congratulations and best wishes to you both! Before you blissfully embark on your honeymoon, though, you need to think about some financial matters.

Chances are, you've been thinking a lot about money as you ponder how much to spend and how to pay for your wedding. We leave that up to you, with only a warning to think long and hard before taking on a lot of debt to pay for your special day.

With some planning, you can put on a lovely wedding without a $30,000 price tag. Many websites, blogs, apps, and articles can help you plan a wedding that won't break your budget. Here are few of our favorite articles:

- "Ten Ways I Trimmed $21,000 Off My Wedding Budget" (lifehacker.com/ ten-ways-i-trimmed-21-000-off-my-wedding-budget-1183546801)

- "8 Websites to Help You Save Money on the Cost of a Wedding" (makeuseof.com/ tag/8-websites-help-save-money-cost-wedding)

- "The 7 Best Wedding Planning Apps Brides and Grooms Should Download Now" (techtimes.com/articles/52507/20150515/best-wedding-planning-apps-brides-grooms- download-now.htm)

A large number of divorces are caused by financial problems. Sometimes these problems are a result of a gambling or another type of addiction. Often, though, financial problems occur because the couple doesn't work together on their financial health.

If you're planning to marry, it's absolutely essential that you and your intended sit down and carefully and thoroughly discuss how you'll handle your finances after the wedding. You should establish some goals to work toward together and be sure you know about each other's debts, spending patterns, and investments. Talk about your college debt, credit card debt, or other liabilities. Get familiar with one another's credit scores, and understand what each of you earns and saves. As a married couple, you'll need to work together to handle your finances.

You also need to decide how you'll set up your bank accounts as a married couple. It's not necessary to have joint accounts, although most married couples have at least some of their money pooled. Some couples, especially when both people are earning, keep both separate accounts and joint accounts. Separate accounts give individuals freedom and independence, while joint accounts offer the convenience of allowing either spouse to sign a check or make online payments. This is a decision you and your partner need to discuss and figure out based on what works best for the two of you.

MONEY PIT

Love might be blind, but your understanding of your partner's financial situation shouldn't be. You'll be in for an unpleasant surprise if you find out your new husband owes $10,000 for something you knew nothing about. If one of you does have a lot of debt or other financial problems, discuss those problems and reach an agreement—before the wedding—on how you're going to handle them.

While contemplating marriage, be sure to consider your spouse-to-be's financial personality. Learn your partner's attitudes concerning savings and the best means for saving money for your future together. Do you have 401(k) plans? Any stocks? What about savings bonds you got as gifts when you were a kid? Talk about saving to buy a house. What about saving for kids?

Talk, too, about how you'll operate within a budget, and together plan the budget you'll use. You don't want the stresses of adjusting to married life to be aggravated by a misunderstanding of how you'll be handling your finances. Iron out as many financial considerations as possible before the wedding to avoid conflicts afterward.

You also should discuss how your marriage will affect your employer benefits. If one of you has a much better package than the other, set it up so you're both covered by the better deal, if possible. Consider health benefits, retirement savings plans, and anything else that might affect your financial situation. Check to see whether either employer offers compensation to an employee who gives up benefits to be covered by the partner's plan.

Pay attention to your insurance policies, too, ensuring you have what you need. And you'll need to think about setting up wills, trusts, and powers of attorney, as applicable. (You learn more about those topics in Chapter 20.)

DOLLARS AND SENSE

Start an emergency fund if you don't already have one. When you're footloose and fancy-free, you're the only one you have to worry about. Now you have the additional responsibility of another person, so start saving whatever you can to put back 3 to 6 months' worth of living expenses in case of an emergency.

What About Prenups?

Prenuptial agreements—those handy little plans that spell out how assets will be divided in the event the marriage fails—used to be primarily for people with lots of money. But even if you don't have tons of money, some matrimonial lawyers and financial advisers strongly recommend a prenup, especially if one person has a child or children from a previous marriage or relationship. A prenuptial agreement also might make sense if one partner owns a business or makes a lot more money than the other. Such an agreement could be important if one partner has major assets independently and doesn't want to risk losing them.

> **DEFINITION**
>
> A **prenuptial agreement,** or prenup, is a legal document that protects your financial interests if a marriage breaks up.

The average cost of hiring an attorney to draw up a traditional prenuptial agreement ranges from $1,500 to $3,000, depending on the complexity and the amount of assets to be considered. Prenuptial agreements also are available online from sources like LegalZoom (legalzoom.com), an online legal document provider. For $995, you can get a basic prenuptial agreement you fill out and then send in for a LegalZoom document reviewer to look over. You'll have to pay more if your wedding is less than 2 weeks away.

Whether or not to have a prenuptial agreement is something you and your fiancé have to decide together. If you can't agree on the need for one, or if you feel your partner is pressuring you to have one and you don't want it, it might be a good idea to get some financial or relationship counseling before the wedding. It might just be a matter of not fully understanding the other's concerns or wishes.

Filing Jointly or Separately?

The American tax system is far from simple, and it's long been a thorny issue for some couples as they marry. The taxes a couple has to pay after marriage might be higher or lower than the combined amount they would have paid if they had remained single. If the amount is more, it's referred to as the *marriage penalty*. If it's less, it's called a *marriage bonus*.

Typically, a marriage penalty happens when two people who make about the same amount of money marry. This is true for both low- and high-income couples because combining salaries and doubling your taxable income can push a couple into a higher tax bracket. It used to be that the deduction a married couple took didn't even come close to adding up to the total of the deductions of two people filing separately, but tax revisions have gone a long way toward closing the gap.

A marriage bonus typically occurs when a couple with very unequal salaries files jointly. The amount earned by the person with the lower income generally isn't enough to put the couple into a higher tax bracket. Because income tax brackets for married individuals are much wider than those for single filers, the couple might actually fall into a lower bracket and pay less in taxes.

To see which way is more advantageous to you, run your returns both ways—jointly and separately—through a tax program such as TurboTax before filing.

And Baby Makes Three

Life happens, and kids very often are a part of life. They can be the best thing to ever happen to you, but they are expensive—very expensive. If you have a child or two, are thinking of having a child, or are expecting a baby soon, you need to consider some child-related financial implications.

No one can tell you exactly how having a baby will affect your life. Suffice it to say, however, it will never be the same. Your sleeping schedule will change. Your relationship with your spouse will change. Your expectations, hopes, and dreams will change. And if you're lucky, you'll experience a profound, life-changing love for your baby.

Your financial situation also will change, starting with the income you may lose due to time off during pregnancy and after the baby is born. If your employer doesn't offer paid maternity or paternity leave, check at work to see if you're covered by short-term disability insurance, which might cover you for time off due to pregnancy and childbirth. If short-term disability won't kick in, you could take time off under the Family and Medical Leave Act, but your employer doesn't have to pay you when you're gone.

 DOLLARS AND SENSE

If you've decided to go the adoption route, it's possible, but not necessarily so, you'll encounter some significant expenses. Public agency adoptions can cost nearly nothing, while private or intercountry adoptions can cost as much as $40,000, according to the U.S. Department of Health and Human Services.

The next financial hurdles to clear are the medical bills for the pregnancy and birth. Check the provisions of your health insurance policy to find out exactly what pregnancy and childbirth expenses are covered and what you might have to pay for yourself. Don't forget to consider any deductibles or co-pays you might be responsible for. If you have to pick up some or even all of the cost, many hospitals and birthing centers will work with you on setting up a payment plan.

Not only are babies expensive to birth, they're also expensive after they arrive in the world. A crib, a stroller, a high chair, a baby swing, car seats, mobiles, sheets, diapers, lotions, … the list goes on and on, and there's more baby gear being invented by the minute. You definitely need furniture and equipment that's safe and durable, but you don't need the Ralph Lauren baby sheet and comforter ensemble available for $125 at Nordstrom. Your baby will sleep just as soundly on the $14.99 version from Target. Also, don't overlook your local consignment shop, yard sales, or online sites like craigslist for baby equipment. You can find a lot of barely used gear around for much less than new costs if you look.

As you might know, childcare is expensive. If you're planning to go back to work after your baby is born, you'll need to carefully consider your options for finding someone to watch Junior. Unless you're lucky enough to have Grandma watch the baby, you can plan on spending some serious dollars for good childcare.

But there is some good news: childcare expenses, with limitations, can be deducted when you file your income tax. To take the deduction, you only need to report the provider's Social Security or taxpayer identification number and address to the IRS.

Divorce and Financial Issues

Marriage is not a perfect or foolproof institution, and sometimes it ends in divorce. If your marriage is failing, or has failed, it's urgently important that you protect your assets and make the best of a bad situation. It might seem insensitive to focus on finances when you're splitting up, particularly if you have a child or children who need your care and attention. But ignoring your financial situation during this time could negatively affect you—and your kids—for years to come.

Often, when divorce occurs, one or both parties is emotionally devastated. Obviously, that's not a good place to be and can make just getting through the day incredibly difficult. The emotional aspects of divorce can be extremely frustrating and consuming, but it's important to pay attention to the entire divorce scenario, which includes your finances.

If you don't have a lot of assets, dividing up what you do have might not be so difficult. If you have a prenuptial agreement, as discussed earlier in this chapter, the division of property should be pretty straightforward. If you don't have a prenup and you have considerable assets, or suspect the division of whatever property you have won't be agreeable or easy, you probably need to hire an attorney.

When it comes to dividing property, you'll need to be realistic about what you'll be able to afford. If you and your spouse were both contributing to mortgage payments, you might not be able to afford them on your own, meaning you might not be able to keep your house. The same may apply to vehicles, vacation property, and other assets.

While you're dividing property, you'll also need to consider how to divide debt. Be sure you get the full story on any debt your spouse has incurred. Many divorces are the result of financial problems, which sometimes occur without the knowledge of one of the partners. Laws regarding the obligation of one spouse to the other in the event of debt vary, but it's always better to confront the reality of your financial situation and decide how to best deal with it.

DOLLARS AND SENSE

Divorce laws vary greatly from state to state, so it's essential that you know what laws apply to you. You can find your state's laws online, but it's a good idea to consult with an attorney—and sooner rather than later, especially if you have children.

If you are required to pay alimony, maintenance, or child support to your ex, or you are to be the recipient of any of those payments, be sure you understand the tax implications. Alimony payments are considered taxable income, but the payer can usually deduct them from his or her income. Child support, however, is neither taxable nor deductible. Marital support becomes alimony in the year of the divorce, so be aware of the tax consequences.

Retirement savings may be affected by divorce as well. In the event that one spouse worked and had a retirement plan and the other spouse had no income or had been in an employment situation that did not include a plan, the property settlement can divide the retirement savings into two parts—one for the employee and one for the spouse. Tax penalties that would apply for an early withdraw from a retirement fund under different circumstances do not apply when an account is divided due to divorce. A court order known as a qualified domestic relation order (QDRO) is needed to make a nontaxable division.

Finally, you'll need to take action regarding credit cards, bank accounts, financial accounts, insurance policies, wills, and any other pending legal agreements. Depending on the circumstances of your divorce, you might have to take steps to prevent your former spouse from gaining access to your bank accounts or credit cards. Be sure all the necessary paperwork is completed to ensure your accounts and policies remain safe.

Clearly, divorce is a difficult and complicated action, which we can only begin to cover here. If you're facing divorce, you should learn everything you can on your own. But unless there's a compelling reason not to, also consult with a qualified attorney who can lead you through the proceedings.

Borrowing Money from Family or Friends

Married or not, at some point of your life, you might find yourself in a position where it makes sense to borrow money from a family member or friend. And although these types of loans have been lifesavers for many, they also can be dangerous.

If you plan to borrow money from a family member or friend to use as a down payment on a house, get your catering business off the ground, pay off the last of your student loans, help with expenses if you take extended unpaid leave after having a baby, or for any other purpose, proceed carefully.

POCKET CHANGE

The National Association of Realtors reports that about 7 percent of home buyers get loans from family members or friends to finance their homes or use as a down payment. And according to the National Small Business Association, 14 percent of business owners receive help from someone they know to help meet expenses.

When you borrow money from a bank or other lender, you have a legal obligation to pay back the money, based on specific terms.

Borrowing from a friend or family member should be no different. You and the lender should have everything in writing, with an agreement that outlines the terms of the loan. Include the interest rate, if there is one; the penalty for late payments; what will happen if the loan recipient defaults; in what installments payments will be made; and so forth. Consider having the agreement notarized, which will make it more legally enforceable in the event of default. When you have an agreement in place, stay in touch with the person who loaned you the money. If your loan payment is going to be late, be sure you let the lender know, and explain the reason.

Family members and friends often are happy to loan money to a deserving relative or friend, but relationships have been irrevocably damaged when the recipient of the loan defaulted.

DOLLARS AND SENSE

There may be some tax benefits for a person who has loaned money for someone else's mortgage. If you borrow money for a home from a family or member or friend, suggest that they check out National Family Mortgage (nationalfamilymortgage.com) to see if they might benefit.

The Least You Need to Know

- Living single and bringing in a paycheck is a tempting time to spend, spend, spend, but it's also a great time to save.
- Living together without being married can affect your finances. Consider these effects before making a commitment.
- Getting married might involve changes to your taxes, insurance, and bank accounts.
- A baby is an expensive proposition, but there are ways to keep expenses under control.

- If you find yourself facing divorce, work carefully to protect yourself financially.
- When borrowing money from a family member or friend, be sure everything is in writing and everyone agrees on the terms of the loan.

CHAPTER 19

Choosing Life Insurance

When you're young and getting started financially, the thought of buying life insurance might not have even crossed your mind.

A 2015 survey by LIMRA, an insurance research and consulting firm, showed that fewer than 20 percent of millennials say they're likely to buy life insurance. What's more, 3 out of 10 said saving for vacation was a bigger priority than life insurance, and 60 percent reported that paying cable, internet, and cell phone bills was more important.

In this chapter, we look at why you might need life insurance and explore ways to find a policy that makes sense for you.

In This Chapter

- You need life insurance
- Different types of life insurance
- Choosing the insurance that makes sense for you
- Knowing how much insurance you need
- Finding a good policy you can afford

Nearly Everybody Needs Life Insurance

If you are young and healthy with no dependents and no debt, maybe you don't need life insurance. For everyone else, life insurance is a good idea.

The point of life insurance is to provide for those who depend on you. Your life insurance also would be used to pay off any debt you owe. So if you have college debt, credit card debt, a car loan, mortgage, or any other type of debt, think about who would be responsible for paying it if you died and whether having to pay off your debt would negatively impact their finances. If your parents cosigned a loan for you, they would be responsible for it if you died. Think about how well they'd be able to handle that financial responsibility at this point of their lives.

If you have a job that includes benefits, you might be covered for life insurance through an employee-provided group policy. If so, be sure you understand the terms of the insurance and how much would be paid out in the event of your death. Also, find out if it's possible for you to increase your coverage if you pay for additional insurance. You might be able to get an affordable rate as part of a group policy.

If it's just you, you should have enough life insurance to cover your funeral and other final expenses and any outstanding loans. If you're married but have no kids, you should have life insurance if your spouse would have to dramatically change his or her lifestyle if you died. If you have kids and support a family, you definitely need life insurance.

Let's look at different kinds of life insurance and what kind might make sense for you.

Term Life Insurance Versus Cash Value

In general, there are two basic types of life insurance: *term life insurance* and *cash value insurance* (also known as permanent, whole-life, variable, or universal insurance). Most people benefit more from term insurance than cash value insurance when they're young. Cash value insurance, which is actually a type of investment vehicle, might make sense for older people who use it as part of their estate planning, or for families who want to pass along life insurance to their heirs.

 DEFINITION

Term life insurance is a policy in which you pay an annual premium in exchange for a predetermined amount of money that will be paid to your beneficiaries if you die during the term you're insured. **Cash value insurance** combines a life insurance policy with a type of savings or investment account, and you actually earn interest, or appreciation, on part of the money you pay into the plan.

Term life insurance is the least-expensive kind of life insurance. In exchange for your annual premium, term life gives a predetermined amount of money to your beneficiaries if you die during the term you're insured. All you need to do is continue to pay the premium. The premium keeps increasing as you get older, however, and someday it might become prohibitive. It's a good idea to review your policies periodically to be sure they make sense for you.

Cash value insurance combines life insurance with a sort of savings or investment account. Your premiums not only ensure your survivors receive money if you die, but in addition, some of the money from the premiums is credited to an account that should increase in value as long as you keep paying premiums.

Which Type Makes Sense for You?

Cash value insurance might sound like a better deal because you think you'll be getting something back from it. An agent who sells cash value life insurance will tell you that after you pay on the policy for so many years (usually 15 or 20), your policy will be all paid up and you won't have to make more payments. The problem is that cash value insurance is much more expensive than term to buy when you're young, and the only reason you might be able to stop paying premiums at a certain time is because you've already paid in a great amount of premiums.

There's an argument for buying a cash value policy at a young age. When you buy term life insurance, you need to provide proof of insurability to get a new policy when the current term expires. If it turns out you're uninsurable due to an emerging disease or other medical problem, you could end up without life insurance. A cash value policy can't be cancelled as long as you continue to make the premium payments.

Agents love cash value life because they get a much higher commission selling it than they do term policies. For that reason, some agents might try to steer you in that direction. Don't let an agent or broker talk you into buying cash value insurance, though. At this point in your life, unless there are special circumstances, it's not likely you'll need it.

 DOLLARS AND SENSE

Cash value insurance can cost up to eight times as much as term life insurance for the same amount of coverage. Unless special circumstances exist, like if you're very wealthy and anticipate an estate tax problem if you should die, term insurance is a better deal for young people.

How Much Life Insurance Do You Need?

Knowing how much life insurance you need isn't always easy to determine. As stated, if you're single or married with no children, you can get away with less than if you have a family to support.

To ensure that your family can continue the lifestyle to which they are accustomed, you'll need to have a look at several things. Other than your mortgage, what kind of debt do you have? If you have debt, you need to have enough life insurance to pay it off, in addition to being able to continue to support your family. The next thing to consider is how much money you spend every month. Look at your bank statements or use a personal budget software package to determine how much you need each month.

This is important because you can't ensure your family will have enough money to live comfortably if you don't really know how much money that requires. The point of having life insurance is to protect your family and help them achieve the goals you would have been working toward if you had continued to earn.

MONEY PIT

Never decide to buy a certain amount of life insurance because it's what your brother or best friend has. Everyone's circumstances are different. For example, your brother might need only half the amount of insurance you do.

In addition to long-term financial goals, your spouse would need to have money to fill in the gap left by the loss of your salary. Your household bills and expenses would remain relatively the same, after all.

The rule of thumb used to be to buy life insurance equal to 10 times your yearly salary. If you earn $50,000 a year, you'd buy $500,000 worth of life insurance. Many financial experts, however, say that rule is outdated and doesn't consider certain factors like debt, savings, and whether you already have a group life insurance policy through work. Also, that rule implies that if one spouse stays at home to care for children and has no income, there is no need for life insurance. Most financial advisers agree both parents should be insured.

If you want to get an idea of the amount of life insurance you should buy, use this formula:

1. Calculate how many years your family would need replacement income for your salary. Using the year your youngest graduates from high school as an end date probably is reasonable.

2. Multiply your salary by the number of years your family would need replacement income for your salary.

3. Add to that number the balance of your mortgage; the total of all other debt such as college loans, car loans, and credit card debt; and funeral costs.

4. Add to that an estimated amount for the cost of college for your children. (You can find a college cost calculator at the College Savings Plans Network website at collegesavings .org/college-cost-calculator.)

5. Subtract from that number the amount of savings you have in place, including retirement savings, college funds already saved, and proceeds from group life insurance.

After you've done the math, you'll know how much life insurance you need.

Let's look at an example: Tom, 36, and Kate, 34, have been married for 5 years and have two daughters, ages 4 and 2. Tom earns $60,000 a year, and Kate, who works part-time, earns $27,000 a year. To figure out how much life insurance he should buy, Tom would …

1. Calculate the number of years before his younger daughter graduates from high school. That's 16.

2. Multiply his salary, $60,000, by 16. That comes to $960,000.

3. Add to $960,000 the amount of his mortgage and all other debt. Tom has a mortgage for $150,000, credit card debt of $2,000, a car loan for $12,000, and college loan debt of $8,000. The median cost of a funeral with a casket is $7,000. All those costs total $179,000. When added to the $960,000, Tom's number is now at $1,139,000.

4. Calculate and add the cost of college for his girls to his total. The college calculator tells him it will cost about $410,000 for his daughters to attend an in-state, public university for 4 years, including room and board. When added to the previous total, Tom's number is up to $1,549,000.

5. Subtract their $18,000 savings and Tom's $175,000 group life insurance benefit at work from his total. Tom needs to have a term policy worth $1,356,000.

Kate would calculate her needs the same way, taking into consideration costs associated with childcare and whether she would move into a full-time job.

Shopping for Life Insurance

You'll want to shop around before choosing a life insurance policy to ensure you get a good price from a reliable company.

You can get instant quotes from different insurance companies by using an online insurance broker like AccuQuote (accuquote.com), LifeInsure.com (lifeinsure.com), or FindMyInsurance (findmyinsurance.com). All you do is enter your basic information such as your age, health status, and the amount of insurance you want, and you'll be given policy prices from numerous companies. When you see the quotes, you can request an application and get more information about the plan if you want.

POCKET CHANGE

Using Tom from our previous example, when we submitted his information to FindMyInsurance, estimated costs for a 30-year term policy worth $1,400,000 came in from about 20 different companies showing he would have to pay about $110 a month or $1,223 a year for his life insurance.

When you've identified a company that offers a good price, check the insurance company's rating on a site like TheStreet (thestreet.com) or Standard & Poor's insurance ratings (standardandpoors .com).

Here are TheStreet's top 10 picks for life insurance in 2016:

- State Farm Life Insurance Company (statefarm.com)

- American Family Life Insurance Company (amfam.com)

- Country Life Insurance Company (countryfinancial.com)

- State Farm Life and Accident Assurance Company (statefarm.com)

- Massachusetts Mutual Life Insurance Company (massmutual.com)

- Guardian Life Insurance Company of America (guardianlife.com)

- New York Life Insurance and Annuity Corporation (newyorklife.com)

- Southern Farm Bureau Life Insurance Company (sfbli.com)

- USAA Life Insurance Company (usaa.com)

- Northwestern Mutual Life Insurance Company (northwesternmutual.com)

Obtaining a life insurance policy probably will require a physical exam or at least a visit from a nurse for a blood pressure check and various other tests. When you've secured a life insurance policy, maintain the best health possible in case you need to shop for new coverage.

As with any insurance, the hope is that you won't need it. In the meantime, you'll have the peace of mind of knowing your family will be taken care of in the event of your death.

The Least You Need to Know

- If you haven't thought about life insurance yet, you probably should.
- Term life insurance makes the most sense for the majority of younger people.
- You'll need to consider many factors when determining how much life insurance you need.
- Comparing policies and costs can help you find the insurance you need at an affordable cost.

CHAPTER 20

Wills, Powers of Attorney, and Health-Care Directives

When you're young and just getting started on your own, the thought of wills, powers of attorney, and health-care directives probably seem as foreign to you as using a walker or researching retirement communities. Life moves pretty fast, however, and it's best to be prepared.

In this chapter, we explore these legal documents and explain why they're important for everyone.

In This Chapter

- Why you need a will
- Getting a will is easy
- Setting up a power of attorney
- The importance of an advance health-care directive

Everyone Should Have a Will

It happens. A 36-year-old father of two loses control of his car along a rural road and crashes through a fence into a tree, killing himself and his wife.

Because the couple was young and hadn't thought about getting a will, several things kick into play—none of them good. First, the state chooses guardians for their kids, meaning the children could be uprooted and sent off to another state to live with their grandparents instead of moving down the street to their aunt's house, which would have been the parents' wish.

Next, the distribution of any assets the couple had accumulated is in question because they had left no instruction regarding who should get them. That includes their house, cars, bank accounts, investments, and any other property they may have had.

According to the online legal technology company Rocket Lawyer, 64 percent of Americans do not have a will. Very few people in their 20s and 30s have wills, which is understandable … but not smart. If you die without a will, or *intestate,* there's no guarantee who will inherit your assets. Even if you don't have a lot, wouldn't you rather determine who gets it than have the state decide?

DEFINITION

Dying **intestate** means dying without having prepared and executed a will to determine who receives your assets.

Having a will is particularly important if you have kids. There should be no excuses if you fall into that category. If you're married and die without a will, your assets generally go to your spouse. If you're single and childless, it's likely the state will decide which relatives get your assets.

So why is it that more than half of all American adults don't have a will? Rocket Lawyer surveyed people about why they didn't have one. Here are their responses:

- 57 percent said they simply hadn't gotten around to doing it.

- 22 percent felt there was no need to hurry to make a will.

- 17 percent didn't see any need to have a will.

- 14 percent didn't make a will because they didn't want to think about dying.

The Advantages to Having a Will

In addition to directing who gets your stuff and appointing a guardian for your children, a will serves a number of other purposes. You can ...

- Name an *executor.*

- Name a property manager for property left to your children. If you leave property to minor children, an adult needs to manage it. A will gives you a vehicle for appointing someone you trust to manage your property until your children are of age.

- Transfer real property, such as your home, to another person.

- Appoint someone to take care of your pet.

- State your wishes concerning burial, cremation, and the type of sendoff you want. This can be extremely helpful to your loved ones.

- Designate money or property to be given to a charity or cause that's particularly important to you.

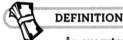

DEFINITION

An **executor,** or a personal representative, is someone who oversees the distribution of your property and ensures the terms of your will are followed after you die. If you don't have an executor, the court will appoint someone to do the job.

Creating Your Will

You can have a lawyer make a will for you, or you can make it yourself. You'll need to sign it after you write it and have two witnesses sign as well. If you want to have a lawyer do your will and you don't have a lawyer, you can contact your local bar association and ask for the name of someone who can help you.

You also can download software, sometimes for free, to create your own will. LegalZoom offers a last will and testament online, and Quicken's WillMaker software walks you through the process of making a will—much like a tax software program. You fill out a form, which is reviewed for completeness and consistency. Some companies offer a guarantee that your will is legally acceptable but may charge extra for that service.

If you do your own will, it's advisable to have it reviewed by an attorney. And if you use a software program, be sure it's legal in your state. The program should specify in which states it can be used.

Powers of Attorney

At this point of your life, having a *durable power of attorney* (and an advance health-care directive, discussed next) is arguably even more important than having a will. A durable power of attorney is a legal document in which you designate someone to handle your financial business for you in the event that you are unable to do so.

> **DEFINITION**
>
> A **durable power of attorney** enables you to designate another person to handle your financial transactions if you become incapacitated and are unable to do so.

If you're in a car accident and temporarily unable file your tax return, pay your mortgage, and take care of your bills, the person you appoint as your power of attorney can do those things for you. Also, if you would become permanently incapacitated—a terrible thing to think about, but it happens—having a power of attorney eases the way for loved ones. The person who you designate will handle your financial affairs should you become incapacitated, so it's important to assign someone who is capable and who you trust will follow your wishes and instructions.

Advance Health-Care Directive

If you know the name Terri Schiavo, you'll realize why it's important to have an *advance health-care directive.*

> **DEFINITION**
>
> An **advance health-care directive** is a legal document that spells out your wishes regarding health-care decisions and appoints someone to make health-care decisions on your behalf if you are unable to do so.

In 1990, the 26-year-old Florida woman fell into a vegetative state after suffering cardiac arrest. Her parents believed their daughter would recover and fought to keep her alive, while her husband argued that she would not have wanted to exist in her current state and wanted to disconnect his wife's feeding tube.

The long, public battle that ensued was heart-wrenching, and it lasted for 15 years while the courts, the Florida state legislature, and then-Florida Governor Jeb Bush all weighed in. Schiavo's feeding tube eventually was removed, and she died in 2005 at the age of 41.

Having an advance health-care directive can spare your family years of anguish.

There are two parts to an advance health-care directive:

- Living will
- Health-care proxy

Living Will

A living will enables you to state your wishes regarding end-of-life medical care. It kicks in when you unable to communicate your wishes.

In a living will, you stipulate whether or not you want medical professionals to take actions such as resuscitating you if your heart stops beating, if you want mechanical breathing if you're unable to breathe on your own, a feeding tube if you're unable to eat on your own, or ongoing dialysis if your kidneys cease functioning.

It's hard to think about end-of-life care at this stage of your life, and hopefully you'll never need a living will. But accidents happen, embolisms occur, and fatal infections can take over. Having your wishes in place can make a situation like this much easier for family members and friends as they struggle to make seemingly impossible decisions.

You also can include in a living will your wishes to have your organs donated after your death, if applicable.

Health-Care Proxy

Appointing a health-care proxy is not something to do without giving the matter a significant amount of consideration.

A health-care proxy, also referred to as a health-care surrogate or durable medical power of attorney, is a legal document in which you designate someone to handle decisions concerning your medical treatment and care. The person you appoint then has the authority to make medical decisions if you are unable to do so, such as if you were in a coma or had suffered a head injury that made it impossible for you to express your preferences regarding your medical treatment.

You can see how important it is to appoint a representative who fully understands your wishes regarding treatment and whom you trust to fully uphold those wishes. Making medical decisions for a loved one can be an extremely difficult and emotionally wrenching job. Ideally, you'll appoint someone who is comfortable interacting with health-care providers in a medical setting.

Generally, you'll appoint just one person as your health-care proxy. You might, however, consider appointing one or more alternates in case your primary representative is not available for some reason.

> **DOLLARS AND SENSE**
>
> Regulations regarding legal documents such as wills, powers of attorney, and health-care directives vary from state to state. It's best to check with a lawyer when dealing with all important legal documents to ensure they're done correctly and in adherence to your state's laws.

The Least You Need to Know

- It might be difficult to think about, but executing a will puts you in charge of who inherits your assets and other major decisions.
- A power of attorney is an important tool in the event that you are unable to handle financial decisions and transactions on your own.
- A living will enables you to state your wishes regarding your end-of-life health care.
- If you are unable to make your own decisions regarding your medical care, you can appoint a representative to do so for you via a health-care proxy.

Looking to Your Future

As you get a little further into adulthood, you'll need to start thinking about your future and how you're going to support yourself and possibly a family. And while you're doing that, you also need to be looking ahead and thinking about retirement.

Employer-sponsored 401(k) plans are a great way to get your retirement savings on track, especially if your employer matches some of your contributions. If you don't have a 401(k) where you work, you should look at investing money into an individual retirement account (IRA).

Part 8 helps you understand how these plans work. You also learn when it's smart to seek the advice of a financial professional and what kind of help is available.

CHAPTER 21

401(k)s and IRAs

At your age, retirement probably seems like a concept for consideration in the distant future—certainly not today. However, although you are decades away from retirement, it's a topic that should be at the forefront of your financial planning. Most financial experts agree you need to have *more than $1 million* saved to ensure a comfortable retirement.

The average yearly expenses for a person between the ages of 65 and 74 were around $46,000 a year in 2013, according to the Bureau of Labor Statistics. Those costs will no doubt be significantly higher in 30 or 40 years when you are ready to retire. And it may be that you're not starting to save as early as you would have been able to do otherwise because of high amounts of student loans and other debt that needs to be repaid.

In This Chapter

- Planning for your retirement, now
- Why it's better to start saving early
- The importance of funding your 401(k)
- Building retirement savings in IRAs

Fortunately, systems are in place that enable you to start saving for your retirement early, and they don't require you to contribute huge amounts of money—although you certainly should save as much possible. As with any savings, even a little bit of money is better than nothing.

In this chapter, we look at two popular retirement savings vehicles, 401(k)s and individual retirement accounts (IRAs), both of which offer tax advantages when left in place until you reach the age when you're eligible to withdraw funds.

Why Every Year Counts

It used to be that most people who worked had pensions provided by their employers. Between their pension checks and Social Security payments, retirees had enough money to live comfortably.

Times have changed though, and pensions are a thing of the past for the most part. In addition, the Social Security system may be targeted for restructuring, and there are questions about the certainty of its future. With the average length of retirement at 18 years according to the U.S. Census Bureau, anyone who wants to ensure a comfortable future should be saving now.

Studies show most people will require about three fourths as much money to maintain their standard of living during retirement as they required before retiring. Of course, all kinds of factors go into that estimate, which is, remember, an average, and with the increase in prescription drug costs and Medicare supplement insurance premiums increasing at a rate much greater than inflation, this number may increase in the years ahead. At this point, there is no way to know what your retirement years will bring. You can't predict what your health will be like in 40 years or what other circumstances will be affecting your life.

Remember these two important facts about saving for retirement:

- The earlier you start, the easier it is to accumulate the money you'll need.
- Little savings can add up over the years to make big savings.

If you find it hard to believe that a couple years makes a big difference in what you'll be able to save, let's look at an example: if you invest $5,000 when you're 25 at an annual rate of return of 6 percent and let it sit until you're 60, you'll have $38,430. But if you wait until you're 35 to invest $5,000 at the same rate of return, you'll have only $21,459 when you turn 60. If you wait until you're 45 to invest the money, you'll have only $11,983.

It makes more sense, and in the long run is much easier on your wallet, to start saving money as early as possible. Retirement seems eons away when you first start working, but the years pass by quickly, and you'll have other financial commitments along the way.

401(k) Plans

Although they've only been around since the 1980s, *401(k) plans*—or *403(b) plans*, if your employer is a nonprofit organization—have become one of the most widely used and popular vehicles for retirement savings. 401(k)s offer tax advantages because your savings aren't taxed until you withdraw them. As of 2016, you can contribute up to $18,000 a year into a 401(k) account, and your employer can match some or all of your savings.

> **DEFINITION**
>
> A **401(k) plan** is one of the most popular and widely used types of retirement savings plans. It enables employees to contribute a portion of their paychecks to a company-sponsored investment plan. A **403(b) plan** is similar to a 401(k), except it's offered only by hospitals, schools, and nonprofit employers. Assets from 403(b) plans normally are held with an insurance company, often in an annuity format.

Participation in 401(k)s

The Great Recession affected nearly everything financial, including 401(k) plans. Participation in 401(k)s dropped off during the recession, when jobs were hard to get and any type of investment seemed uncertain. Many employers who had been matching their employees' 401(k) contributions stopped that practice as well.

A turnaround got underway in 2014, however, according to a 2015 Bank of America Merrill Lynch analysis of 2.5 million people participating in retirement plans the company administers. The data showed that 64 percent more employees between the ages of 18 and 34 began contributing to 401(k)s in 2014 compared to the same age group the previous year. Matching contributions by employers was on the upswing, too. With that increase in participation, overall participation in 401(k)s among American workers with access to plans stands at nearly 80 percent.

The increase is attributed to a more robust job market and belief that the economy is stronger. Younger workers also have responded favorably to automatic enrollment plans with automatic contribution increase features. That's good news. Younger employees have the most opportunity to benefit from participation in retirement plans because they have more time for their investments to grow before they need them.

To encourage participation among employees, the Pension Protection Act of 2006 made it possible for employers to automatically enroll new employees in their 401(k) plans. Your company can attempt to enroll you as often as once a year, requiring you to opt out if you don't want to invest.

Companies that offer the automatic opt-in choose a default investment fund and savings rate. Unless you opt out, you will have a set percentage of your pay invested. However, you are free to change funds and rates of deferrals. Your company can automatically increase the amount of your default contribution every year to encourage more savings, which is good because it increases your investment.

 MONEY PIT

If your company has an automatic 401(k) enrollment plan, be sure you find out what the default contribution is. Some automatic plans default your contribution at 3 percent even though you could contribute much more. If your employer is matching your contribution, you could be missing out on free money by not maximizing your contribution.

Taking Advantage of an Employer Match

In addition to providing flexibility, 401(k)s sometimes also offer a great savings incentive by way of an employer match. The amount of the match varies greatly from company to company. If you're really lucky, your employer will match your contribution dollar for dollar up to a certain percentage of your paycheck. The most typical match is for every dollar an employee contributes up to 6 percent, the employer throws in 50 percent. By taking advantage of the match, you get an automatic 50 percent return on your money.

Companies trying to attract new hires in competitive marketplaces may offer matches or partial matches to contributions up to 10 percent or even higher. Not taking advantage of those opportunities while they're available can have a real negative effect on your retirement.

Some firms, but fewer than ever, match an employee's contributions with company stock. Company stock can be a good thing, but it isn't *always* a good thing.

If you're with a company that's matching your 401(k) contributions with company stock, be sure to keep a close eye on the value of your account.

POCKET CHANGE

Even with the employer-match incentive, it's estimated that 1 in every 4 employees does not contribute the maximum amount to get the full benefit of the employer's match.

Investing in Your 401(k)

What happens to your money after it goes into the 401(k)? You get to decide where it should be invested by choosing from a list of investment options provided through your employer plan. If your employer has the 401(k) account in various mutual funds or a family of funds (which provide a variety of fund choices within the same company), you could divide your money between stocks and bonds with perhaps some fixed-interest rate investments or money market funds thrown in for good measure.

Understandably, selecting investments can be a daunting proposition for someone who knows next to nothing about investments. But experts say the process of choosing these options has served as a crash course for a lot of young people who otherwise would know nothing about investing money. They say selecting investments is not that complicated if you keep it simple.

Employers are prohibited by the Department of Labor from offering investment advice regarding their employees' 401(k)s and can be held liable if they do. Financial advisers, however, have come up with some guidelines to direct employees in investing their 401(k) plans. Your employers' 401(k) should have a financial adviser you can talk with about your allocation.

Most advisers suggest investors in their 20s and 30s put at least 60 percent of their money in a large U.S. company stock fund such as the T. Rowe Price Capital Appreciation Fund. The rest, they say, could be divided among international stocks, small company stocks, and bonds. Your company should provide meetings about the various investment choices and how they pertain to you. If it doesn't, ask to have the service provided because it's required by law. You must understand your choices; your future depends on it.

Keep in mind that your 401(k) money is a long-term investment, and you shouldn't plan to use it until your retirement. This makes it conducive to equities—what most people consider the stock market—where you have to accept that your money is in for the long haul and be willing to ride out the market's ups and downs.

DOLLARS AND SENSE

For whatever reason, some workers feel resentful when money is taken out of their paychecks for their 401(k). If you are, think about this: if, between the ages of 25 and 35, you contribute $5,000 a year to your 401(k) and average an 8 percent yearly return on your money, when you reach age 65, you'll be really happy you saved that money because you'll have accumulated nearly $900,000 from just 10 years of savings.

When to Adjust Your Contributions

It's likely that when you first start contributing to a 401(k) it will be at a minimal level. And that's okay because some contribution is always better than none. Just remember that you always should contribute enough to get a company match, as discussed earlier.

It is imperative, however, to increase your contribution level as you get raises. Remember, you can contribute up to $18,000 a year, so be sure to increase your contribution as much as you're able to as your salary increases. It's easy to save what you never see, and the salary increases are new money to you, so put some or all of it away for your retirement instead of making bigger contributions to Uncle Sam. If you keep increasing your contribution level by 1 or 2 percent a year, over time, you'll have a lot more money put aside for your retirement than you ever imagined possible, without much pain at all.

Another easy way to build up your 401(k) is to contribute all or part of a bonus into it—your account gets a nice contribution, even when your paycheck doesn't change. This is a great way to supplement your annual contribution level.

> **MONEY PIT**
>
> It doesn't happen often, but it's possible to overinvest in a 401(k) plan and exceed the limit of $18,000 a year. This most often occurs when an employee changes jobs and doesn't inform his or her new employer of contributions already made. If this happens, you could face IRS penalties and double taxation on your contributions.

The idea of contributing 5, 10, or 15 percent of your salary is daunting, but gradually increasing your contribution levels makes your account balance grow a step at a time.

Tax Advantages of 401(k) Plans

Historically, a great advantage of 401(k) plans is that the money you put into them is both pretax money and tax-deferred money. That means you win twice. Your 401(k) contributions are taken out of your salary before your salary is taxed for federal income taxes. The contributions are still subject to Social Security taxes, and some states subject the contributions to state and local income taxes. Still, not having to pay federal income tax on the money you contribute is a great benefit.

The money you contribute also is tax-deferred, which means you don't pay any tax on it, or the money it earns for you, until you withdraw it, either prematurely or during retirement. An individual in the 25 percent tax bracket pays 25¢ less tax on every $1 invested in a 401(k). Here's another way of looking at it: if you're in the 25 percent tax bracket and invest $100 per month in your 401(k), your federal tax liability is $300 less per year than if you didn't invest in the 401(k).

Employers now are able to offer Roth 401(k)s. The money you invest in a Roth 401(k) is post-tax, with only the employer contributions and the earnings tax-deferred. This can be a good investment for people in their 20s and 30s who generally fall into lower tax brackets. By investing in a Roth 401(k), your contributions go in post-tax, but when it's held for at least 5 years and not touched until you reach age 59½, the earnings can be withdrawn tax free.

If you believe you could end up being in a higher tax bracket after retirement, paying taxes on the contribution now and withdrawing in a higher bracket later leads to a net savings on the amount in the Roth 401(k).

 DOLLARS AND SENSE

> A Roth 401(k) is a great way for an individual whose income is too high for a Roth IRA to invest in a Roth.

Managing Your 401(k) When Changing Jobs

It's likely you'll have numerous employers during your years of working. And every time you change employers, you'll need to address your 401(k) plan.

Basically, you have four options when changing jobs:

- Roll over the account to your new company's plan.

- Leave the account where it is.

- Cash out the account.

- Roll over the account to an IRA.

If you transfer your 401(k) account to the plan your new company offers, your savings are held in the same place and can continue to grow. There are no tax implications or early withdrawal penalties, and the money keeps growing for your future. Just be sure your new employer's plan allows for a rollover; some do not.

You also can leave your 401(k) plan in place with your old employer, if that's permitted, and if it's *cash neutral,* which means there would not be a transaction that would require net cash. Some plans allow you to maintain the account without changes indefinitely, while others require that you transfer your assets within a particular time period. There probably will be a cost to you when you transfer.

DEFINITION

Cash neutral is a strategy that does not require net cash for a transaction but instead relies on simultaneous buying and selling.

Cashing out your 401(k) account generally is not a good idea, as the whole point of it is to preserve funds for your retirement. If you're under the age of 59½, you'll probably get slammed with a 10 percent early withdrawal penalty, plus you'll have to pay taxes on the distribution. Unless there's a compelling reason to liquidate the account, it's always better to keep the money in a retirement account.

Another option is to roll over your money into a traditional individual retirement account (IRA). (You read about IRAs later in this chapter.) Once your money is safely within an IRA, you can choose different investment options with the account or convert the account to a Roth IRA.

Be sure to consider all these options carefully and think about which makes the most sense for you. The whole point is to enable your money to grow so it's available when you need it.

Understanding Vesting

Vesting is the length of time you're required to work for a company before you're entitled to the funds your employer has put into your retirement account on your behalf. There are two types of vesting:

- Cliff vesting
- Graduated vesting

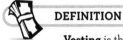

DEFINITION

Vesting is the length of time required for an employee to work for a company before he or she is entitled to all the employer's contributions to the plan.

Cliff vesting (usually 5 years) means you must work for your employer for 5 years before you're entitled to the matching funds placed in your 401(k). If you change jobs after only 2 years and your company has 5-year cliff vesting, you'll only have your own contributions available to move elsewhere. This portability is what makes 401(k)s so popular. If you leave this employer after 5 years, you receive the employer's match as well as your own contributions.

DOLLARS AND SENSE

When you're thinking of changing jobs, consider whether to change immediately or to wait a bit until you're vested. Always know how much of your retirement plan is employer matched and how much you have to lose if you leave.

With graduated vesting, you're partially vested after 2 years, but you must stay with your employer for 6 years before you're 100 percent vested. The following table outlines the schedule.

Years Employed	Percent Vested
After 2	20
After 3	40
After 4	60
After 5	80
After 6	100

When you change jobs, whether you're vested or not, you have your contribution to your 401(k). You can withdraw these funds (but don't forget income tax liability and penalty), roll them over into an IRA, or even possibly roll them over into your new employer's 401(k) plan.

If your new employer has a 401(k) plan, see if you can transfer directly from your former employer's 401(k) plan to your current employer. If you can't, roll the funds into a separate IRA and then roll them into your new 401(k) later, if permitted.

Getting Money Early from Your 401(k)

Unfortunately, sometimes it's absolutely necessary to get money from your 401(k) account before you are of the eligible age of 59½. In certain situations, you may withdraw from your 401(k) for hardship, but you must demonstrate real need to your employer to be able to do so. In some cases, your employer will let you borrow against your 401(k) plan and deduct the repayment from your paycheck. The money you repay goes right back into your account, and you pay yourself, not a bank, with the principal and interest.

If you withdraw your 401(k) money before the eligible age, expect some stiff financial consequences. You'll pay a 10 percent penalty, and the money is taxable, which can be a significant blow at tax time. The IRS directs that people who withdraw funds from their 401(k) plans have 20 percent withheld from the money to be used for tax payment. The problem is, that amount usually isn't enough money to pay for both the penalty and the taxes owed on the withdrawal.

For example, if you withdrew $5,000 from your 401(k) plan and had the standard 20 percent withheld ($1,000), you would receive $4,000. But if you were a taxpayer in the 24 percent bracket, you'd owe $1,200 in taxes, plus $500 for the penalty, for a total of $1,700. The 20 percent taken out wouldn't cover those costs, and you'd be $700 short on April 15. Not a nice surprise!

Still, the 401(k) is your money, and you can get it if you have a real need—and if you're willing to pay the penalties.

Individual Retirement Accounts (IRAs)

As of the beginning of 2016, anybody who earns any money working can contribute up to $5,500 a year in an *individual retirement account* (IRA).

> **DEFINITION**
>
> An **individual retirement account** is a retirement savings plan into which you can contribute up to $5,500 per year (as of 2016). Funds can grow tax-deferred until they're withdrawn at retirement.

An IRA is a tax-deferred type of retirement savings plan, meaning you don't pay taxes until you withdraw money from the fund. Of course, this money can only be contributed if you work. If you make $5,500 a year mowing lawns and shoveling snow but never report a penny of it, those earnings don't make you eligible to contribute to an IRA. (They could, however, get you in trouble with the IRS!)

IRAs used to be the hotshot investment vehicles. Things changed, though, when lawmakers dumped all kinds of restrictions on them in 1986. Back in the good old days, anybody could deduct his or her IRA contributions. Now the money you contribute might be tax-deductible, but it might not be.

Contributing to an IRA

Currently, if you earn less than $5,500 a year, the maximum amount you can contribute is the amount you've earned. If you earn $1,650 scooping ice cream at Ben & Jerry's, for example, that's the amount you can stash in an IRA. If you have no income but do receive alimony, you're eligible to contribute to an IRA. And as of 2016, if you're married but not working, your spouse can contribute up to $5,500 a year for you, or $11,000 total for the family.

Let's look at how it breaks down. If you're single and do not have an employer-sponsored retirement plan, you can put up to $5,500 a year in an IRA. The full contribution is a dollar-for-dollar deduction from your taxable income on your income tax return.

The incremental increases as of 2016 and beyond are as follows:

- Under age 50: $5,500

- Over age 50: $6,500

After 2016, the limit may increase in increments of $500 annually to keep pace with inflation.

If you're single, covered by an employer-sponsored plan, and your annual adjusted gross income is $61,000 or less in 2016, you can contribute up to $5,500 to your IRA and deduct the full amount. If your income is between $61,001 ($98,001 for joint filers) and $70,999 ($117,999 for joint filers), the deduction is prorated. If you make more than $71,000 a year, you can contribute, but you get no deduction.

If you're married and file jointly, have an employer-sponsored plan, and your annual adjusted gross income is $98,000 or less, you can deduct the full amount. The figure is prorated from $98,000 to $118,000. After $118,000, you can't take any deduction.

For workers over age 50, there's a "catch-up" provision for those contributing to an IRA. In 2016, workers who are over age 50 can contribute an extra $1,000 (for a total of $6,500) to an IRA.

If your spouse doesn't have a retirement plan at work and you file a joint tax return, your spouse can deduct his or her full $5,500 contribution until your joint income reaches $184,000. After that, the deduction is prorated until your joint income is $194,000, at which time you can't deduct the IRA contribution.

Even if you can't deduct the contributions, they still help out with taxes because the income earned within the IRA is *tax-deferred*. It's not as great as *tax-deductible*, but it's the next best thing. IRAs are good savings vehicles, but if your IRA contributions aren't deductible, be sure you take advantage of the programs on which you can get a tax deduction, such as 401(k)s, first.

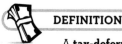

DEFINITION

A **tax-deferred** investment is one on which you'll pay no tax on income or gain until you withdraw the money. A **tax-deductible** investment is one that reduces the amount of your current taxable income.

Roth IRAs

The *Roth IRA,* a variation on the basic IRA, has been popular since it was introduced in 1998. The Roth IRA is different from the traditional one in several ways, and many financial experts agree it is better than the traditional IRA for people with the right circumstances, especially for those in their 20s and 30s.

DEFINITION

A **Roth IRA** is an IRA in which the funds placed into the account are nondeductible. If held more than 5 years, the original funds withdrawn are received tax-free, but the earnings are subject to a penalty if withdrawn before age 59½.

Your contribution to a Roth IRA is made with after-tax money, as opposed to pretax money you invest in a traditional IRA. This means you don't have to pay tax on the income and appreciation on a Roth IRA. If you have at least 20 years in which to let the funds grow, a Roth IRA probably is the best choice.

When you contribute to a regular, deductible IRA, you put in an amount, let's say $5,500, before you pay tax on that money. When you take your contributions and your earnings out at retirement, you have to pay taxes on that money. With a Roth IRA, your $5,500 contribution comes out of income you've already paid taxes on (that is, earnings), and the contributed funds grow tax-free. If the funds are held for at least 5 years and you're at least 59½ when you claim them, you never pay tax on the money withdrawn.

Yep, that's right. If you follow the rules and hold the funds within the Roth for 5 years, you never have to pay tax on the account again. That means you get all the earnings on that $5,500 completely tax-free, which is a very appealing feature of the Roth. Contributions to a Roth IRA, however, are not tax-deductible.

You can get your Roth money without penalty any time after you reach 59½ years of age, but you're not required to take it out when you reach 70½, as you are with traditional IRAs. You can just let that money sit there if you want to, continuing to grow, tax-free. You can even leave the money and *all* the earnings there to pass on, tax-free, to your heirs.

There are income limits to Roths, though. If your income is more than $132,000 and you're single, you can't get a Roth IRA. If you and your spouse have a combined income of more than $193,000, you're not eligible for a Roth IRA.

DOLLARS AND SENSE

If you have a traditional IRA, you might want to consider switching it to a Roth. You can do this if your income (single) is under $133,000. You'll be taxed on the money you're converting, but advisers say you're still better off to move it, especially if you're under 50 years old. If you don't understand the implications, check with a financial adviser.

SEP-IRAs

If you are self-employed, you should consider a *SEP-IRA*, or a Simplified Employee Pension IRA. SEP-IRAs are not very complicated and are a great deal for a person who is self-employed or owns a business with only a few employees.

> **DEFINITION**
>
> A **SEP-IRA,** or a Simplified Employee Pension IRA, is a retirement plan for self-employed persons or small company employers in which contributions of up to $53,000 a year or 25 percent of income, whichever is higher, are permitted.

SEP-IRAs allow people who are self-employed or are owners of small companies to add more funds to a retirement account than they can with a traditional IRA. As with other types of IRAs, the interest you make in a SEP-IRA is not taxed until you take out the money.

If you work for yourself, you can contribute up to about 13.04 percent of your income, or up to $53,000, into a SEP-IRA every year. The money you contribute is deducted from your taxable income, so your contribution can save you a lot on federal and maybe also state taxes, depending on where you live. You can open and contribute to a SEP-IRA up until the day of your tax-filing deadline.

SEP-IRAs are advantageous for people who need to save on their own. They might sound intimidating, but you can have a SEP-IRA anywhere you could have a regular IRA. It just requires a little additional paperwork. Ask your tax preparer or financial consultant about changing your IRA to a SEP-IRA.

The disadvantage of a SEP-IRA for a small business owner is that you are required to contribute the same percentage of income you contribute for yourself for each of your employees, which can be a daunting proposition.

Timing Your IRA Contributions

Most people start thinking about funding their IRAs when they meet with their accountants in April. Funding an IRA at that time of year is better than never, but you should know that the earlier you stash some money in your IRA, the better.

If you fund an IRA in January or February, the funds begin to work, tax-deferred, with gains starting immediately and accumulating for the entire year. You get 12, maybe 15 months of deferral by funding your IRA in January, rather than waiting until it's time to file your tax return in April.

If it's not financially feasible to fund your IRA all at once, you might consider contributing some money each month, beginning in January. To fund your IRA to the allowable limit, you'd make monthly payments of $458. If you break it down ever further, you'd pay $105.76 a week. Smaller, more frequent payments often are easier than making a large payment all at once.

POCKET CHANGE

Another type of IRA, an *educational IRA*, is set up to fund education expenses.

The Least You Need to Know

- It's important to start saving for retirement early because it gives your money more time to grow.
- Contributing funds to an employer-sponsored 401(k) plan is a convenient and popular means of building up a retirement fund.
- If your employer matches your contributions up to a certain percentage, it's important that you try to contribute at least as much as the employer matches.
- When shopping for an IRA, compare information about different types of plans available before choosing the one for you.
- Consider spreading out contributions to your IRA over the year to avoid having to come up with one large lump sum.

CHAPTER 222

Working with Professional Financial Advisers

If you know nothing about your personal finances, probably the worst thing you can do is go out and hire a financial adviser, assuming she'll take care of everything and you'll never have to think about your finances again. On the surface, it sounds like a good idea: let somebody else worry about it, right?

The problem with hiring a financial adviser when you have no knowledge of your own finances is that you're placing a lot of trust, and some of your most valuable assets, in the hands of a person you may know nothing about—or even someone who you *do* think you know something about. You've heard about the Bernie Madoff story, right? Or the adviser whose kids swam on the same team as her clients' kids while she was ripping off their parents for a big part of their savings?

In This Chapter

- Finding someone to help you with your investments
- What to ask before hiring a financial adviser
- Knowing who to stay away from
- Monitoring your financial adviser's actions

It also could be that the financial "expert" you hire is not an expert at all. Basically, just about anybody can claim to be a financial adviser. Finances, investments, taxation, and the like are all very complicated topics that take years of education to acquire the knowledge to do the job well. Not everyone can be an expert, and it's imperative that you find someone who has the knowledge you're looking for.

Millennials, many of whom endured the Great Recession and are fighting their way out of student debt, are not lining up at traditional financial advising firms the way members of previous generations did. Your generation likes to do things differently, and many are skeptical of capital markets and financial advisers. So while not denying that they need financial advice, many young adults are looking for it in some nonconventional ways … and some financial services providers are getting on board.

Know Thy Finances, Know Thy Adviser

All this gloom-and-doom financial adviser talk isn't meant to scare you off from hiring someone to help you with your finances if you've gotten to the point where you need it. Nearly everybody can use some help sometimes. The point is, the more you know about your personal finances, the easier it will be for you to find a qualified, trustworthy *financial adviser.*

DEFINITION

A **financial adviser** is a broad term for a professional you hire to help you make decisions about your finances.

When you understand your finances, you'll be able to ask intelligent questions of your potential advisers and understand their answers. You'll know what they're talking about when they throw out phrases like *full-service broker* or *fee-only adviser.* You won't feel stupid asking questions about your own money because generally, you'll know exactly what you're talking about. Armed with prior knowledge, you'll work together with the adviser to put your money to the best possible use.

A financial adviser is called an *adviser* because it's her job to *advise* you on the best uses of your money. Ultimately, however, it's your money, and you're in charge of what happens to it.

Do I Need a Financial Adviser?

You might need a financial adviser for many reasons. Maybe you're faced with a complicated financial situation regarding the sale or purchase of a property, or perhaps you want some advice about which stocks and bonds to buy. Maybe you're setting up a college fund or getting really serious about your retirement fund. Or it could be that you earned a big bonus you'd like to maximize in some sort of investment.

The reason for, and point at which, you seek help with your finances is entirely up to you. Whether you're leaving a job and deciding what to do with the $5,800 you have in your 401(k), or you've inherited $200,000 from your grandmother, you might feel that you need some financial advice from time to time.

MONEY PIT

Some unethical financial advisers try to take advantage of emotionally distraught people. If you're going through an upsetting time and need financial advice, be careful. Seek all the advice you need, but try to avoid making any major decisions until you've had a chance to think clearly about them. And consider taking someone who is more clear-headed with you when you talk to your adviser. He or she can then remind you of what was discussed if you need it.

Understanding Fiduciary Responsibility

Financial advisers are divided into two groups: those who have a fiduciary obligation to put you first (this includes most Registered Investment Advisers) and those who work for a brokerage firm and cannot be a fiduciary (this includes stockbrokers and sometimes insurance agents). The fiduciary relationship is a legal relationship between two or more persons in which the adviser …

- Provides the highest ethical advice.

- Acts at all times with a higher standard of care and legal manner for your sole benefit and interests.

- Advises you exactly what the charges will be and how they will be paid. This is known as *full disclosure*, which is different from just handing you a contract. With full disclosure, you know exactly what you are paying for the advice.

Fiduciary advisers, who unfortunately represent only 1 in 12 investment advisers, have a duty to avoid any situation in which their personal interests and fiduciary duty to their clients conflict and a duty not to profit from their fiduciary position without disclosure of the fees charged.

The Who's Who of Financial Advisers

When discussing some of the different kinds of financial advisers, the issue can become a little bit complicated. A financial adviser by any other name may, or may not, be a financial adviser.

We explain some of the common classes of financial advisers in the following sections. Just remember that the type of adviser you need depends on your circumstances, and you should never hire someone just because she has a title you think sounds impressive.

DOLLARS AND SENSE

Many millennials say they prefer a financial adviser who is more like a coach or collaborator than someone who simply dispenses traditional advice. This generation tends to have different financial goals than their parents did, and they look for someone who understands their attitudes and priorities.

Financial Planners

The term *financial planner* often is used to describe anyone who offers financial advice or services. It also frequently is used interchangeably with *financial adviser.*

Financial planners, as the name implies, are people who design financial plans of action. They may design and carry out the plan, or their clients may choose to execute the plans they design.

Financial planner is a very broad categorization, so if you're looking to hire one, be sure you know what credentials or other titles may come along with it. For starters, financial planners can be certified—or not.

Certified Financial Planners

A very large group of people in this country are called *certified financial planners.* They've all earned the Certified Financial Planning (CFP) credential, a national certification that requires certificants to have a fiduciary relationship with their advisees.

Earning the CFP credential involves working through a home-study program and passing a cumulative, 6-hour test. Designees must have 3 years of financial work experience and promise to adhere to a code of ethics. Work experience should include financial planning, investments, or banking. CFPs are also required to take 30 hours of continuing education courses every 2 years to stay current on industry happenings.

Financial Consultants

Another type of financial planner is the *financial consultant.* The financial consultant provides an overview of financial information and options so you can choose the products that make the most sense for you.

Financial consultants generally won't produce a plan for your finances, only information and advice. The assumption is that the consultant is fee-only. (She won't receive a commission on any products sold.) Be sure to ask your consultant how she will be paid.

DOLLARS AND SENSE

There's a wide range of training and expertise among financial advisers. You can be sure a certified financial planner is trained and qualified, but some designations only require several short classes for certification. Be sure to ask about a potential adviser's background, training, and experience before you agree to work with them.

Bank Customer Service Representatives

A bank *customer service representative* (CSR) is another type of financial planner, usually trained by the bank where she's employed. The CSR's job is to bring deposits into the bank, either as CDs, money market funds, trust accounts, or other types of accounts.

The CSR also is expected to direct clients' money to a subsidiary company that sells mutual funds or annuities—one in which the bank receives either a commission or a percentage of the management fee. Because you will be guided to purchase a load fund—that is, one that charges a sales commission—you do indirectly pay a fee to these consultants. Always ask how much a CSR is paid per investment.

Certified Public Accountants/Personal Financial Specialists

More and more *certified public accountants* (CPAs) are becoming financial consultants. The American Institute of Certified Public Accountants now has a special designation, called a *personal financial specialist* (PFS), for CPAs who have 3 years of financial planning experience and pass a 6-hour test. Unless you purchase a product, CPAs usually are paid on an hourly basis.

Many people depend on their CPA for financial help, regardless of whether or not the CPA is designated a PFS.

Insurance Agents

You might not normally think of an *insurance agent* as a financial planner, but some agents specialize in financial planning. They usually have either a CLU (Chartered Life Underwriter) or ChFC (Charter Financial Consultant) designation, or both. These are designations by the American College in Bryn Mawr, Pennsylvania, given to persons who complete and pass an eight-course program. Often, the program of study can be designed in the agent's area of expertise.

CLUs and ChFCs need continuing education. The designations, although not mandatory to do financial planning, show a level of expertise and experience.

Money Managers

Finally, a *money manager* is a financial adviser who, after reviewing your parameters, risk tolerance, and total financial picture, agrees to handle your funds, makes trades on your behalf, and buys and sells stocks and bonds for you. A money manager normally is employed by investors who have a substantial amount of money.

Money managers typically receive a percentage of the market value of their client's account as compensation (approximately 1 percent of the value of the assets on an annual basis). As an example, a money manager who has $200,000 under management and charges an annual fee of 1 percent would earn $2,000 per year from your account. She probably would charge the fee quarterly, which is $500 per quarter or $166.67 per month.

POCKET CHANGE

A new trend in how financial advisers are paid, especially among advisers who cater to millennials, is a monthly fee. An adviser will charge a fee each month to make and manage a financial plan, with the thought that young people are used to making monthly payments for services such as cable or gym fees.

Most money managers have a CFA (Certified Financial Analyst) designation. Look for this designation when you're thinking about hiring a money manager.

Finding a Reputable Financial Adviser

If you're like most millennials, you are tuned in and constantly in touch. You know what your friends are doing, what celebrities are doing, what's hot, and what's not. You share information and are transparent in your likes and dislikes. This connectedness can be extremely helpful when looking for help, whether you need a doctor, hair stylist, lawyer, plumber, or financial adviser.

It's easy to find information on services, fees, expertise, skill, reliability, and other traits. Websites can help you find a financial adviser, and it's always a good idea to seek advice from colleagues, friends, and family members who have worked with advisers. If you have a lawyer, he may be able to recommend a good financial planner as well.

You should be aware that an increasing number of financial advisers are not accepting clients who do not have significant wealth. Some will only agree to work with you if you have a certain amount of money—sometimes $100,000 or more. Certainly other advisers cater to clients with less money, and some smart advisers are catering to younger adults with the intention of forging long-term relationships as their clients' wealth increases.

The Garrett Planning Network's website (garrettplanningnetwork.com) offers a map showing advisers who don't require their clients to have a ton of money. Online service LearnVest (learnvest.com) offers a one-time set-up fee and low monthly cost that gives you unlimited email access to a certified financial planner.

Meeting with Potential Advisers

It's important to find somebody who understands and shares your views and philosophies on investments and financial planning, so don't hire someone without first having a meeting to get to know that person. Remember, you should have some good financial information and understanding under your belt before the meeting because you've been doing your homework and reading about investments and other financial matters that may affect you.

When you're with your prospective adviser, you need to ask some questions. But let's get one thing very clear before we start: don't forget, even for a minute, that *you* are the person who will be hiring the financial adviser, and *you* will be paying her fees. It's not the other way around. Many people are intimidated by professionals because they feel stupid or uninformed around them. News flash! That's why you're meeting with the adviser in the first place. It's understood that she has more expertise in the finance area than you do, and hopefully you can benefit from her knowledge. That's the point, right? You don't need to impress the financial adviser; she needs to impress you.

Here are some questions you should ask the financial advisers you consider:

How long have you been in this business?   As with most professions, experience is important. You want to find someone who fully understands the financial industry and all its nuances and who has lived through the ups and downs of the market. You also should look for someone who understands you, your generation, and your financial goals.

How have you prepared for this job?   You'll want to know about your potential adviser's education and previous job experience.

What was your job before you became a financial adviser?   Look for a logical progression, such as moving into a financial adviser position from a banking job. If the progression doesn't seem logical, ask for an explanation.

Can you put me in touch with some other clients whose financial situations are similar to mine?   References are very important. If you talk to other clients and don't get all the information you're looking for, don't be afraid to ask the candidate for more names.

In addition to these questions, ask to see their Uniform Application for Investment Adviser Registration, or as it's more commonly known, their Form ADV, Part II A and B. This provides a financial planner's background and tells whether they or their firm have been in any trouble in the past with the law or with investment regulatory offices. If an adviser refuses to make this form available, it should set off warning bells.

POCKET CHANGE

Some financial advisers cater to particular groups of people, including millennials, claiming they can better serve their needs with specialized advice. American Express has trained some of its advisers to handle the particular financial needs of gays and lesbians. Several large financial firms offer specialized advice for women, college students, nonprofit groups, and so forth. Some planners also cater to ethnic groups, such as African Americans or Asians.

Finding an Adviser Online

Many brokers are online these days, with more and more showing up all the time. *Robo-advisers* also are becoming increasingly popular. These investment platforms provide automated online investment advice and use algorithms to determine asset allocations and automated rebalancing for investors.

DEFINITION

A **robo-adviser** is an online wealth management tool that offers automated portfolio management advice. Advice is algorithm-based and does not require a human financial planner.

With robo-advisers, each client's portfolio is structured to achieve optimal returns at every level of risk. A key investing approach robo platforms use is to invest in low-cost ETFs that minimize embedded investment costs. Because they utilize technology rather than active management by a human financial adviser, robo-advisers charge significantly lower fees than what most financial advisers typically charge.

Many young people like robo-advisers, partly due to the lower costs and also because of their affinity for and trust in technology. Plus, robo-advisers are available to investors who are just starting out with limited funds and tend to not be particularly attractive clients to financial firms.

If you're going to employ an online adviser, either the human variety or a robo-adviser, do your homework and compare both services offered and fees charged. Here are some things to look for:

- Quality trade executions

- Online newsletters and reports to keep you informed about what's happening in the financial world

- 24-hour telephone service

- Personal access to representatives in case you need face-to-face service

- Customized stock alerts to let you know when something is happening that might affect your account

Also, be sure to find out the various ways in which you can access your accounts. Is an interactive voice response phone system or online chat feature available? In addition, look for apps that enable you to access your accounts from your phone or tablet.

Here are some popular online brokers, all of which offer some robo services:

- TD Ameritrade (tdameritrade.com)

- Vanguard Online (vanguard.com)

- Charles Schwab (schwab.com)

- Fidelity Investments (fidelity.com)

Emerging robo-advisers include the following:

- Wealthfront (wealthfront.com)

- WiseBanyan (wisebanyan.com)

- Personal Capital (personalcapital.com)

Go with Your Gut

There's one more important factor to consider when you're choosing a financial adviser: your gut. Some people click, and others don't. Although you should never hire somebody just because you like him, you probably shouldn't hire somebody you just don't like either.

> **DOLLARS AND SENSE**
>
> Every financial adviser should be able to show you a code of ethics he or she adheres to. Don't be afraid to ask about it. If the adviser can't or won't show it to you, you probably should look elsewhere.

The investing goals of today's young adults vary from those of their parents, and it's important to find an adviser who understands your goals and knows what's important to you. If you love to travel and are adamant that you don't want to wait until you're retired to see the world, find an adviser who will help you achieve your travel goals while still ensuring your retirement account is healthy.

If you like somebody, and you feel confident she's a good and competent professional, you might have a match. You need someone who will take the time to talk with you, teach you, answer any and all of your questions, and be there for you. If you don't like someone, it probably will be very hard to work together effectively, even if she's considered the best financial adviser in the business.

Ultimately, the decision is up to you. Consider all the factors, throw in your gut feeling, and go for it.

Financial Adviser Red Flags

We don't need to tell you that if you see a "financial adviser" operating out of their car, it's not a good plan for you to get involved with him. But other, subtler things should set off warning bells, too:

- Exorbitant fees
- Conflict of interest concerning products and services
- Less-than-notable track records

Let's review each in more detail so you know what to look for—and avoid.

Too-High Fees

Chances are, you don't have a lot of spare cash sitting around you don't know what to do with. That's why you have to be sure up front what a financial adviser charges and what you get for that fee.

Find out whether the adviser is fee-only or if she gets a commission for the financial products she sells. If you can, stick with someone who doesn't sell on commission (more on that in the next section). Then, find out what her hourly fee is. Rates vary greatly, so shop around. You don't want to sign up with somebody and find out later that her rate is $500 an hour.

If the hourly fee seems too high (expect to pay between $150 and $300 an hour), call some other advisers in your area and compare rates. Remember that fee-only financial planners charge you every time you ask for advice or information. That's how they make their living. If you choose a fee-only adviser, be sure you're billed regularly. That will let you know exactly what you're paying for and help you decide whether the advice is worth the money.

If your financial adviser works on commission and receives a fee from the annuity company from which she gets the products she sells, you won't know how much she's earning on your investment unless you ask. Do ask. She must tell you the commission she received, if you inquire. If she doesn't, find another adviser. Even if you aren't actually paying the fee, you should know how much the adviser is making for the advice or help you receive.

The following table compares a standard brokerage fee schedule and an online brokerage.

Stock Commissions

	200 Shares	**300 Shares**	**500 Shares**	**1,000 Shares**
Full-service brokerage	$130	$165	$225	$308
Internet trading	($5 to $10 per trade)			

If it appeals to you, explore robo-adviser or other online brokerage options, where the fees are likely to be much lower. You might not get the personal touch you'd get with an in-person adviser, but going robo is great when you first start to invest.

DOLLARS AND SENSE

Always find out when you set up an initial appointment with a financial adviser whether the meeting is free. Many, but not all, advisers offer a free consultation for prospective clients.

Conflicts of Interest

If a financial adviser stands to make big money on commissions from selling certain types of financial products, watch out. You might be pressured to buy products that are more beneficial to your adviser than they are to you. An adviser who does this is more salesperson than financial adviser, and that's not what you need. Some of the best financial consultants available are commissioned salespeople; you just need to understand how they're paid and ask if there's a product available with a smaller commission.

When you first meet with someone you think you might hire, ask whether or not she gets a commission from products she sells. If she says she doesn't but you're getting a bad feeling, you can check her out.

All advisers are required to register with the Securities and Exchange Commission (SEC) in Washington or their state SEC, and they all must fill out the Uniform Application for Investment

Adviser Registration, or Form ADV, Part II A and B. Ask the adviser for a copy of that form. If she says she doesn't have one, you can call the SEC to be sure she's registered.

Every adviser also must be registered with her state SEC, and you should be able to get a copy of your adviser's registration form from that agency.

You also can check out the status of any certified financial planner by using the verification function on the website of the Certified Financial Planner Board of Standards at cfp.net/utility/ verify-an-individual-s-cfp-certification-and-background.

Past Bad Behavior

Form ADV contains information about whether an adviser has had problems in the past, such as being sanctioned, named in a lawsuit, had complaints filed against her, or had her license suspended. If you want to check your adviser's track record, check on her with the SEC, both in Washington and in your state office. They can tell you if they've received any complaints about this adviser.

POCKET CHANGE

Contact the U.S. Securities and Exchange Commission at 800-732-0330 or by logging on to sec.gov.

You also can check out a potential adviser at the Investment Adviser Public Disclosure's website at adviserinfo.sec.gov.

Or call the Better Business Bureau or even the insurance commissioner in your state.

More Financial Adviser Don'ts

After you've found and hired a financial adviser, she might do some things you don't like, such as take off every Friday afternoon to head for the beach or recommend you put money in an investment that ends up in the tank.

But there are some things your financial adviser should never, ever do. If she does, you need to find yourself a new adviser, and you might want to consider taking legal action.

MONEY PIT

Most financial advisers are diligent and honest and want to do their best for their clients. As in any profession, though, you'll find some who are out to make a quick buck. These are the people who bring the sleaze factor to the profession. If you keep in mind that the sleaze factor exists, you'll be more likely to avoid it.

Misrepresentation

If your adviser tells you the mutual fund you're buying carries no commission for her, but you find out later (in the prospectus mailed to you by the brokerage firm) that she made big bucks by selling it to you, that's *misrepresentation*. It's also misrepresentation if the adviser tells you to go ahead and put your money in a particular investment because you're guaranteed to make 20 percent and you end up losing most of your principal.

DEFINITION

Misrepresentation occurs when an adviser falsifies or leaves out facts in relation to an investment, leading you to believe something that is not true.

If she would have said, "I think this might be a good investment for you. Why don't we try it?" you couldn't charge that you'd been a victim of misrepresentation. But an adviser should never tell you something is guaranteed unless she can provide a guarantee in writing. Your adviser should always give you the pros and cons of an investment and tell you exactly how the risk relates to your objectives. If she doesn't, consider it a sign she may be conducting less-than-ethical business.

Another kind of misrepresentation is personal misrepresentation. If you find out your adviser has told you she's something or someone she's not, you should ask her about it, check out her most recent ADV, and, if you still feel uncomfortable, find someone new.

Who Has Custody of Your Money?

Regardless of what type of adviser you have, she should never have custody—or personal access—to your money. Having custody means the adviser would be able to move your money into her business account, after which who knows what might happen to it.

You don't want your money in your adviser's account (known as commingling), even if only for a few days. Always make investment checks payable to the brokerage house, insurance company, or whatever, but never to your adviser.

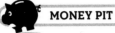

MONEY PIT

Some shady advisers move your investments all over the place, earning commissions at your expense. That's called *churning and burning,* and you don't have to stand for it.

"May I Borrow a Few Bucks?"

A definite no-no for any adviser is asking you for a loan, or suggesting that you go into business together. After commingling funds, borrowing money from a client for her business or personal needs is the most unconscionable act an adviser can perform.

If an adviser ever asks you for funds, contact her boss or the SEC. It's a particularly egregious situation.

Ignoring You or Keeping You Out of the Loop

If you read about a money market fund that gives you just what you've been looking for and you call your adviser and tell her you want to put $3,000 in it, she should complete the transaction. Unless she's a money manager (and she should do it anyway), your adviser is obligated to follow your instructions. Now, if she feels it is an inappropriate investment for you, she should tell you why and also put her response into writing, but she should still follow your instructions.

She may try to advise you not to put your money in that particular fund, and if you trust her, you'd do well to listen. Still, if you insist, she must place your money where you tell her. It is, after all, *your* money.

If you find out your adviser has been buying and selling your investments without your approval, you have a legitimate complaint. Terminate your relationship immediately. A money manager or broker has two types of investment relationships: discretionary and nondiscretionary. If your relationship is nondiscretionary, an investment should never be made without your agreement. If your adviser has discretion, you should have a formal agreement, and you should fully understand the discretionary relationship and what it costs.

If your financial adviser always has an excuse to get out of a meeting with you or doesn't keep you informed about what's going on, you need to ask why. Your adviser should meet with you either on a regular basis or certainly upon your request.

If you feel that your financial adviser has cheated you or has done something unethical, you can look for help by contacting a securities lawyer. Or you can seek *arbitration.* You can do this either by hiring an attorney to represent you in arbitration, or by representing yourself in arbitration.

DEFINITION

Arbitration is the hearing and determination of a dispute between parties by a third party.

Before you hire an attorney, contact the Financial Industry Regulatory Authority (FINRA) at 301-590-6500 or finra.org. FINRA's website lets you file a complaint online.

If you're thinking of representing yourself, contact the American Arbitration Association. It will send you the materials you'll need to prepare your own case, if that's the route you choose. Call 212-716-5800 to request the package, or log on to adr.org.

If you go into arbitration, you and your adviser will each present your side of the matter to an arbitration panel. A three-member panel will hear the case and then decide on a solution. Its solution is final and can't be appealed.

The Least You Need to Know

- Although you might be able to handle most aspects of your personal finances on your own, at times you might need some help.
- You need to know what types of financial advisers are available and where to find someone you can trust before you can choose one.
- Don't be afraid to ask your potential adviser specific questions about her experience, qualifications, and references.
- Avoid advisers who overcharge, look for big commissions at your expense, have poor track records, or embody the "sleaze factor."
- Keep an eye out for the things your financial adviser should never do.
- If you feel you've been cheated by your financial adviser, you may have some recourse.

Glossary

401(k) plan   A retirement plan into which you can contribute a portion of your current salary, usually before taxes. Contributions can grow tax-deferred until you withdraw them upon retirement.

403(b) plan   A retirement plan similar to a 401(k), except it's offered only by hospitals, schools, and nonprofit employers.

adjustable-rate mortgage (ARM)   A mortgage set up with an interest rate that can change at specific intervals as determined under the initial contract.

adjuster   An individual who inspects damage as reported on an insurance claim and determines a settlement amount for the claim.

advance health-care directive   A legal document that spells out your wishes regarding health-care decisions and appoints someone to make health-care decisions on your behalf.

affidavit of domestic partnership   A written, sworn document stating that two people live together in a long-term relationship and agree to share each other's financial responsibilities and be accountable for each other's common welfare.

annual fee   A charge you agree to pay to a bank or credit card company for the privilege of holding its card.

arbitration   The hearing and determination of a dispute between parties by a third party.

balanced mutual fund   A mutual fund wherein the primary objective is to buy a combination of stocks and bonds. These middle-of-the-road funds balance their portfolios to achieve both moderate income and moderate capital growth. These funds tend to be less volatile than stocks-only funds. On average, balanced funds tend to be invested as 45 percent bonds and 55 percent stocks.

bankruptcy   The legal status of a person or other entity who is unable to repay owed debts to creditors.

bear market   An extended period of general price decline in the stock market as a whole.

beneficiary   The person who is named to receive the proceeds from an investment vehicle, trust, or contract. A beneficiary can be an individual, a company, or an organization.

blue-chip stock   Stock of large-cap companies that generally comes with a lower-than-average risk.

bond   A debt instrument. The issuer promises to pay the investor a specified amount of interest for a period of time and repay the principal at maturity.

bond fund   A mutual fund that invests in bonds and passes current income to its shareholders, with capital gains as a secondary objective. Some bond funds purchase long-term securities providing a relatively high current yield but varying substantially in price with changes in interest rates. Other funds choose short-term securities having lower yields but fluctuating little in value.

budget   A schedule of income and expenses, commonly broken into monthly intervals and typically covering a 1-year period.

bull market   An extended period of generally rising prices in the market as a whole.

capitalized cost   In leasing, the cost a leasing company pays for a vehicle.

career counselor   A certified individual who can help you clarify your career goals, assess your abilities and aptitudes, provide information about different careers, develop an individualized career plan, help you create a résumé, and teach you skills and strategies for job hunting.

cash neutral   A strategy that does not require net cash for a transaction but instead relies on simultaneous buying and selling.

cash value life insurance   Insurance for which part of the premium is used to provide death benefits, and the remainder is available to earn interest. Cash value life insurance is a protection plan and a savings plan that charges significantly higher premiums than term insurance.

certificate of deposit (CD)   A type of savings investment in which money is invested for a specified amount of time and the investor is guaranteed a certain amount of interest.

certified financial planner (CFP)   A designation indicating that a financial planner has completed extensive training, passed a rigorous test, is certified by the Certified Financial Planner Board of Standards, and held to a high standard of integrity.

certified public accountant (CPA)   A designation by the American Institute of Certified Public Accounts indicating that an individual meets certain work experience requirements and has passed an exam.

churning and burning   To trade securities very actively in a brokerage account to increase brokerage commissions rather than customer profits. Brokers may be tempted to churn accounts because their income is directly related to the volume of trading undertaken by their customers. Churning is illegal and unethical.

co-payment   The amount the insured person is responsible to pay at each time of service under a health insurance contract.

collateral   Something of value put up as security for a loan to ensure the lender won't lose the money loaned.

collision and comprehensive coverage   Types of auto insurance that pay to repair or replace your car if it's in an accident, regardless of whether or not the collision is your fault.

commercial bank   Financial institutions, either chartered by the federal or state governments, that take deposits, loan money, and provide other services to individuals or corporations.

commingling   The unethical practice of a financial adviser mixing his or her own funds with those of clients, making it difficult to determine who owns the funds.

compound interest   Interest paid on interest from previous periods in addition to the principal. Essentially, compounding involves adding interest to principal and any previous interest to calculate interest in the next period. Compound interest may be figured daily, monthly, quarterly, semiannually, or annually.

consumer confidence   A measure of how consumers feel at a given time about the current state of the economy.

cosigner   Someone who assumes responsibility if you can't pay off your credit card debt. Also known as a *guarantor.*

credit history   The record of an individual's past events that pertain to credit previously given or applied for.

credit report   An extensive document that details your credit history.

credit score   A number based on data in your credit report that represents your overall credit-worthiness. *See also* FICO score.

credit union   A nonprofit, cooperative financial institution providing credit to its members who share a common bond, such as an employer or trade. Credit unions often pay slightly higher rates of interest on passbook-type savings accounts and charge lower rates on consumer loans.

customer service representative (CSR)   A front-line bank employee who opens checking and savings accounts, certificates of deposit, and so forth.

debit card   A card you use for purchases that deducts money from your checking account, unlike a credit card, which requires you to pay for purchases at a later date.

debt settlement   An agreement that allows you to pay less than you owe to a creditor in order to settle your debt. Debt settlement usually is very detrimental to your credit score and credit history. Also known as *debt arbitration* or *debt negotiation.*

deductible   The amount the insured person must pay before an insurance company pays a claim.

depression   A critical downturn in economic activity that lasts for 2 or more years and is characterized by high unemployment, diminished available credit, reduced trade and commerce, high rates of bankruptcies, debt defaults, and other factors. *See also* Great Depression.

disability   The inability to work because of a physical or mental condition.

discretionary expenses   Expenses incurred for nonessentials; money spent as a person chooses.

disposition charges   Expenses charged to the lessee at the end of the lease for selling the vehicle or property leased.

diversification   The acquisition of a group of assets in which returns on the assets are not directly related over time. Proper investment diversification, requiring a sufficient number of different assets, is intended to minimize risk associated with investing.

dividend   A share of a company's net profits, distributed by the company to a class of its stockholders, and paid in a fixed amount for each share of stock held. Dividends are usually fixed in preferred stock; dividends from common stock vary as the company's performance shifts.

durable power of attorney   A legal document that enables you to designate another person to handle your financial transactions should you become incapacitated and unable to do so.

dwelling coverage   The part of your homeowner's insurance that covers the structure in which you live.

emergency fund   Money saved for use to cover routine and nonroutine expenses in the event that you would lose your job or become unable to work, thereby losing your income.

employed part-time for economic reasons   People who want to work full-time but can't find full-time jobs.

employer-sponsored benefit plan   A benefit or package of benefits an employer provides for employees.

equity   The value of your ownership in property or securities. The equity in your home is the difference between the current market value of the home and the money you still owe on the mortgage. The term *equity* is used interchangeably with *stocks*.

escrow   The holding of assets (for example, securities or cash) by a third party that delivers the assets to the grantee or promisee on the fulfillment of some condition. Some parts of mortgage payments are held in escrow to cover expenses like taxes and insurance. Down payments are also held in escrow until settlement.

exchange   A marketplace for the purpose of trading financial instruments such as securities, derivatives, and commodities. An exchange can be an electronic platform or a physical location. Exchanges are for the purpose of assuring fair and orderly trading.

exchange traded fund (ETF)   A group of securities representing a mutual fund that are traded in the stock market throughout the day at the market value at that time.

executor   Someone who oversees the distribution of your property and ensures the terms of your will are followed after you die. If you don't have an executor, the court will appoint someone to do the job. Also known as a *personal representative*.

Fannie Mae   A security issued by the Federal National Mortgage Association (FNMA) that is backed by insured and conventional mortgages. Monthly returns to holders of Fannie Maes consist of interest and principal payments made by homeowners on their mortgages.

fee-only adviser   A financial adviser who is paid a fee by clients rather than earning commission from the sale of a particular product.

FICO score   A scoring model used to determine credit risk for those seeking mortgages. FICO mortgage scores range from 300 to 850, with higher scores pointing to lower credit risks. The FICO score is used by the three national credit bureaus: TransUnion, Equifax, and Experian. *See also* credit score.

finance charge   A fee you pay when you borrow money or use credit.

financial adviser   A professional who guides individuals to arrange and coordinate their financial affairs. Also known as *financial consultant* or *financial planner*.

fixed expenses   Expenses such as rent, utilities, and car payments that occur on a regular basis.

fixed-rate mortgage (FRM)   A mortgage in which the annual interest charged does not vary throughout the period of the loan.

foreclosure   When a lender claims a property on which the loan has been defaulted.

Freddie Mac   A security issued by the Federal Home Loan Mortgage Corporation (FHLMC) that is secured by pools of conventional home mortgages. Holders of Freddie Macs receive a share of the interest and principal payments made by the homeowners.

full-service broker   A broker who offers a range of services such as retirement planning, investment advice, tax planning, and estate advice. Full-service brokers receive higher commissions and fees than discount brokers.

gap insurance   Insurance purchased to pay the difference between the value your auto insurance pays if a leased vehicle is stolen or totaled and the amount required to terminate the lease.

Great Depression   The longest-lasting and most severe economic setback in U.S. history, starting with the stock market crash in October 1929 and lasting until 1939.

Great Recession   An economic downturn that resulted from the burst of the U.S. housing bubble and caused a global recession. The recession officially started in December 2007 and lasted until June 2009 in the United States.

gross income   All income except as specifically exempted by the Internal Revenue Code.

growth stock   Stock that is expected to have above-average increases in revenue and earnings.

guarantor   Someone who assumes the responsibility if you can't pay off your credit card debt. Also known as a *cosigner.*

headhunter   Someone who matches you with a company that's looking for someone to fill a particular position. He or she also handles negotiations between a prospective employee and the company.

health maintenance organization (HMO)   A type of health plan that restricts your choice of health-care providers and often costs less than a plan that does not restrict providers. *See also* preferred provider organization (PPO).

homeowner's insurance   Insurance obtained by a property owner to protect the property and its contents. It also provides liability coverage for accidents that occur on the property.

individual retirement account (IRA)   A retirement savings plan in which you can contribute up to $5,500 per year. Funds can grow tax-deferred until you withdraw them at retirement. Contributions may or may not be tax-deductible depending on the income level and participation in other retirement plans.

interest   The fee the bank charges you to use its money to finance what you buy with your credit card.

interest rate   The specific percentage rate a bank or credit card company charges you for interest.

intestate   The condition of dying without having prepared and executed a will to determine who receives your assets.

investment portfolio   The listing and value of all your investments at a given point in time.

lease   A contract under which someone obtains the use of an object, such as a vehicle or property, for a specified time and amount of money.

lending investment   A loan you make with the understanding that you'll get it back, plus interest.

liability coverage   Insurance to cover costs resulting from damage to another person or another person's property for which you are legally responsible.

load fund   A mutual fund with shares sold at a price, including a sales charge (typically 4 to 9.3 percent of the net amount invested). Load funds are sold at a price exceeding their net asset value, but they are redeemed at their net asset value.

loan balance   The total balance that remains on a loan you have.

long-term unemployed   People who have been out of work for 27 weeks or more.

marginally attached to the labor force   People who aren't working but are not considered unemployed because they haven't looked for work within 4 weeks.

market report   A reporting of prices paid for various securities or commodities during a set period of time.

maturity date   The date on which the principal and all remaining interest is due to be paid back on a loan.

misrepresentation   A misstatement or omission of facts by a financial adviser that may negatively affect a client.

money manager   A bank or business responsible for managing a securities portfolio for an individual or institution.

money market fund   A mutual fund that sells shares of ownership and uses the proceeds to purchase short-term, high-quality securities such as Treasury bills, negotiable certificates of deposit, and commercial paper. Income earned by shareholders is received in the form of additional shares of stock in the fund (normally priced at $1 each). Although no fees are generally charged to purchase or redeem shares in a money market fund, an annual management charge is levied by the fund's advisers. This investment pays a return that varies with short-term interest rates. It is relatively liquid and safe, but yields and features vary.

mortgage   A loan for the purpose of financing property. The loan is secured by a lien on the property and comes with conditions regarding the length of time over which it will be repaid, the amount of interest you'll pay on the loan, and other factors.

municipality   A zoned area such as a city, borough, or township that has an incorporated government.

mutual fund   An open-end investment company that invests its shareholders' money in a diversified group of securities of other corporations. Mutual funds are usually professionally managed.

net worth   The amount of wealth calculated by taking the total value of assets owned and subtracting all liabilities.

no-load fund   A mutual fund sold without a sales charge. No-load funds sell directly to customers at net asset value with no intermediate salesperson charging a fee.

nondiscretionary expenses   Expenses, such as mortgage payments and utility bills, an individual must pay.

nonroutine expenses   Budgeted expenses, such as a furnace repair or unexpected medical expenses, that are not regular or customary.

personal finance   Every aspect of one's life that deals with money.

personal financial specialist (PFS)   A credential earned by certified public accounts who specialize in helping clients plan all aspects of their wealth, including estate and retirement planning. PFS accountants must complete continuing professional education and pay an annual fee to use the designation, which is awarded to CPAs who complete study and pass an exam.

points   Prepaid interest paid as a fee to a mortgage lender to cover the cost of applying for the loan; 1 point is 1 percent of the loan's value.

preferred provider organization (PPO)   Health insurance coverage that rewards you for using providers from a specific list of care providers. The difference between an HMO (health mainte-nance organization) and a PPO is that a PPO pays for the services of a nonspecified provider, but an HMO usually does not pay for such services. *See also* health maintenance organization (HMO).

premium   The amount paid, in one sum or periodically, for a contract of insurance.

premium bond   A bond for which the value has increased.

prenuptial agreement   A written agreement by a couple to be married in which financial matters, including rights following divorce or the death of one spouse, are detailed.

principal   The capital sum, as distinguished from interest or profit.

priority obligation   Loans, fees, or bills that are essential and often mandated to pay. Child support is a priority obligation, for example.

property taxes   Taxes assessed on real estate. Most common are municipal and school taxes. Also known as *real estate tax*.

recession   A significant decline in economic activity that affects the entire economy and lasts for longer than a few months. *See also* Great Recession.

refinancing   Reapplying for a new mortgage, usually to receive a lower interest rate. Refinancing is done for consolidation or additional funding.

residual value   The value of a vehicle when it comes off a lease; the value you need to pay to acquire the vehicle.

revolving debt   A type of credit agreement that lets you borrow against a predetermined line of credit when paying for something. Revolving debt is the type of debt used by credit card companies.

robo-adviser   An online financial adviser that provides automated, algorithm-based advice to clients for lower fees than a human adviser would.

Roth IRA   Introduced in 1998, an individual retirement account (IRA) in which the funds placed into the account are nondeductible. If held more than 5 years, all funds withdrawn are received tax-free.

routine expenses   Expenses that occur on a regular basis, such as food costs, dental checkups, church contributions, etc. These expenses may vary in amount, but they occur on a regular basis.

savings and loan (S&L)   The collective name for savings banks and savings and loan associations. S&Ls generally accept deposits from and extend credit primarily to individuals. Also known as *thrift*.

savings ratio   The percentage of your gross income you're able to save within a given time.

securities   Investments that represent evidence of debt, ownership of a business, or the legal right to acquire or sell an ownership interest in a business.

SEP-IRA (Simplified Employee Pension IRA)   A retirement plan for self-employed individuals and small business owners that enables them to save retirement money for themselves and their employees.

share   Any of the equal parts of a company's capital that are sold as stock to investors.

shareholder   A person who owns shares in a corporation.

simple interest   Interest paid on an initial investment only. Simple interest is calculated by multiplying the principal by the annual rate of interest by the number of years involved.

speculating   Taking above-average risks to achieve above-average returns, generally during a relatively short period of time. Speculation involves buying something on the basis of its potential selling price rather than on the basis of its actual value.

spending ratio   The amount of your gross income that goes toward a particular area of expenditures.

stock   Shares of ownership in a company, including common stock of various classes and any preferred stock outstanding.

stock fund   A mutual fund that limits its investments to shares of common stock. Common stock funds vary in risk, from relatively low to quite high, depending on the types of stocks in which the funds are invested.

stock market   The organized securities exchanges for stock and bond transactions. Major exchanges are the New York Stock Exchange (NYSE), the American Stock Exchange (AMEX), and the National Association of Securities Dealers Automated Quotation System (NASDAQ).

target date fund   An age-weighted retirement plan that's normally used by a company that wishes to have a specified sum available for an older employee (usually an owner) at the time of retirement.

tax-deductible   An expense that can be used to offset gross income when calculating your taxable gross income.

tax-deferred   Income that is earned but neither received nor taxed until a later date, when the funds are withdrawn or mature. Tax-deferred assets include those within an IRA, 401(k) plan, 403(b) plan, tax-deferred annuity, tax-deferred life insurance, and others.

term life insurance   Life insurance in which the insurance company pays a specified sum if the insured dies during the coverage period. Term insurance includes no savings, cash values, borrowing power, or benefits at retirement. On the basis of cost, it is the least expensive insurance available, although policy prices can vary significantly among firms.

thrift   A financial institution that derives its funds primarily from consumer savings accounts set up to provide personal mortgages. The term originally referred to those institutions offering mainly passbook savings accounts. The word *thrift* often refers to savings and loan (S&L) associations, but it also can mean credit unions and mutual savings banks. *See also* savings and loan (S&L).

tiered account system   A type of bank account that pays higher interest if your account balance is consistently over a certain amount set by the bank, usually at least $1,000 but many times higher.

Treasury bill   A short-term government security that's purchased at a lower price than the redemption value.

Treasury note   Intermediate-term (1 to 10 years), interest-bearing debt of the U.S. Treasury. Treasury notes are quoted and traded in $\frac{1}{32}$ of a point.

underemployed   A group of people who are skilled but working in low-paying or unskilled jobs.

unemployment compensation   Temporary income you can get in the event that you lose your job due to circumstances that are not your fault.

uninsured motorist coverage   Insurance that protects you in the event you are in an accident with an uninsured or underinsured driver.

variable expenses   Expenses that are changeable, alterable.

warranty   A statement of promise or assurance in connection with a contract or purchase.

Resources

In addition to this book, many other good resources are available to help you keep track of and stay on top of your personal finances. This collection of books, websites, and apps can help you find the resources you need.

Books

Andreana, Lise. *No More Mac 'n Cheese! The Real-World Guide to Managing Your Money for 20-Somethings.* Vancouver: Self-Counsel Press, 2012.

Andrew, Douglas R. *Missed Fortune 101: A Starter Kit to Becoming a Millionaire.* New York: Hachette Book Group, 2008.

Andrew, Douglas R., Emron D. Andrew, and Aaron R. Andrew. *Millionaire by Thirty: The Quickest Path to Early Financial Independence.* New York: Hachette Book Group, 2010.

Anthony, Jason, and Karl Cluck. *Debt-Free by 30: Practical Advice for the Young, Broke, and Upwardly Mobile.* New York: Plume Books, 2001.

Blake, Jenny. *Life After College: The Complete Guide to Getting What You Want.* Philadelphia: Running Press, 2011.

Corley, Thomas. *Change Your Habits, Change Your Life.* Minneapolis: Hillcrest Media Group, 2016.

———. *Rich Habits: The Daily Success Habits of Wealthy Individuals.* Minneapolis: Hillcrest Media Group, 2010.

Frey, Alex. *A Beginner's Guide to Investing: How to Grow Your Money the Smart and Easy Way.* CreateSpace Independent Publishing Platform, 2012.

Kobliner, Beth. *Get a Financial Life: Personal Finance in Your Twenties and Thirties.* New York: Simon & Schuster, 2016.

O'Shaughnessy, Patrick. *Millennial Money: How Young Investors Can Build a Fortune.* New York: St. Martin's Press, 2014.

Palmer, Kimberly. *Generation Earn: The Young Professional's Guide to Spending, Investing, and Giving Back.* New York: Ten Speed Press, 2010.

Reaume, Amanda. *Money Is Everything: Personal Finance for the Brave New Economy.* Berkeley: Callisto Media, Inc., 2015.

Romans, Christine. *Smart Is the New Rich: Money Guide for Millennials.* New York: John Wiley & Sons, 2015.

Sethi, Ramit. *I Will Teach You to Be Rich.* New York: Workman Publishing Co., 2009.

Siegel, Cary. *Why Didn't They Teach Me This in School? 99 Personal Money Management Principles to Live By.* CreateSpace Independent Publishing Platform, 2013.

Torabi, Farnoosh. *You're So Money: Live Rich, Even When You're Not.* New York: Crown Publishing Group, 2008.

Websites

The following websites might interest you as well. Please remember we don't endorse these sites; the authors of the sites are responsible for the content.

AccuQuote
accuquote.com

Affordable Care Act Marketplace
healthcare.gov

Ally Bank
ally.com

America Saves
americasaves.org

American Express
americanexpress.com

American Family Life Insurance
amfam.com

Annual Credit Report
annualcreditreport.com

AOL Money and Finance
aol.com/finance

Bank of America
bankofamerica.com

Bank5 Connect
bank5connect.com

Banking Sense
bankingsense.com

Bankrate
bankrate.com

Barclays
banking.barclaysus.com

Capital One
capitalone.com

CarsDirect
carsdirect.com

Cash Money Life
cashmoneylife.com

CBS MarketWatch
marketwatch.com

Charles Schwab
schwab.com

Chase
chase.com

The Cheat Sheet
cheatsheet.com

CIT Bank
bankoncit.com

Citibank
citicards.com

Citizens Bank
citizensbank.com

CNN Money
money.cnn.com

Common Bond
commonbond.co

Connexus Credit Union
connexuscu.org

Country Life Insurance Company
countryfinancial.com

CreditCards.com
creditcards.com

Darien Rowayton Bank (DRB)
drbank.com

Discover Bank
discover.com

eBay Motors
ebay.com/motors

Edmunds.com
edmunds.com

Equifax Credit Services
equifax.com

Experian
experian.com

ExpertFlyer
expertflyer.com

Fannie Mae
fanniemae.com

Fidelity Investments
fidelity.com

FindMyInsurance
findmyinsurance.com

First Internet Bank of Indiana
firstib.com

FNBO Direct
fnbodirect.com

Forbes
forbes.com

Freddie Mac
freddiemac.com

Guardian Life Insurance Company of America
guardianlife.com

iGObanking.com
igobanking.com

Insurance Information Institute
iii.org

Investopedia
investopedia.com

IRS
irs.gov

Job Mo
jobmo.org

Jobcase
jobcase.com

Jobr
jobrapp.com

Kasasa
kasasa.com

Kelley Blue Book
kbb.com

Kiplinger
kiplinger.com

LegalZoom
legalzoom.com

Lending Club
lendingclub.com

LendKey
lendkey.com

LifeInsure.com
lifeinsure.com

LinkedIn
linkedin.com

LoungeBuddy
loungebuddy.com

MarketWatch
marketwatch.com

Massachusetts Mutual Life Insurance Company
massmutual.com

The Military Wallet
themilitarywallet.com

Mint
mint.com

Modest Money
modestmoney.com

Monster
monster.com

The Motley Fool
fool.com

MSN Money Central
msn.com

MyBankTracker
mybanktracker.com

MyMoney.gov
mymoney.gov

MySavingsDirect
mysavingsdirect.com

National Association of Health Underwriters
nahu.org

National Association of Securities Dealers Automated Quotation System (NASDAQ)
nasdaq.com

National Family Mortgage
nationalfamilymortgage.com

Nationwide Bank
nationwide.com

NerdWallet
nerdwallet.com

New York Life Insurance and Annuity Corporation
newyorklife.com

New York Stock Exchange (NYSE)
nyse.com

Northwestern Mutual Life Insurance Company
northwesternmutual.com

Personal Capital
personalcapital.com

Priority Pass
prioritypass.com

Schwab Bank
schwab.com

Seeking Alpha
seekingalpha.com

Smart About Money
smartaboutmoney.org

SoFi
sofi.com

Southern Farm Bureau Life Insurance Company
sfbli.com

State Farm Life and Accident Assurance Company
statefarm.com

State Farm Life Insurance Company
statefarm.com

SWITCH
switchapp.com

Synchrony Bank
synchronybank.com

TD Ameritrade
tdameritrade.com

TheStreet
thestreet.com

TransUnion Credit Information Services
transunion.com

U.S. Securities and Exchange Commission
sec.gov

USAA Life Insurance Company
usaa.com

Vanguard Online
vanguard.com

Wealthfront
wealthfront.com

Wells Fargo
wellsfargo.com

Wise Bread
wisebread.com

WiseBanyan
wisebanyan.com

Yahoo! Finance
finance.yahoo.com

Apps

More and more good financial apps are being introduced every day, and they can help you do everything from saving your change to figuring out your taxes. Here are some to try.

Acorns
acorns.com

Balance
cwakamo.com/balance

CarMax
carmax.com

Checkbook
appxy.com/checkbook

Credit Karma
creditkarma.com

Digit
digit.co

Edmunds
edmunds.com

Goodbudget
goodbudget.com

Kelley Blue Book Mobile
kbb.com

LearnVest
learnvest.com

Level Money
levelmoney.com

Mint
mint.com

MyBankTracker
mybanktracker.com

Personal Capital
personalcapital.com

Pocket Expense
appxy.com/pocket-expense

PocketGuard
pocketguard.com

Prosper Daily
prosper.com

SnipSnap
snipsnap.it

Spending Tracker
mhriley.com/spendingtracker

Helpful Forms

Legal documents and estate planning aren't topics people in their 20s and 30s typically think about, but they should be on your radar, especially if you're married or married with kids.

In Chapter 18, we explored the idea of a prenuptial agreement. Whether or not you choose to execute one is up to you, but it's worth thinking about. And in Chapter 20, we explain what wills, powers of attorney, and other legal documents are and why you need to have them.

In this appendix, we include some vital documents for your use. (Not all will apply to you.) We suggest you consult a lawyer to review the forms after you've completed them.

Prenuptial Agreement

A prenuptial agreement, sometimes called a premarital agreement, is a contract entered into by two people before the start of a marriage, civil union, or other type of arrangement.

This Agreement is made this _____ day of _____, 20__, between _____, of _____, future husband, and _____, of _____, future wife.

WHEREAS, a marriage is intended to be, soon after the date hereof, solemnized between _____ and _____, and

WHEREAS, each party owns real and personal property which was obtained independently of the other party, and each has made a complete disclosure of his or her property as listed on Exhibit A and Exhibit B attached hereto and made part of this Agreement, and

WHEREAS, each party has been advised and understands his or her rights, and the rights of each party's heirs in the event of the marriage and in the absence of any agreement regarding those marital rights, and

WHEREAS, each party desires to keep all of his or her separate property whether now owned or hereafter acquired, free from any claim of the other party by virtue of the forthcoming marriage, and

WHEREAS, each party declares that he or she has had independent legal advice or the opportunity to secure independent legal advice before entering into this Agreement and that each party acknowledges that he or she fully understands the legal effect of this Agreement, and each party acknowledges the free, knowledgeable, and voluntary execution of the Agreement with no fraud, deceit, or undue influence being exerted and that the same is executed by them with the intent to be bound hereunder, and

WHEREAS, each party desires to set forth his or her mutual agreement and understanding in writing.

NOW, THEREFORE, IT IS AGREED AS FOLLOWS:

1. That all property of any kind or nature, real, personal, or mixed, which belong to a party, shall be and forever remain the individual property of that party (also known hereafter as separate property), including all income therefrom.

2. Each party shall have full right and authority, in all respects the same as if unmarried, to use, enjoy, manage, convey, mortgage, and dispose of all that party's present and future separate property, of every kind and character, including the right and power to freely, without any spousal claim, dispose of the same by gift or by Last Will and Testament.

3. Each party waives and relinquishes any spousal claim, family allowance, election against the other party's Last Will and Testament, or intestate share in the decedent's separate property.

4. Each party waives and relinquishes, in the event of legal separation or divorce, any claim against the separate property of the other party.

5. Neither party intends by this Agreement to limit or restrict his or her right to receive a transfer, conveyance, devise, or bequest from the other.

6. Each party agrees to execute any documents necessary to accomplish the intent of this Agreement.

7. Each party agrees that this Agreement, may, by mutual agreement, be amended, revoked, or rescinded.

8. This Agreement is legally binding upon each party and each party's heirs, personal representatives, successors, and assigns.

9. This Agreement shall take effect only in the event that the parties become legally married to one another.

IN WITNESS WHEREOF, we have subscribed our names to this Prenuptial Agreement, this _____ day of _____, 20__.

Signed: _____

Signed: _____

Reviewed by: _____

Attorney for: _____

Reviewed by: _____

Attorney for: _____

Last Will and Testament—Basic for Single Person

A basic will for a single person normally designates a personal representative for the deceased, instructions for settling debt, and notes on how property should be distributed.

I, _____, of _____, _____, being of sound and disposing mind and memory, do make, publish, and declare this to be my Last Will and Testament, and I hereby revoke all wills and codicils heretofore made by me.

I. Identification, Definitions, Comments

    A. I am a single person.

    B. A beneficiary must survive me by thirty (30) days to be entitled to receive a devise.

    C. "Issue" is to be construed as lawful lineal descendants and include adopted persons. Issue shall receive any devise by representation, not per capita.

II. Debts, Expenses, Encumbrances, Taxes

    A. I direct that my enforceable debts, expenses of my last illness, and funeral and administrative expenses of my estate shall be paid by my personal representative from my residuary estate. At his or her discretion, my personal representative may continue to pay any installment obligations incurred by me during my lifetime on an installment basis or may prepay any or all of such obligations in whole or in part, and my personal representative may, at his or her discretion, distribute any asset encumbered by such an obligation subject to the obligation.

    B. I direct that all inheritance, estate, and succession taxes (including interest and penalties thereon) payable by reason of my death shall be paid out of and be charged generally against my residuary estate without reimbursement from any person.

III. Specific Devises

I devise all my personal effects and household goods to _____. If he or she does not survive me, I devise said property, in equal shares, to _____. If a devisee does not survive me, his or her share devolves to the deceased devisee's issue, or if none survive me, the share devolves, equally, to the surviving devisees.

IV. Residuary Estate

I devise my residuary estate to _____. If he or she does not survive me, I devise my residuary estate, in equal shares, to _____. If a devisee does not survive me, his or her share devolves to the deceased devisee's issue, or if none survive me, the share devolves, equally, to the surviving devisees.

V. Personal Representative

I hereby appoint _____ as personal representative. If he or she cannot serve, I appoint _____ as personal representative. I authorize unsupervised administration of my estate. I request that the personal representative serve without bond, or if a bond is required, that a minimum bond be required. My personal representative shall have all powers enumerated and granted to personal representatives under the Code of the State of _____, and any other power that may be granted by law, to be exercised without the necessity of Court approval, as my personal representative determines to be in the best interest of the estate.

I have signed this Last Will and Testament in the presence of the undersigned witnesses on this _____ day of _____, 20__.

Signed: _____

Testator: _____

The foregoing instrument was at _____, _____, this _____ day of _____, 20__, signed, sealed, published, and declared by the testator to be his or her Last Will and Testament, in our presence, and we, at the testator's request and in his or her presence and in the presence of each other, have hereunto subscribed our names as attesting witnesses.

Witness: _____

Address: _____

Witness: _____

Address: _____

Last Will and Testament—Basic for Married Person with Minor Children

A will for a person who is married and has children is more complicated than one for a single person with no dependents. In addition to designating a personal representative for the deceased and instructions for settling debt and for how property should be distributed, this will addresses guardianship of the children.

I, _____, of _____, _____, being of sound and disposing mind and memory, do make, publish, and declare this to be my Last Will and Testament, and I hereby revoke all wills and codicils heretofore made by me.

I. Identification, Definitions, Comments

A. I am married to _____. I have _____ children: _____, _____, and _____.

B. A beneficiary must survive me by thirty (30) days to be entitled to receive a devise.

C. "Issue" is to be construed as lawful lineal descendants and include adopted persons. Issue shall receive any devise by representation, not per capita.

II. Debts, Expenses, Encumbrances, Taxes

A. I direct that my enforceable debts, expenses of my last illness, and funeral and administrative expenses of my estate shall be paid by my personal representative from my residuary estate. At his or her discretion, my personal representative may continue to pay any installment obligations incurred by me during my lifetime on an installment basis or may prepay any or all of such obligations in whole or in part, and my personal representative may, at his or her discretion, distribute any asset encumbered by such an obligation subject to the obligation.

B. I direct that all inheritance, estate, and succession taxes (including interest and penalties thereon) payable by reason of my death shall be paid out of and be charged generally against my residuary estate without reimbursement from any person.

III. Specific Devises

I devise all my personal effects and household goods to _____. If he or she does not survive me, I devise said property, in equal shares, to _____, _____, and _____. If a child does not survive me, his or her share devolves to the deceased child's issue, or if none survive me, the share devolves, equally, to the surviving children.

IV. Residuary Estate

I devise my residuary estate to _____. If he or she does not survive me, I devise my residuary estate, in equal shares, to _____, _____, and

_____. If a child does not survive me, his or her share devolves to the deceased child's issue, or if none survive me, the share devolves, equally, to the surviving children.

V. Personal Representative

I hereby appoint _____ as personal representative. If he or she cannot serve, I appoint _____ as alternate personal representative. I authorize unsupervised administration of my estate. I request that the personal representative serve without bond, or if a bond is required, that a minimum bond be required. My personal representative shall have all powers enumerated and granted to personal representatives under the Code of the State of _____, and any other power that may be granted by law, to be exercised without the necessity of Court approval, as my personal representative determines to be in the best interest of the estate.

VI. Guardian

I appoint _____ as guardian of the person and property of each of my minor children. If he or she cannot serve as guardian, I appoint _____ as alternate guardian. I request that no bond be required for the guardian; however, if such a bond is required, I request that such bond be nominal in amount.

VI. Miscellaneous

If my spouse and I executed wills at approximately the same time, this Last Will and Testament is not made pursuant to any contract or agreement with my spouse.

I have signed this Last Will and Testament in the presence of the undersigned witnesses on this _____ day of _____, 20__.

Signed: _____

Testator: _____

The foregoing instrument was at _____, _____, this _____ day of _____, 20__, signed, sealed, published, and declared by the testator to be his or her Last Will and Testament, in our presence, and we, at the testator's request and in his or her presence and in the presence of each other, have hereunto subscribed our names as attesting witnesses.

Witness: _____

Address: _____

Witness: _____

Address: _____

Last Will and Testament—with Trust for Minor Children

This will designates a trustee to oversee the residual estate of the deceased for the benefit of the deceased's children. It also addresses guardianship and appoints a personal representative.

I, _____, of _____, _____, do make, publish, and declare this to be my Last Will and Testament, hereby revoking all former wills and codicils.

I. Identification, Definitions, Comments

    A. My spouse is _____. We have _____ children: _____, _____, and _____.

    B. "Survive me" means that the person referred to must survive me by thirty (30) days. If the person referred to dies within thirty (30) days of my death, the reference to him shall be construed as if he had failed to survive me, and all devises made herein to or for the benefit of that person shall be void.

    C. Whenever used herein, words importing the singular include the plural and words importing the masculine include the feminine and neuter, unless the context otherwise requires.

    D. "Issue" of the person referred to means the lawful lineal descendants (except those who are lineal descendants of living lineal descendants) who, at the time they must be ascertained in order to give effect to the reference to them, are either in being or they are in gestation and later born alive. Issue shall take by right of representation, in accordance with the rule of per stirpes distribution. "Issue" includes adopted persons.

II. Debts, Expenses, Encumbrances, Taxes

    A. I direct that my enforceable debts, expenses of my last illness, and funeral and administration expenses of my estate shall be paid by my personal representative from my estate as soon as practicable after my death.

    B. If any real or personal property that passes by reason of my death is encumbered by a mortgage, pledge, or other lien, I direct that such claim not be a charge to or paid as an administrative expense of my estate, but the person receiving such property shall take it subject to all claims.

    C. I direct that the expense of safeguarding, packing, shipping, and delivering any property to a beneficiary be paid as an administrative expense of my estate.

    D. I direct that all transfer, estate, inheritance, succession, and other death taxes (together with any interest and penalty thereon) that shall be payable by reason of my death shall be paid out of and be charged generally against my residuary estate without reimbursement from any person.

III. Specific Devises

I devise all my clothing; jewelry; household goods; personal effects; automobiles; boats; athletic and sporting equipment; any collections of stamps, coins, money, or other thing; all books; manuscripts; antiques; works of art; and all other tangible personal property not otherwise specifically devised, including insurance policies thereon, owned by me at the time of my death, to _____. If my spouse does not survive me, I devise said property, in equal shares, to my children _____. If a child does not survive me, his share devolves to his issue if any survive me; if a child's issue does not survive me, the share shall devolve to the other child.

IV. Residuary Estate

A. I devise my residuary estate to _____. If my spouse does not survive me, I devise my residuary estate to _____, of _____, _____, as trustee, in trust, for the benefit of my children, _____, _____, _____, under the following terms and conditions:

1. If there is one child under age twenty-two (22), the trustee shall hold and administer the trust for the benefit of my children. The trustee may pay to the children or expend on their behalf so much of the net income from the trust as the trustee may deem advisable to provide properly for the children's support, maintenance, health, and education. Any income not distributed shall be added to the principal. The trustee may, in his sole discretion at any time, and from time to time, disburse from the principal of the trust (even to the point of completely exhausting such estate) such amounts as the trustee deems advisable to provide for the support, maintenance, health, and education of the children. In determining the amounts of the principal to be so disbursed, the trustee shall take into consideration any other income or property which the children may have from any other source. For all sums so disbursed, the trustee shall have full acquaintance. All such disbursements from the principal shall be charged against the trust and shall not be charged against any child's share of the principal subsequently divided.

2. When the youngest child becomes age twenty-two (22), the trust estate shall be divided equally among my children, those then living and those predeceased but with issue then living. Any child age twenty-five (25) shall receive his proportionate share upon written request to the trustee; any child who is at least age twenty-two (22) but less than age twenty-five (25) shall receive one third (1/3) of his proportionate share upon written request to the trustee and have the remainder of his share administered according to the provisions of Paragraph 1 herein; if any child does not survive but has issue, his share shall be distributed to his issue, or if there is no issue, his share shall devolve to the other children. If none of the foregoing persons survive to receive final distribution of the trust, the trust estate shall be distributed according to the terms of Paragraph B herein. Notwithstanding the foregoing, the trust shall terminate within twenty-one (21) years of

the last to die of the beneficiaries who were living at my death; upon such termination, the trust estate shall vest in and be distributed as provided for herein.

3. No person paying money or delivering any property to the trustee need see to its application.

4. The trustee is entitled to reasonable compensation for services rendered and to reimbursement for expenses.

5. If, at any time, the aggregate principal value of the trust is ten thousand dollars ($10,000.00) or less, the trustee may in his sole judgment terminate the trust and distribute the assets thereof in the trustee's possession to the beneficiary or beneficiaries, at that time, of the current income.

6. Any interest in any trust created by this instrument shall not be transferable or assignable by any beneficiary, or be subject during his life to the claims of his creditors, including spousal support claims from a separation or dissolution of marriage.

7. The trustee shall have all powers enumerated in the Trust Code of the State of _____, as may be amended, and all other powers granted by law.

B. If none of my children nor their issue survives me, I devise my residuary estate to _____.

V. Personal Representative

I appoint _____ as personal representative of this Last Will and Testament; if he is unable or unwilling to serve, I appoint _____ as personal representative. I request that my personal representative serve without posting bond, or if a bond is required, that a minimum bond be set. My personal representative shall have all powers enumerated in the Probate Code of the State of _____, as may be amended, and all other powers granted by law. In addition to powers conferred by law, I authorize my personal representative to exercise absolute discretion, without the necessity of any notice, petition to or order from any court or being required to report to or obtain the approval of any court.

VI. Guardian

I appoint _____, or if he is unable or unwilling to serve, _____, as guardian of the person and property of each minor child who survives me, during his minority. I request that the guardian be permitted to serve without bond or that the bond be a nominal amount.

IN WITNESS WHEREOF, I have subscribed my name to this, my Last Will and Testament, the preceding pages bearing my initials.

Signed: _____

Testator: _____

The foregoing instrument was at _____, _____, this _____ day of _____, 20__, signed, sealed, published, and declared by the testator to be his Last Will and Testament, in our presence, and we, at the testator's request and in his presence and in the presence of one another, have hereunto subscribed our names as attesting witnesses.

Witness: _____

Address: _____

Witness: _____

Address: _____

Will Information Form

A will information form is intended to collect all the information you need to help determine the contents of your will. Lawyers often ask for a will information form so they can offer the best advice concerning a client's will.

Husband: _____

Wife: _____

Address: _____

Child: _____ Age: _____

Child: _____ Age: _____

Child: _____ Age: _____

Bequests

Property   **Beneficiary**

_____   _____

_____   _____

_____   _____

Cash Amount   **Beneficiary**

_____   _____

_____   _____

_____   _____

Residuary

First: Name and relationship (if does not survive): _____

Name and relationship (if does not survive): _____

Name and relationship: _____

Equally or percent share: _____

Second: Name and relationship (if does not survive): _____

Name and relationship (if does not survive): _____

Name and relationship: _____

Equally or percent share: _____

Third: Name and relationship (if does not survive): _____

Name and relationship (if does not survive): _____

Name and relationship: _____

Equally or percent share: _____

Executor

First: Name and relationship: _____

Name and relationship: _____

Second: Name and relationship: _____

Name and relationship: _____

Guardian

First: Name and relationship: _____

Name and relationship: _____

Second: Name and relationship: _____

Name and relationship: _____

Trust

Beneficiary	**Age**	**Share**
_____	_____	_____
_____	_____	_____
_____	_____	_____

Distribution Alternatives

All at age: _____   One third (1/3) at age: _____

One half (1/2) at age: _____   Balance at age: _____

Trustee

First: Name and relationship: _____

Second: Name and relationship: _____

Codicil

If you want to make changes to your will after you've created it, you'll need to complete a codicil.

Codicil to the Last Will and Testament of _____

I, _____, of _____
_____, do make, publish, and declare this to be the First Codicil to my Last Will and Testament
executed by me on _____, 20__, in the presence of _____ and
_____ as witnesses.

I hereby remove _____ and substitute _____ as primary
guardian, under Article _____ of my Last Will and Testament.

In all other respects, I hereby ratify all the provisions of my Last Will and Testament, dated
_____, 20__.

IN TESTIMONY WHEREOF, I have subscribed my name on this my First Codicil to my Last Will
and Testament all in the presence of the persons witnessing it at my request, on this _____ day of
_____, 20__.

Signed: _____

Testator: _____

The foregoing instrument was signed, published, and declared by _____ to be his
or her First Codicil to his or her Last Will and Testament, in our presence, in the testator's presence,
and in the presence of one another, and at the testator's request, we signed our names as witnesses to
the codicil this _____ day of _____, 20__.

Witness: _____

Address: _____

Witness: _____

Address: _____

Pet Care Trust Agreement

A pet care trust agreement appoints someone to care for your pet or pets in the event of your death.

This Trust Agreement is made this _____ day of _____, 20__, at

_____, _____, between _____, the Settlor,

and _____, also serving as the Original Trustee under this Agreement.

The Settlor desires to create a Trust for the purpose of caring for and providing for the benefit and use of my pet _____, by the name of _____, and this trust shall be administered for said pet as enumerated herein:

1. The Settlor has delivered to the Trustee the property indicated in Exhibit A attached hereto, receipt of which is acknowledged by the Trustee of the Trust by signing and dating Exhibit A. That property and any other property that may be received by the Trustee from the Settlor as additions to this Trust shall be held and disposed of by the Trustee in accord with the terms stated in this Agreement.

2. The income generated by this Trust shall be paid to _____, who has agreed to take over the care and custody of my _____ and provide him or her with a loving home.

3. If the income generated by this Trust is not sufficient to provide the necessary care for my pet, the Trustee at his or her sole discretion may use the Trust principal for my pet's benefit.

4. My Trustee shall confer on a regular basis with my pet's caregiver to ensure there are adequate funds to provide for the appropriate care. Funds may be used to provide special dietary food, veterinary examination and treatment costs, medicines, possible operations, and professional grooming.

5. The Trust shall continue until the death of my _____. Upon the death of my pet, his or her remains will be cremated and disposed of according to the instructions provided the pet's caregiver. The Trust shall pay for the cost of this cremation.

6. The Settlor may, by signed instrument delivered to the Trustee, revoke this Agreement in whole or in part or amend it, but no amendment changing the powers, duties, or compensation of the Trustee shall be effective unless approved in writing by the acting Trustee.

7. The Trustee may resign by giving the Settlor written notice thirty (30) days in advance of the effective date of the Trustee's resignation. If there is no Successor Trustee designated, the personal representative of the estate of _____ shall designate a Successor Trustee. The Successor Trustee shall continue to hold title to all assets in the Trust until appropriate distribution can be lawfully made.

8. _____, as the Original Trustee, and all Successor Trustees under this Agreement shall have all powers enumerated under the Trust Code of the State of _____ and any other power that may be granted by law, to be exercised with the necessity of Court approval, as my Trustees, in their sole discretion, determine to be in the best interests of the beneficiaries. Said powers are to be construed in the broadest possible manner and shall include the following and shall pertain to both principal and income, but shall in no way be limited thereto:

   A. To retain any property received from the Settlor without liability for loss due to lack of diversification or nonproductivity.

   B. To invest and reinvest the Trust estate in any kind of real or personal property without regard to any law restricting investment by Trustees and without regard to current income.

   C. To sell any Trust property, for cash or on credit, at public or private sales; to exchange any Trust property for other property; and to determine the prices and terms of sales and exchanges.

   D. To take any action with respect to conserving or realizing upon the value of any Trust property, and with respect to foreclosures, reorganizations, or other changes affecting the Trust property; to collect, pay, contest, compromise, or abandon demands of or against the Trust estate, wherever situated; and to execute contracts, notes, conveyances, and other instruments, including instruments containing covenants and warranties binding upon and creating a charge against the Trust estate.

9. The following provisions govern the administration of this Trust as established by the Settlor.

   A. Any named Trustee of this Trust is relieved from any requirement as to routine Court accountings that may now or may hereafter be required by the statutes in force in any jurisdiction, although he or she is not precluded from obtaining judicial approval of his or her accounts. The Trustee shall be required to account on at least an annual basis to the pet's caregiver.

      This instrument and the dispositions hereunder shall be construed and regulated and their validity and effect shall be determined by the laws of the State of

      _____.

   B. Any Trustee shall be entitled to reasonable compensation for services rendered in administering and distributing the Trust property, which shall be paid in accordance with an hourly rate if the Trustee is an individual. If the Trustee is a corporate fiduciary, it shall be compensated in accordance with its current fee schedule. During the administration of this Trust, the Trustee shall be entitled to reimbursement for expenses.

C.   No person paying money or delivering property to a given Trustee need see to its proper application by the Trustee.

D.   In the event that _____ dies, resigns, or is unable to serve as Trustee of this Trust, _____ is nominated to serve as Successor Trustee under this Trust Agreement. The Successor Trustee shall automatically assume his or her position as Successor Trustee upon the signing of an oath, without the necessity of any Court order or approval of the same.

10.   In the event that there is any balance remaining in this Trust, the balance held in the Trust shall be paid to _____, and said Trust shall terminate.

IN WITNESS WHEREOF, I, _____, have hereunto signed my name as Settlor and as the Original Trustee of this Agreement on the _____ day of _____, 20___.

Settlor: _____

Trustee: _____

Witness: _____

Witness: _____

Appointment of Health-Care Power of Attorney

A health-care power of attorney appoints a representative to make decisions regarding your health care in the event that you are unable to do so.

I, _____, name _____ as representative to act for me in matters affecting my health, in particular to:

(1) Consent to or refuse health care for me.

(2) Employ or contract with servants, companions, or health care providers for me.

(3) Admit or release me from a hospital or health-care facility.

(4) Have access to records, including medical records, concerning my condition.

(5) Make anatomical gifts on my behalf.

(6) Request an autopsy.

(7) Make plans for the disposition of my body.

I authorize my representative to make decisions in my best interest concerning the withdrawal or withholding of health care. If at any time, based on my previously expressed preferences and diagnosis and prognosis, my representative is satisfied that certain health care is not or would not be beneficial, or that such health care is or would be excessively burdensome, then the representative may express my will that such care be withheld or withdrawn and may consent on my behalf that any or all health care be discontinued or not instituted even if my death results.

My representative must try to discuss this decision with me. However, if I am unable to communicate, my representative may make such a decision for me, after consultation with my physician or physicians and other relevant health-care providers. To the extent appropriate, my representative may also discuss this decision with my family and others, to the extent they are available.

I understand my rights under the Health Insurance Portability and Accountability Act of 1996 (HIPAA) and hereby declare and authorize my representative to have the authority to obtain any health-care information to the same extent I would be able to obtain my own health-care information.

Dated: _____, 20__

Signed: _____

Printed: _____

_____ has been personally known to me, and I believe him or her to be of legal age and capable of making decisions regarding his or her health care.

I am competent and at least 18 years of age.

Witness: _____

Dated: _____, 20___

Witness: _____

Dated: _____, 20___

Health-Care Power of Attorney—Minor Child

This document is used to appoint a representative to make decisions regarding your child or children's health care if you are unable to do so.

I, _____, as parent of _____ and _____,
name _____ as representative to act for me in matters affecting each of my children's health, in particular to:

(1) Consent to or refuse health care for my child.

(2) Employ or contract with servants, companions, or health care providers for my child.

(3) Admit or release my child from a hospital or health-care facility.

(4) Have access to records, including medical records, concerning my child's condition as if I requested those records, being fully aware of federal and State of _____ health-care privacy laws. I understand my child's rights under the Health Insurance Portability and Accountability Act of 1996 (HIPAA) and hereby declare and authorize my child's representative to have the authority to obtain any health-care information to the same extent I would be able to obtain my child's health-care information.

Dated: _____, 20___

Signed: _____

Printed: _____

_____ has been personally known to me, and I believe him or her to be of legal age and capable of making decisions regarding the health care of my child.

I am competent and at least 18 years of age, and I am not a relative of the grantor or his or her children.

Witness: _____

Dated: _____, 20___

Witness: _____

Dated: _____, 20___

Health-Care Information Authorization

This form authorizes that information about your health care can be shared with a designated person or persons.

Name: _____

Address: _____

Spouse: _____

Address: _____

Health-Care Power of Attorney

Primary representative: _____

Address: _____

Secondary representative: _____

Address: _____

Any restrictions on authority? _____   Explain: _____

Burial instructions to be included? _____   List: _____

Living Will

Living will: _____ Yes/_____ No

    Artificially supplied nutrition/hydration: _____ Yes/_____ No

    Health-care representative to decide: _____ Yes/_____ No

Out-of-hospital do not resuscitate declaration: _____ Yes/_____ No

Life-prolonging declaration: _____ Yes/_____ No

Durable Power of Attorney

Health-care decisions by grantee of power: _____ Yes/_____ No

Grantee of durable POA: _____

Grantee of health-care POA: _____

Release of Health Care Information To:*

Spouse: _____

Child: _____

Other: _____

Grantee of any health-care decision must be given this information, usually provided in that document.

Life-Prolonging Procedures Declaration

A life-prolonging procedures declaration specifies your wishes to have your life prolonged with appropriate measures in the event that you are unable to make that decision known.

Declaration made this _____ day of _____, 20___. I, _____, being at least eighteen (18) years of age and of sound mind, willfully and voluntarily make known my desire that if at any time I have an incurable injury, disease, or illness determined to be a terminal condition, I request the use of life-prolonging procedures that would extend my life. This includes appropriate nutrition and hydration; the administration of medication; and the performance of all other medical procedures necessary to extend my life, to provide comfort care, or to alleviate pain.

In the absence of my ability to give directions regarding the use of life-prolonging procedures, it is my intention that this declaration be honored by my family and physician as the final expression of my legal right to request medical or surgical treatment and accept the consequences of refusal.

I understand the full import of this declaration.

Signed: _____

Printed: _____

City, county, and state of residence: _____

The declarant has been personally known to me, and I believe him or her to be of sound mind. I did not sign the declarant's signature above for or at the direction of the declarant.

I am not a parent, spouse, or child of the declarant. I am not entitled to any part of the declarant's estate or directly financially responsible for the declarant's medical care. I am competent and at least eighteen (18) years of age.

Witness: _____

Dated: _____, 20___

Witness: _____

Dated: _____, 20___

Living Will Declaration

A living will declaration specifies your wishes to not have your life prolonged under certain circumstances if you are unable to make that decision known.

Declaration made this _____ day of _____, 20___. I, _____, being at least eighteen (18) years of age and of sound mind, willfully and voluntarily make known my desires that my dying shall not be artificially prolonged under the circumstances set forth below, and I declare:

If at any time my attending physician certifies in writing that: (1) I have an incurable injury, disease, or illness; (2) my death will occur within a short time; and (3) the use of life-prolonging procedures would serve only to artificially prolong the dying process, I direct that such procedures be withheld or withdrawn and that I be permitted to die naturally with only the performance or provision of any medical procedure or medication necessary to provide me with comfort care or to alleviate pain, and, if I have so indicated below, the provision of artificially supplied nutrition and hydration (indicate your choice by initialing or making your mark before signing this declaration):

_____ I wish to receive artificially supplied nutrition and hydration, even if the effort to sustain life is futile or excessively burdensome to me.

_____ I do not wish to receive artificially supplied nutrition and hydration, if the effort to sustain life is futile or excessively burdensome to me.

_____ I intentionally make no decision concerning artificially supplied nutrition and hydration, leaving the decision to my health-care representative appointed under the laws of the State of _____.

In the absence of my ability to give directions regarding the use of life-prolonging procedures, it is my intention that this declaration be honored by my family and physician as the final expression of my legal right to refuse medical or surgical treatment and accept the consequences of refusal.

I understand the full import of this declaration.

Signed: _____

Printed: _____

City, county, and state of residence: _____

The declarant has been personally known to me, and I believe him or her to be of sound mind. I did not sign the declarant's signature above for or at the direction of the declarant. I am not a parent, spouse, or child of the declarant. I am not entitled to any part of the declarant's estate or directly financially responsible for the declarant's medical care. I am competent and at least eighteen (18) years of age.

Witness: _____

Dated: _____, 20__

Witness: _____

Dated: _____, 20__

Out-of-Hospital Do Not Resuscitate Declaration and Order

This form indicates that you would not want to be resuscitated under certain circumstances if you were stricken when you were outside a hospital setting.

Declaration made this _____ day of _____, 20___. I, _____, being at least eighteen (18) years of age and of sound mind, willfully and voluntarily make known my desires that my dying shall not be artificially prolonged under the circumstances set forth below, and I declare:

If at any time my attending physician certifies in writing that: (1) I have an incurable injury, disease, or illness; (2) my death will occur within a short time; and (3) the use of resuscitation would be unsuccessful or within a short period I would experience repeated cardiac or pulmonary failure and the use of resuscitation would serve only to artificially prolong the dying process, I direct that, if I experience cardiac or pulmonary failure in a location other than an acute care hospital or a health-care facility, cardiopulmonary resuscitation procedures be withheld or withdrawn and that I be permitted to die naturally. My medical care may include any medical procedure necessary to provide me with comfort care or to alleviate pain.

I understand that I may revoke this Out-of-Hospital Do Not Resuscitate Declaration at any time by a signed and dated writing, by destroying or canceling this document, or by communicating to health-care providers at the scene the desire to revoke this declaration.

In the absence of my ability to give directions regarding the use of life-prolonging procedures, it is my intention that this declaration be honored by my family and physician as the final expression of my legal right to refuse medical or surgical treatment and accept the consequences of refusal.

I understand the full import of this declaration.

Signed: _____

Printed: _____

City, county, and state of residence: _____

The declarant has been personally known to me, and I believe him or her to be of sound mind. I did not sign the declarant's signature above for or at the direction of the declarant.

I am not a parent, spouse, or child of the declarant. I am not entitled to any part of the declarant's estate or directly financially responsible for the declarant's medical care. I am competent and at least eighteen (18) years of age.

Witness: _____

Dated: _____, 20___

Durable General Power of Attorney

A durable general power of attorney appoints someone to handle your affairs if you are unable to do so.

KNOW ALL PERSONS PRESENT, that I, _____, a resident of _____, _____, have made, constituted, and appointed and do hereby make, constitute, and appoint _____, a resident of _____, _____, as my true and lawful attorney-in-fact and in my name and stead to do and perform all acts and exercise all powers and general authority with respect to all of the following designated transactions and matters as fully described in the State of _____ Powers of Attorney Act, applying to all powers of attorney created and specified therein, as amended, to wit:

Real property transactions; tangible personal property transactions; bond, share, and commodity transactions; banking transactions; pensions and retirement accounts; business operating transactions; insurance transactions; beneficiary transactions; gifts; family maintenance matters and actions; benefits from military service matters and actions; records, reports, and statement matters and actions; estate transactions; health care powers matters and actions; and general authority with respect to delegating authority and general authority with respect to all other matters.

IN WITNESS WHEREOF, I have hereunto set my hand and seal this _____ day of _____, 20__.

Signed: _____

Printed: _____

State and county: _____   Social Security number: _____

Before me, the undersigned Notary Public within and for said County and State, personally appeared _____, who signed in my presence the foregoing Durable Power of Attorney and acknowledged the execution thereof to be his or her voluntary act and deed.

Witness my hand and notarial seal this _____ day of _____, 20__.

Signed: _____

Printed: _____

County of residence: _____   Commission expiration: _____

Limited Power of Attorney

A limited power of attorney designates an agent who is authorized to perform certain, but not all, tasks on your behalf. For instance, if you would want someone to handle paying your bills if you are not able to do so but not make financial decisions regarding your investments, that would be a limited power of attorney.

KNOW ALL PERSONS PRESENT, that I, _____, a resident of _____, _____, have made, constituted, and appointed and do hereby make, constitute, and appoint _____, a resident of _____, _____, as my true and lawful attorney-in-fact and in my name and stead to do and perform all acts and exercise all powers and general authority with respect to all of the following designated transactions: _____ _____, as provided for by Section _____ of the Code of the State of _____.

A person may rely in good faith upon any representations and authority of my attorney-in-fact regarding any transaction within the attorney-in-fact's authority as stated herein.

This Limited Power of Attorney and actions taken by my attorney-in-fact properly authorized hereunder shall be binding upon me, my heirs, successors, assigns, legatees, guardians, and personal representatives.

My attorney-in-fact, acting in good faith and under the authority stated herein, is hereby released and forever discharged from any and all liability and from all claims by me, my heirs, successors, assigns, legatees, guardians, and personal representatives.

This Limited Power of Attorney is effective as of _____, and shall terminate upon _____.

IN WITNESS WHEREOF, I have hereunto set my hand and seal this _____ day of _____, 20___.

Signed: _____

Printed: _____

State and county: _____   Social Security number: _____

Before me, the undersigned Notary Public within and for said County and State, personally appeared _____, who signed in my presence the foregoing Limited Power of Attorney and acknowledged the execution thereof to be his or her voluntary act and deed.

Witness my hand and notarial seal this _____ day of _____, 20___.

Signed: _____

Printed: _____

County of residence: _____   Commission expiration: _____

Revocation of Durable Power of Attorney

If you change your mind about the person you appointed to handle your affairs, you'll need to fill out a revocation of durable power of attorney form.

_____ hereby states that he or she hereby revokes the appointment of _____ to serve as attorney-in-fact.

That the date of the Durable Power of Attorney appointing _____ to serve as his or her attorney-in-fact was _____.

That the authority granted to _____ to serve as attorney-in-fact is no longer in effect and he or she shall have no authority to make any further decisions on behalf of the grantor.

That the Durable Power of Attorney was/was not recorded on _____, at the Office of the _____, County of _____, State of _____, as document number _____.

IN WITNESS WHEREOF, I have hereunto set my hand and seal this _____ day of _____, 20__.

Signed: _____

Printed: _____

State and county: _____   Social Security number: _____

Before me, the undersigned Notary Public within and for said County and State, personally appeared _____, who signed in my presence the foregoing Revocation of Durable Power of Attorney and acknowledged the execution thereof to be his or her voluntary act and deed.

Witness my hand and notarial seal this _____ day of _____, 20__.

Signed: _____

Printed: _____

County of residence: _____   Commission expiration: _____

Index